D0457982

We Are the Change
We Seek

We Are the Change We Seek

The Speeches of Barack Obama

Edited by E. J. Dionne Jr.
and Joy-Ann Reid

BLOOMSBURY

NEW YORK · LONDON · OXFORD · NEW DELHI · SYDNEY

Bloomsbury USA
An imprint of Bloomsbury Publishing Plc

1385 Broadway	50 Bedford Square
New York	London
NY 10018	WC1B 3DP
USA	UK

www.bloomsbury.com

BLOOMSBURY and the Diana logo are trademarks of Bloomsbury Publishing Plc

First published 2017

ISBN: HB: 978-1-63286-946-3
          ePub: 978-1-63286-948-7

LIBRARY OF CONGRESS CATALOGING-IN-PUBLICATION DATA
Names: Obama, Barack. | Dionne, E. J., editor. | Reid, Joy-Ann Lomena, editor.
Title: We Are the Change We Seek : The Speeches of Barack Obama / E.J. Dionne Jr. and Joy-Ann Reid, [editors].
Description: New York : Bloomsbury USA, 2017. | Includes bibliographical references.
Identifiers: LCCN 2016043968 | ISBN 9781632869463 (hardback)
Subjects: LCSH: Obama, Barack. | United States—Politics and government—2009– | United States—Politics and government—2001–2009. |Speeches, addresses, etc., American. | BISAC: BIOGRAPHY & AUTOBIOGRAPHY / Presidents & Heads of State.
Classification: LCC E891.5 .O335 2017 | DDC 973.932092—dc23
LC record available at https://lccn.loc.gov/2016043968

2 4 6 8 10 9 7 5 3 1

Typeset by RefineCatch Limited, Bungay, Suffolk
Printed and bound in the U.S.A. by Berryville Graphics Inc.,
Berryville, Virginia

To find out more about our authors and books visit www.bloomsbury.com. Here you will find extracts, author interviews, details of forthcoming events and the option to sign up for our newsletters.

Bloomsbury books may be purchased for business or promotional use. For information on bulk purchases please contact Macmillan Corporate and Premium Sales Department at specialmarkets@macmillan.com.

To my wife, Mary Boyle, and our children, James, Julia, and Margot, who will always remember braving the cold to witness history on January 20, 2009.

To my husband, Jason Reid, and my children, Winsome, Jmar, and Miles, who were lucky enough to know for certain that someone who looks like them can be president.

And to John Lewis, who made it possible.

CONTENTS

Introduction

"LET US MARCH"

Barack Obama and the Audacity of Persuasion
E. J. Dionne Jr. and Joy-Ann Reid

BARACK OBAMA ENTERED the White House in January
2009 confronting as dismal a constellation of circumstances as any president since Franklin Roosevelt: a global
financial meltdown that would come very close to being an
economic collapse, skyrocketing rates of unemployment, and
unpopular wars in Iraq and Afghanistan that showed no signs
of being resolved. Despite his fervent campaign promise to ease
the country's political divisions, he discovered that he faced a
Republican opposition intent on taking back power by
stymieing his program, challenging his mandate to govern, and
leaving his dreams of harmony stillborn.

Over time, this meant that Obama had to use his rhetorical
gifts to confront and defeat his political adversaries. When
circumstances required, Obama could be a highly effective
partisan, which further embittered his opponents. Even at his
most eloquent, Obama would never win over those who saw
him as a dangerous philosophical antagonist.

Yet Obama never dropped the idea that beneath the surface
of seething conflict, a country that had elected him as its first

African American president was not as torn as it seemed to be. For his supporters—and, increasingly, as his term concluded, for Americans who had grown weary of the endless partisan wars—Obama remained a figure intent on evoking Abraham Lincoln's appeal to the "better angels of our nature." By the time his presidency neared an end, even some among his opponents conceded, sometimes grudgingly, that Obama had a calm fluency they would miss.

Obama always understood that when it came to moving people through the spoken word, he had "it." He acknowledged as much in 2009 to Harry Reid, then the Senate Majority Leader, after Reid described an Obama floor speech as "phenomenal." In his memoir, Reid said he would "never forget his response."

"I have a gift, Harry," Obama said in a way that seemed quite matter of fact.

Reid insisted that Obama spoke these words "without the barest hint of braggadocio or conceit, and with what I would describe as deep humility."

The account was published after Obama had become president and Reid, the loyal Democrat, may have been going out of his way to make sure the new president was not seen as arrogant in his certainty about his eloquence. Yet there was a plausibility to Reid's claim because Obama's cool detachment often allowed him to tote up his own list of virtues and shortcomings dispassionately. He had simply concluded that being able to persuade, move, and inspire counted as one of his most important assets. He was right about this.

It is surprising that rhetorical genius is not and has never been essential to a successful presidency. Over the last century, the list of presidents we mark out as especially gifted speakers is not long—Franklin Roosevelt, John F. Kennedy, Ronald Reagan, Bill Clinton, and Obama.

Roosevelt and Kennedy belong on the list not only because they spoke powerfully, but also because each mastered a new medium that had come to dominate politics—radio in FDR's case, television in JFK's. The demands of the two were different. Radio was warmly intimate, television friendly toward the coolly ironic. Reagan, liberals would always say, profited from his acting skills and from years on the speaking circuit, but he also excelled because he knew his own mind and had a clear sense of where he wanted to move the country. Clinton shared with Reagan a gift for making coherent arguments and the sure knowledge that making those arguments again and again was a central task of a successful presidency. At the 2012 Democratic National Convention, Clinton used his abilities to press the case on behalf of Obama, once his wife's bitter rival, winning from the man he now supported a new title, "Explainer in Chief." Proving that even Obama could sometimes be outshone rhetorically, Clinton's case for Obama's reelection was widely seen as more persuasive than the one the president made for himself.

In his choice of oratorical ancestors, Obama's first love was Lincoln, a sensible choice for a politician from Illinois who had declared his presidential candidacy in Lincoln's adopted hometown of Springfield, and whose election as the first African American president fulfilled the work of the Great Emancipator. (It did so in a way that might have shocked Lincoln, who, especially early in his career, shared many of the racial prejudices of his time.) Obama had something else in common with Lincoln:

a view that the trajectory of American history pointed toward justice and inclusion. Here, Obama also followed Martin Luther King Jr. Lincoln, King, and Obama all believed that the best way to redeem the American promise was to insist that from the country's origins, this promise was inherent in its founding documents, the Declaration of Independence especially. Obama bound himself to the American past in order to change the future.

There was also a great deal of Roosevelt in Obama, both Franklin and Theodore. Obama, like Clinton, saw himself as the president of a new progressive era that shared in common with the original Progressive Era an imperative to deal with radical economic and social changes. If the early progressives sought to write new rules for a country that had moved from farm to factory and from rural areas to big cities, latter-day progressives would bring order and a greater degree of fairness to a nation even more metropolitan, both suburban and urban, and that was replacing manufacturing work with toil in the technological, scientific, and service economies. In one of the most important speeches of Obama's presidency, in Osawatomie, Kansas, Obama hitched himself firmly to Teddy Roosevelt's intellectual and political legacies.

A president who took over in the midst of the greatest economic catastrophe since the Great Depression could not avoid embracing FDR, and he also had FDR thrust upon him. A cover of *Time* magazine depicted Obama as an FDR look-alike, with a confident smile and a jaunty cigarette holder at his lips. It seemed appropriate for a man who struggled with his smoking habit.

There were certainly some echoes of JFK, particularly in

Obama's generational rhetoric. If JFK was the young voice of the World War II generation, Obama was the first president not touched by the turmoil of the 1960s and he saw himself as liberating the country from many of that era's assumptions, struggles, and discords. Despite what his conservative enemies often said about him, Obama, like Kennedy, was mistrustful of ideology and could sometimes be very tough on allies to his left. (His Osawatomie speech was, in part, an effort to rekindle their faith in him.)

Perhaps the most unexpected reference point for Obama, given the philosophical divide between them, was Reagan. But Obama's respect for the Gipper shouldn't surprise. They shared something unusual in our history: Both had used a single speech to push themselves into the highest reaches of American politics. It is hard to find other politicians who have done the same. William Jennings Bryan with his "Cross of Gold" speech in 1896 came closest.

In Reagan's case, the speech that launched a political career was "A Time for Choosing," a broadcast Reagan made on behalf of Barry Goldwater's failing presidential campaign on October 27, 1964. It is doubtful that the speech changed many minds—Goldwater went down to an historically resounding defeat—but it marked Reagan out as a conservative hero into our day. Using the telling quip, the engaging story, and the apt (if sometimes misleading) statistic, Reagan made modern conservatism sing. By the time Reagan closed (with Lincoln's "the last best hope on earth" formulation), the millions of conservatives who watched him that night knew that they had found the man who would lead them to the White House. Sixteen years later, he did.

Obama opened his door to the American political imagination with a very different speech, his keynote address to the
Democratic National Convention on July 27, 2004. What we
remember is its call for national unity, its insistence that "there's
not a liberal America and a conservative America; there's a
United States of America." Also: "There's not a black America
and white America and Latino America and Asian America;
there's the United States of America." A country that, it seemed
at the time, yearned for unity had found its champion.

What's forgotten is that the speech was also a partisan address
with a political purpose. In a sense, it embodied tensions that
were present throughout Obama's rise to office and his time in
the White House. Obama always had to go back and forth
between his conciliatory hopes and his need to win pitched
battles with a Republican party that resisted his overtures.

If Reagan sought to sharpen ideological divisions, Obama
saw ideological divisions themselves—especially around social
and moral issues—as both the product of Republican strate-
gizing and a drag on liberal and Democratic hopes. The lead-in
to Obama's peroration on behalf of unity, after all, was an
attack on Republican divisive designs. "Now even as we speak,"
Obama said, "there are those who are preparing to divide us,
the spin masters and negative ad peddlers who embrace the
politics of anything goes." Obama was dividing the country in
his own way: between those who would divide the country for
political purposes and those who would not.

This spoke to what was an ongoing Obama project: to
defang cultural issues along with racial and religious divisions
by way of encouraging white working-class and middle-class
Americans to support progressives and Democrats who had

their economic interests at heart. The Red/Blue America speech included a paean to a progressive view of the economy and pledges on behalf of those "losing their union jobs" and decent wages. Ironically, Donald Trump, Obama's archenemy, would appeal to precisely such voters in 2016. Two of Obama's most important addresses, on religion before the Call to Renewal conference in 2006, and on race after the controversies surrounding his pastor, the Reverend Jeremiah Wright, were designed to close two of the widest divides in American politics—to the advantage, Obama hoped, of progressives.

"Secularists are wrong when they ask believers to leave religion at the door before entering the public square," he said in the first speech. As for Wright, he criticized his pastor for "having a profoundly distorted view of this country—a view that sees white racism as endemic and that elevates what is wrong with America with all that we know is right with America." Given the profound divisions that grew during the Obama years, it is paradoxical and even tragic that Obama dedicated so much of his rhetorical firepower to the task of conciliating religious white conservatives to his vision, only to look on as those divisions deepened. Even gifted preachers can fail in their task of conversion.

Obama had something else in common with Reagan, or hoped to. He, like Reagan, wished to realign American politics. Reagan had moved politics to the right. Obama wanted to be just as effective in reversing the tide. During his primary campaign against Hillary Clinton, Obama gave an interview to the *Reno Gazette-Journal* in which he said pointedly: "I think Ronald Reagan changed the trajectory of America in a way that Richard Nixon did not and Bill Clinton did not." Aligning his opponent's husband with Nixon was probably no accident. But most telling were his words about Reagan. "He put us on a fundamentally different path because the country was ready for it," Obama said. "I think he tapped into what people were already feeling. Which is: we want clarity, we want optimism, we want a return to that sense of dynamism and entrepreneurship that has been missing."

The interview would prove to be an excellent guide to Obama's rhetorical strategy for the next eight years. Obama's approval ratings at the end of his term suggested that a majority of the country was, indeed, ready for the change he promised, even if a large minority would continue to resist.

And there was one aspect of Obama's rhetorical approach that was distinctly his own, or perhaps more accurately, that he shared not with past presidents but with the civil rights heroes: an acknowledgment that the task of bending history was long, arduous, and full of disappointments. That is where hope came in, and always would. Obama would insist that even in moments of disappointment, despair was not an option—not only because despair was useless, but also because it denied possibilities that would always exist.

"Hope is not blind optimism," Obama said early in the 2008 campaign. "It's not ignoring the enormity of the task ahead or the roadblocks that stand in our path. It's not sitting on the sidelines or shirking from a fight. Hope is that thing inside us that insists, despite all evidence to the contrary, that something better awaits us if we have the courage to reach for it, and to work for it, and to fight for it."

So Obama was constantly reminding his own side to count up the victories won, successes earned, possibilities realized. He told students at Howard University in 2016 that "to deny how far we've come would do a disservice to the cause of justice, to the legions of foot-soldiers, to . . . your mothers and your dads, and grandparents and great-grandparents, who marched and toiled and suffered and overcame to make this day possible."

Obama's conservative detractors regularly accused him of "apologizing" for America. In truth, he was constantly making the case for America, the America that always had the capacity to change and "perfect" itself. Like his theological hero, Reinhold Niebuhr, Obama understood human frailty—"original sin" in Christian theological terms—but also the human capacity for transcendence. He calculated that frailty into all his endeavors, political and rhetorical. He was, like Niebuhr, resolutely a realist. But he kept placing his bets on transcendence and hope. "Yes, we can" was a clever political slogan, but it also went to the heart of the case he would make again and again.

IT IS CERTAINLY a habit of presidents to speak in historical terms and to place their own exertions into the flow of the long American story. But few other presidents (Lincoln was one) have been more insistent than Obama on offering a running class in American history and its meaning. This, wrote the historian James Kloppenberg in his book *Reading Obama*, reflected how Obama saw the complicated lessons of America's saga as a roadmap for where it should move next:

> Obama has amalgamated American traditions usually—but incorrectly—thought to be distinct. He has learned congruent lessons from multiple sources. Democracy works

best when rights are balanced against responsibilities. Democracy requires compromise, not because it is the path of least resistance but because people can learn from each other, and because lasting change demands widespread popular assent. Change in America is a work of decades, not months or even years. Obama also learned, from absorbing all these lessons, that a culture's only home is to be found in its tortured history.

This explains why Obama regularly comes back (as Bill Clinton also did) to the idea from the Constitution's Preamble of a "more perfect union." In Obama's rhetoric, "perfect" is as often a verb as it is an adjective describing some optimal state. The assumption is always that the United States has not yet reached its goal, but that it gets nearer to it by the decade. "Fifty years from Bloody Sunday, our march is not yet finished, but we're getting closer," he declared on the fiftieth anniversary of the march in Selma. "Two hundred and thirty-nine years after this nation's founding our union is not yet perfect, but we are getting closer. Our job's easier because somebody already got us through that first mile. Somebody already got us over that bridge."

He offered the same idea playing off the double meaning of "perfect" in his address about the Wright controversy: "This union may never be perfect, but generation after generation has shown that it can always be perfected."

There is in Obama's worldview an assumption very similar to the idea that Václav Havel brought to Congress when he addressed it in 1990. "As long as people are people, democracy, in the full sense of the word, will always be no more than an ideal," Havel declared. "One may approach it as one would the horizon in ways that may be better or worse, but it can never be fully attained. In this sense, you, too, are merely approaching democracy." The journey toward a goal is in itself a goal. Thus did Obama describe to the graduating students at Howard University in 2016 what he most admired about the champions of the civil rights era. "They knew," he said, "that even if they won, that would just be the beginning of a longer march to equality."

Obama has also regularly historicized himself, as he did at Osawatomie, and as he always did in referring to what might be seen as an American miracle: that a country riven from the beginning by racial injustice came to elect an African American as president of the United States.

It was during Obama's presidency that a sharp divide in how Americans absorb and interpret their history became as clear as it has ever been—owing, perhaps, to the inescapable contrast between Obama's view and the attitude taken by his conservative opponents, especially members of the Tea Party.

Simply put, some Americans are more inclined to look toward the past and others toward the future. Some speak of our nation's manifest virtues as rooted in old values nurtured by a deposit of ideas that we must preserve against all challengers. Others focus on our country's proven capacity for self-correction and change.

As a result, one stream of reverence for our founders flows from a belief that they have set down timeless truths. The alternative view lifts them up as political and intellectual adventurers willing to break with old systems and accepted ways of thinking.

Many Americans, no doubt, blend these views into their own forms of patriotism, but most of us tilt in one direction or the other. Obama clearly celebrates America's capacity to change, and in this, he stands in the tradition of FDR, who spoke at Thomas Jefferson's home at Monticello on July 4, 1936, to insist that the inventors of our experiment created a nation that would never fear change.

What, he asked, had the founders done? "They had broken away from a system of peasantry, away from indentured servitude," Roosevelt explained. "They could build for themselves a new economic independence. Theirs were not the gods of things as they were, but the gods of things as they ought to be. And so, as Monticello itself so well proves, they used new means and new models to build new structures."

Not the gods of things as they were, but the gods of things as they ought to be: Thus the creed of the reformer. The purpose of the past is to serve the present and future. History is about testing institutions against standards and adapting them, as Roosevelt put it, to "enlarge the freedom of the human mind and to destroy the bondage imposed on it by ignorance, poverty, and political and religious intolerance."

There is a straight line between Roosevelt's understanding of our tradition and President Obama's as he expressed in Selma. "What greater expression of faith in the American experiment than this, what greater form of patriotism is there than the belief that America is not yet finished," Obama declared, "that we are strong enough to be self-critical, that each successive generation can look upon our imperfections and decide that it is in our power to remake this nation to more closely align with our highest ideals?"

Yet Obama's gift also carried burdens. He was graded on a tough curve when his eloquence failed him, when a speech was not up to a standard that came to be applied to him the moment he stepped down from that convention podium in 2004. He was, at times, the victim of what Mario Cuomo, the eloquent governor of New York, saw as a version of the "dumb blonde syndrome." When a politician spoke particularly well, Cuomo argued, it was assumed that talking was all he could do. Obama joked in 2008 that opponents derided his supporters because they had fallen for a silver tongue. To laughter, he mimicked his foes: "They just like him because he talks good."

The lofty confidence he called upon his supporters to embrace was the object of scorn, too. Obama liked to say that he stood accused of being a "hope monger." It didn't bother him, and particularly in 2008 but at many points since, he sought to relive at the level of presidential politics his work as a community organizer. He saw his task as engaging citizens in the hard work of democracy. "Change will not come if we wait for some other person or if we wait for some other time," he said on the night of the Super Tuesday primaries in 2008. "We are the ones we've been waiting for. We are the change we seek."

He carried another burden as well. Whether he was acting as consoler or cajoler in chief, the country's first black president was regularly called upon to interpret moments of racial crisis and his efforts drew both effusive praise and searing criticism. That he became a positive reference point for tens of millions of Americans and a negative one for tens of millions of others was, perhaps, inevitable. A black man raised by a white mother and white, Midwestern grandparents, he was also an African American husband and father who always bore in mind his duty as a role model and a hero for young African Americans, particularly young black men. He had responsibilities around race unlike those of any of his predecessors.

In carrying out these charges, Obama reached back to the hopeful, multiracial creed of civil rights Christianity. His emphasis on hope; his talk of struggle, organizing, and movement-building; his frequent references to "the fierce urgency of now"—all openly echoed the vocabulary of a civil rights cause steeped in the Scriptures. He invoked the side of Martin Luther King Jr. most associated with conciliatory themes, not the angrier King who, toward the end of his life, drew sharp criticism from conservatives for his resolute opposition to the Vietnam War. It was this latter King whom Wright echoed, creating the storm to which Obama was forced to respond.

Returning to the rhetoric of the early civil rights era suited Obama's temperament and worldview, and it had practical advantages. The early movement, and particularly King's preaching, centered not primarily on the defeat of adversaries, but on their conversion. The conversion theme and the quest for a cross-racial "beloved community" fit well with Obama's core message of political and racial reconciliation. "We need to take faith seriously," Obama wrote in *The Audacity of Hope* (its title coming from one of Wright's sermons), "not simply to block the religious right but to engage all persons of faith in the larger project of American renewal." The spiritual resonances of civil rights rhetoric helped give his 2008 campaign the feeling of a religious revival and offered a grounding to his appeal to hope.

This Obama was heard often during his time in office, nowhere more movingly than in Charleston, South Carolina, in his eulogy for the Reverend Clementa Pinckney after a massacre in an African American church. It ended with the president spontaneously singing "Amazing Grace," the way a preacher might sing the lines of his sermon, to a chorus of stunned hallelujahs.

KLOPPENBERG POINTS TO one important aspect of the Obama worldview that on occasion clashed with his hopeful view of the country and its future. Kloppenberg, who was writing at a low point in Obama's presidency, saw in Obama the philosophical pragmatism of William James and John Dewey. Even if nearly all politicians like to call themselves "pragmatic," pragmatism itself is a cool philosophy, not a hot ticket to rhetorical heights:

> Pragmatism is a philosophy for skeptics, a philosophy for those committed to democratic debate and the critical assessment of the results of political decisions, not for true believers convinced that they know the right course of action in advance of inquiry and experimentation . . . The flexibility of pragmatist philosophy, which helps explain Obama's intellectual acuity and suppleness, may paradoxically undercut his ability to inspire and persuade the American electorate and the United States Congress at a time when strident rhetoric and unyielding partisanship have displaced reasoned deliberation and commitment to problem solving.

Kloppenberg sympathized with Obama's struggle, but Obama was required to deal with the political circumstances he was given, not the circumstances he wished for. While we have collected in this volume some of his most persuasive, effective, and moving speeches, there were important times during his presidency when his rhetorical gifts failed him—indeed, when he didn't seem to deploy them at all. He was remarkably (and, to his supporters, surprisingly) ineffective in making the case for two of his major achievements, the economic stimulus and the health care program that bears his name. These failures haunted him throughout the presidency. He often seemed to treat the stimulus, wrote Jonathan Alter in his account of Obama's first year, "as if it was a dog's breakfast concocted by someone else." His arguments for Obamacare shifted as the battle for the program dragged on, and he was trapped in a vicious circle: the failure to advance an effective case for the program made it unpopular, which meant that he stayed away from a robust defense of it lest making it a central issue that would harm him politically.

At times, Obama seemed to lose his gifts of persuasion entirely. In his memoir *Believer*, David Axelrod, his senior adviser and a loyal friend, writes of a planning meeting for which he prepared a video that included parts of the 2004 convention speech and some of the inspiring moments of the 2008 campaign. "I finished with more recent footage, documenting a restrained president sharing the details of his deficit reduction policies and what they would mean for some distant fiscal year. It was a clinical and bloodless performance, lacking both passion and a sense of advocacy."

"We need you to be *that* guy again," Axelrod told his boss, referring to the Obama who had been "passionate and purposeful."

Yet he regularly did become *that* guy again. Obama earned his reputation as an orator precisely because he could use speeches to solve political problems and seize the nation's attention. His 2007 Jefferson-Jackson dinner speech in Iowa really did set Democrats in the state afire. His speech during the Wright controversy did put it behind him. His speech at Osawatomie lifted him from the mire of budget fights and reignited the loyalties of his progressive supporters. The sobriety of his Nobel Peace Prize address softened criticism from those who said he had not yet earned the prize—partly because he chose to acknowledge this himself. If his speeches and eulogies after the many episodes of gun violence during his term failed to move Congress to pass sane gun legislation, they did provide a rallying point for Americans who yearned to put the country on a different path. And whether at Notre Dame or in Selma, he maintained his faith that a country divided by race, religion, culture, and politics would endure to move forward because "America is not some fragile thing."

This collection reflects our best judgment of which of Obama's speeches are most likely to endure, including the best known and most widely remembered. It is also an effort to present several sides of the man, the politician, the preacher, and the commander in chief. It begins with his 2002 talk at a rally in Chicago where he opposed the Iraq War and thus (without knowing it at the time) found the issue that would allow him to win the Democratic presidential nomination six years later. It ends with his final address before the United Nations General Assembly in September 2016, a speech that functions as a recounting of Obama's domestic and foreign achievements while in office as well as an affirmation of his belief in the power of the democratic idea.

A week before Election Day in 1960, Adlai Stevenson, another Illinois Democrat who won many Democratic hearts for his eloquence during two unsuccessful campaigns for the presidency, introduced John F. Kennedy at a rally in Los Angeles. A speechmaker praised by his admirers for appealing to the intellect, Stevenson was raising up a young man who had the even greater gift of inspiring passionate commitment.

"Do you remember," Stevenson said, "that in classical times when Cicero had finished speaking, the people said, 'How well he spoke,' but when Demosthenes had finished speaking, the people said, 'Let us march.'"

It is not clear that any American politician can compare to either Cicero or Demosthenes. It is something we can never really know. But on his best days, Obama could inspire Americans in large numbers to believe that it was worth marching, worth engaging in a political system they often scorned. He did not unite the country as he had hoped because it remained divided on the very question to which Obama devoted so much energy. Many Americans truly believed that greatness was something to be regained. Obama believed it lay ahead.

His message took many forms, but he regularly came back to the idea that the country could be perfected if only its citizens would embrace the task. We suspect that Americans will return to his speeches because ours is a country in which there will always be a market for hope.

"WHAT I AM OPPOSED TO IS A DUMB WAR"

Speech against the Iraq War
CHICAGO, ILLINOIS, OCTOBER 2, 2002

On October 2, 2002, the same day that a resolution authorizing military action in Iraq was introduced in the U.S. Congress, a young Illinois state senator delivered an impassioned speech at an anti-war rally in Chicago. Barack Obama railed against what he saw as a "dumb" and "rash" war being waged by "armchair, weekend warriors in this administration." The press paid little attention to Obama's remarks at the time, but he galvanized the crowd and established himself in the Chicago progressive community as a rising star. Years later, taking a principled stance against the Iraq War would serve Obama well as he campaigned against former Senator Hillary Clinton for the Democratic Party's nomination for president.

LET ME BEGIN by saying that although this has been billed as an anti-war rally, I stand before you as someone who is not opposed to war in all circumstances. The Civil War was one of the bloodiest in history, and yet it was only through the crucible of the sword, the sacrifice of multitudes, that we could begin to perfect this union, and drive the scourge of slavery from our soil. I don't oppose all wars.

My grandfather signed up for a war the day after Pearl Harbor was bombed, fought in Patton's army. He saw the dead and dying across the fields of Europe; he heard the stories of fellow troops who first entered Auschwitz and Treblinka. He fought in the name of a larger freedom, part of that arsenal of democracy that triumphed over evil, and he did not fight in vain. I don't oppose all wars.

After September 11, after witnessing the carnage and destruction, the dust and the tears, I supported this administration's pledge to hunt down and root out those who would slaughter innocents in the name of intolerance, and I would willingly take up arms myself to prevent such tragedy from happening again. I don't oppose all wars. And I know that in this crowd today, there is no shortage of patriots, or of patriotism.

What I am opposed to is a dumb war. What I am opposed to is a rash war. What I am opposed to is the cynical attempt by Richard Perle and Paul Wolfowitz and other armchair, weekend warriors in this administration to shove their own ideological agendas down our throats, irrespective of the costs in lives lost and in hardships borne.

What I am opposed to is the attempt by political hacks like Karl Rove to distract us from a rise in the uninsured, a rise in the poverty rate, a drop in the median income—to distract us from corporate scandals and a stock market that has just gone through the worst month since the Great Depression. That's what I'm opposed to. A dumb war. A rash war. A war based not on reason but on passion, not on principle but on politics. Now let me be clear—I suffer no illusions about Saddam Hussein. He is a brutal man. A ruthless man. A man who butchers his own people to secure his own power. He has repeatedly defied UN resolutions, thwarted UN inspection teams, developed chemical and biological weapons, and coveted nuclear capacity. He's a bad guy. The world, and the Iraqi people, would be better off without him.

But I also know that Saddam poses no imminent and direct threat to the United States or to his neighbors, that the Iraqi economy is in shambles, that the Iraqi military a fraction of its former strength, and that in concert with the international community he can be contained until, in the way of all petty dictators, he falls away into the dustbin of history. I know that even a successful war against Iraq will require a U.S. occupation of undetermined length, at undetermined cost, with undetermined consequences. I know that an invasion of Iraq without a clear rationale and without strong international support will only fan the flames of the Middle East, and encourage the worst, rather than best, impulses of the Arab world, and strengthen the recruitment arm of al Qaeda. I am not opposed to all wars. I'm opposed to dumb wars.

So for those of us who seek a more just and secure world for our children, let us send a clear message to the president today. You want a fight, President Bush? Let's finish the fight with bin Laden and al Qaeda, through effective, coordinated intelligence, and a shutting down of the financial networks that support terrorism, and a homeland security program that involves more than color-coded warnings. You want a fight, President Bush?

Let's fight to make sure that the UN inspectors can do their work, and that we vigorously enforce a non-proliferation treaty, and that former enemies and current allies like Russia safeguard and ultimately eliminate their stores of nuclear material, and that nations like Pakistan and India never use the terrible weapons already in their possession, and that the arms merchants in our own country stop feeding the countless wars that rage across the globe. You want a fight, President Bush?

Let's fight to make sure our so-called allies in the Middle East, the Saudis and the Egyptians, stop oppressing their own people, and suppressing dissent, and tolerating corruption and inequality, and mismanaging their economies so that their youth grow up without education, without prospects, without hope, the ready recruits of terrorist cells. You want a fight, President Bush? Let's fight to wean ourselves off Middle East oil, through an energy policy that doesn't simply serve the interests of Exxon and Mobil.

Those are the battles that we need to fight. Those are the battles that we willingly join. The battles against ignorance and intolerance. Corruption and greed. Poverty and despair. The consequences of war are dire, the sacrifices immeasurable. We may have occasion in our lifetime to once again rise up in defense of our freedom, and pay the wages of war. But we ought not—we will not—travel down that hellish path blindly. Nor should we allow those who would march off and pay the ultimate sacrifice, who would prove the full measure of devotion with their blood, to make such an awful sacrifice in vain.

"THE AUDACITY OF HOPE"

Keynote Address at the 2004 Democratic National Convention

BOSTON, MASSACHUSETTS, JULY 27, 2004

Having already served nearly eight years in the Illinois state senate, Barack Obama launched a campaign in 2003 for the U.S. Senate. Starting out as a distinct underdog, he won a crowded Democratic primary with 53 percent of the vote, more than double the next closest candidate. The buzz around Obama's landslide primary victory earned him the attention of presidential hopeful John Kerry, and in June, the Kerry campaign informed Obama that he had been chosen to deliver the keynote address at the Democratic Convention in Boston. The core message of Obama's speech—"the audacity of hope"—was a phrase his pastor, Reverend Jeremiah A. Wright Jr., had used in a sermon. Obama would later distance himself from Wright's often fiery rhetoric, but at the time, this simple expression encapsulated perfectly the vision for the future Obama offered to the American people: that, emerging from the highly polarizing Bush years, the country might obliterate the divides between red and blue America

and rebuild "the United States of America." A
national political career was born with this speech.

O N   B E H A L F   O F   the great state of Illinois, crossroads of a
nation, land of Lincoln, let me express my deep gratitude
for the privilege of addressing this convention. Tonight is a
particular honor for me because, let's face it, my presence on
this stage is pretty unlikely.

My father was a foreign student, born and raised in a small
village in Kenya. He grew up herding goats, went to school in
a tin-roof shack. His father, my grandfather, was a cook, a
domestic servant to the British.

But my grandfather had larger dreams for his son. Through
hard work and perseverance my father got a scholarship to study
in a magical place, America, that's shone as a beacon of freedom
and opportunity to so many who had come before him.

While studying here my father met my mother. She was
born in a town on the other side of the world, in Kansas.

Her father worked on oil rigs and farms through most of the
Depression. The day after Pearl Harbor, my grandfather signed
up for duty, joined Patton's army, marched across Europe. Back
home my grandmother raised a baby and went to work on a
bomber assembly line. After the war, they studied on the GI
Bill, bought a house through FHA and later moved west, all
the way to Hawaii, in search of opportunity.

And they too had big dreams for their daughter, a common
dream born of two continents.

My parents shared not only an improbable love; they shared
an abiding faith in the possibilities of this nation. They would

give me an African name, Barack, or "blessed," believing that in a tolerant America, your name is no barrier to success.

They imagined me going to the best schools in the land, even though they weren't rich, because in a generous America you don't have to be rich to achieve your potential.

They're both passed away now. And yet I know that, on this night, they look down on me with great pride.

And I stand here today grateful for the diversity of my heritage, aware that my parents' dreams live on in my two precious daughters.

I stand here knowing that my story is part of the larger American story, that I owe a debt to all of those who came before me, and that in no other country on Earth is my story even possible.

Tonight, we gather to affirm the greatness of our nation not because of the height of our skyscrapers, or the power of our military, or the size of our economy; our pride is based on a very simple premise, summed up in a declaration made over two hundred years ago: "We hold these truths to be self-evident, that all men are created equal, that they are endowed by their Creator with certain inalienable rights, that among these are life, liberty and the pursuit of happiness."

That is the true genius of America, a faith in simple dreams, an insistence on small miracles; that we can tuck in our children at night and know that they are fed and clothed and safe from harm; that we can say what we think, write what we think, without hearing a sudden knock on the door; that we can have an idea and start our own business without paying a bribe; that we can participate in the political process without fear of retribution; and that our votes will be counted—or at least, most of the time.

This year, in this election, we are called to reaffirm our values and our commitments, to hold them against a hard reality and see how we are measuring up, to the legacy of our forebearers and the promise of future generations.

And fellow Americans, Democrats, Republicans, independents, I say to you, tonight, we have more work to do, for the workers I met in Galesburg, Illinois, who are losing their union jobs at the Maytag plant that's moving to Mexico, and now they're having to compete with their own children for jobs that pay seven bucks an hour; more to do for the father I met who was losing his job and choking back the tears wondering how he would pay $4,500 a month for the drugs his son needs without the health benefits that he counted on; more to do for the young woman in East St. Louis, and thousands more like her, who has the grades, has the drive, has the will, but doesn't have the money to go to college.

Now, don't get me wrong, the people I meet in small towns and big cities and diners and office parks, they don't expect government to solve all of their problems. They know they have to work hard to get ahead. And they want to.

Go into the collar counties around Chicago, and people will tell you: They don't want their tax money wasted by a welfare agency or by the Pentagon.

Go into any inner-city neighborhood, and folks will tell you that government alone can't teach kids to learn.

They know that parents have to teach, that children can't achieve unless we raise their expectations and turn off the television sets and eradicate the slander that says a black youth with a book is acting white. They know those things.

People don't expect government to solve all their problems.

But they sense, deep in their bones, that with just a slight change in priorities, we can make sure that every child in America has a decent shot at life and that the doors of opportunity remain open to all. They know we can do better. And they want that choice.

In this election, we offer that choice. Our party has chosen a man to lead us who embodies the best this country has to offer. And that man is John Kerry.

John Kerry understands the ideals of community, faith, and service because they've defined his life. From his heroic service in Vietnam to his years as prosecutor and lieutenant governor, through two decades in the United States Senate, he has devoted himself to this country. Again and again, we've seen him make tough choices when easier ones were available. His values and his record affirm what is best in us.

John Kerry believes in an America where hard work is rewarded. So instead of offering tax breaks to companies shipping jobs overseas, he offers them to companies creating jobs here at home.

John Kerry believes in an America where all Americans can afford the same health coverage our politicians in Washington have for themselves.

John Kerry believes in energy independence, so we aren't held hostage to the profits of oil companies or the sabotage of foreign oil fields.

John Kerry believes in the constitutional freedoms that have made our country the envy of the world, and he will never sacrifice our basic liberties nor use faith as a wedge to divide us.

And John Kerry believes that in a dangerous world, war must be an option sometimes, but it should never be the first option.

You know, a while back, I met a young man named Seamus in a VFW hall in East Moline, Illinois. He was a good-looking kid, 6´2˝, 6´3˝, clear eyed, with an easy smile. He told me he'd joined the Marines and was heading to Iraq the following week.

And as I listened to him explain why he had enlisted—the absolute faith he had in our country and its leaders, his devotion to duty and service—I thought, this young man was all that any of us might ever hope for in a child. But then I asked myself: Are we serving Seamus as well as he's serving us?

I thought of the nine hundred men and women, sons and daughters, husbands and wives, friends and neighbors who won't be returning to their own hometowns. I thought of the families I had met who were struggling to get by without a loved one's full income or whose loved ones had returned with a limb missing or nerves shattered, but still lacked long-term health benefits because they were Reservists.

When we send our young men and women into harm's way, we have a solemn obligation not to fudge the numbers or shade the truth about why they are going, to care for their families while they're gone, to tend to the soldiers upon their return, and to never, ever go to war without enough troops to win the war, secure the peace, and earn the respect of the world.

Now, let me be clear. Let me be clear. We have real enemies in the world. These enemies must be found. They must be pursued. And they must be defeated.

John Kerry knows this. And just as Lieutenant Kerry did not hesitate to risk his life to protect the men who served with him in Vietnam, President Kerry will not hesitate one moment to use our military might to keep America safe and secure.

John Kerry believes in America. And he knows that it's not enough for just some of us to prosper. For alongside our famous individualism, there's another ingredient in the American saga, a belief that we are all connected as one people.

If there's a child on the south side of Chicago who can't read, that matters to me, even if it's not my child.

If there's a senior citizen somewhere who can't pay for their prescription drugs and having to choose between medicine and the rent, that makes my life poorer, even if it's not my grandparent.

If there's an Arab-American family being rounded up without benefit of an attorney or due process, that threatens my civil liberties.

It is that fundamental belief—I am my brother's keeper, I am my sister's keeper—that makes this country work.

It's what allows us to pursue our individual dreams, yet still come together as a single American family: E pluribus unum— "Out of many, one."

Now even as we speak, there are those who are preparing to divide us, the spin masters and negative ad peddlers who embrace the politics of anything goes.

Well, I say to them tonight, there's not a liberal America and a conservative America; there's the United States of America.

There's not a black America and white America and Latino America and Asian America; there's the United States of America.

The pundits like to slice and dice our country into red states and blue States: red states for Republicans, blue States for Democrats. But I've got news for them, too. We worship an awesome God in the blue states, and we don't like federal agents poking around our libraries in the red states.

We coach little league in the blue states and, yes, we've got some gay friends in the red states.

There are patriots who opposed the war in Iraq, and there are patriots who supported the war in Iraq.

We are one people, all of us pledging allegiance to the stars and stripes, all of us defending the United States of America.

In the end, that's what this election is about. Do we participate in a politics of cynicism, or do we participate in a politics of hope?

John Kerry calls on us to hope. John Edwards calls on us to hope. I'm not talking about blind optimism here, the almost willful ignorance that thinks unemployment will go away if we just don't think about it, or the health care crisis will solve itself if we just ignore it.

That's not what I'm talking about. I'm talking about something more substantial. It's the hope of slaves sitting around a fire singing freedom songs; the hope of immigrants setting out for distant shores; the hope of a young naval lieutenant bravely patrolling the Mekong Delta; the hope of a millworker's son who dares to defy the odds; the hope of a skinny kid with a funny name who believes that America has a place for him, too.

Hope in the face of difficulty, hope in the face of uncertainty, the audacity of hope: In the end, that is God's greatest gift to us, the bedrock of this nation, a belief in things not seen, a belief that there are better days ahead.

I believe that we can give our middle class relief and provide working families with a road to opportunity.

I believe we can provide jobs for the jobless, homes to the homeless, and reclaim young people in cities across America from violence and despair.

I believe that we have a righteous wind at our backs, and that as we stand on the crossroads of history, we can make the right choices and meet the challenges that face us.

America, tonight, if you feel the same energy that I do, if you feel the same urgency that I do, if you feel the same passion that I do, if you feel the same hopefulness that I do, if we do what we must do, then I have no doubt that all across the country, from Florida to Oregon, from Washington to Maine, the people will rise up in November, and John Kerry will be sworn in as president. And John Edwards will be sworn in as vice president. And this country will reclaim its promise. And out of this long political darkness a brighter day will come.

"HOW FAR WE'VE COME"

Remarks at John Lewis's Sixty-fifth Birthday Gala
ATLANTA, GEORGIA, FEBRUARY 21, 2005

Barack Obama's admiration for John Lewis is well-known, even breaking through the rancor that would part Obama from much of the black political establishment in 2008. That foundation was laid in part in 2005, when then-Senator Obama traveled to Atlanta to laud Lewis on his sixty-fifth birthday. He would tell an NAACP Freedom Fund banquet in Detroit three months later that, as he sat between Ethel Kennedy and Coretta Scott King at the ceremony, both women turned to him and said, "We're looking forward to hearing you speak," to which Obama thought: What an intimidating thing! *Intimidated or not, Obama delivered a moving treatise on Lewis and his fellow civil rights activists' personal heroism, their sacrifices and their struggles, as they paved the way for full and authentic citizenship for African Americans.*

IT'S AN HONOR to be here tonight to celebrate one of the most courageous and compassionate Americans of our time. Happy birthday, John.

When I was first asked to speak here, I thought to myself, never in a million years would I have guessed that I'd be serving in Congress with John Lewis.

And then I thought, you know, there was once a time when John Lewis might never have guessed that he'd be serving in Congress. And there was a time not long before that when people might never have guessed that someday, African Americans would be able to go to the polls, pick up a ballot, make their voice heard, and elect that Congress.

But we can, and I'm here, because people like John Lewis believed. Because people like John Lewis feared nothing and risked everything for those beliefs. Because they were willing to spend sleepless nights in lonely jail cells, endure the searing pain of billy clubs cracked against their bones, and face down death simply so that all of us could share equally in the joys of life.

How far we've come because of your courage, John.

How far we've come from the days when the son of sharecroppers would huddle by the radio as the crackle of Dr. King's dreams filled his heart with hope. He was often forced to leave school to work in the fields and the public library was off-limits to his kind, and yet young John Lewis sought knowledge. His parents were never the type to complain or try to stir up any trouble, and yet their son sought justice.

And so he organized, even when so many tried to stop his efforts. He spoke truths, even when they tried to silence his words. And he marched, even when they tried to knock him down again and again and again.

The road John chose for himself was not easy. But the road to change never is.

I think it's simple for us to look back forty years and think that it was all so clear then. That while there may be room for moral ambiguity in the issues we debate today, civil rights was different. That people generally knew what was right and what was wrong, who the good guys and the bad guys were. But the moral certainties we now take for granted—that separate can never be equal, that the blessings of liberty enshrined in our Constitution belong to all of us, that our children should be able to go to school together and play together and grow up together—were anything but certain when John Lewis was a boy.

And so there was struggle and sacrifice, discipline and tremendous courage. And there was the culmination of it all one Sunday afternoon on a bridge in Alabama.

I've often thought about the people on the Edmund Pettus Bridge that day. Not only John and Hosea Williams leading the march, but the hundreds of everyday Americans who left their homes and their churches to join it. Blacks and whites, teenagers and children, teachers and bankers and shopkeepers—a beloved community of God's children ready to stand for freedom.

And I wonder, where did they find that kind of courage? When you're facing row after row of state troopers on horseback armed with billy clubs and tear gas . . . when they're coming toward you spewing hatred and violence, how do you simply stop, kneel down, and pray to the Lord for salvation? Truly, this is the audacity of hope.

But the most amazing thing of all is that after that day—after John Lewis was beaten within an inch of his life, after people's heads were gashed open and their eyes were burned and they watched their children's innocence literally beaten out of them . . . after all that, they went back to march again.

They marched again. They crossed the bridge. They awakened a nation's conscience, and not five months later, the Voting Rights Act of 1965 was signed into law.

And so it was, in a story as old as our beginnings and as timeless as our hopes, that change came about because the good people of a great nation willed it so.

Thank you, John, for going back. Thank you for marching again.

Thank you for reminding us that in America, ordinary citizens can somehow find in their hearts the courage to do extraordinary things. That in the face of the fiercest resistance and the most crushing oppression, one voice can be willing to stand up and say that's wrong and this is right and here's why. And say it again. And say it louder. And keep saying it until other voices join the chorus to sing the songs that set us free.

Today, I'm sure you'll all agree that we have songs left to sing and bridges left to cross. And if there's anything we can learn from this living saint sitting beside me, it is that change is never easy, but always possible. That it comes not from violence or militancy or the kind of politics that pits us against each other and plays on our worst fears; but from great discipline and organization, from a strong message of hope, and from the courage to turn against the tide so that the tide eventually may be turned.

Today, we need that courage. We need the courage to say that it's wrong that one out of every five children is born into poverty in the richest country on Earth. And it's right to do whatever necessary to provide our children the care and the education they need to live up to their God-given potential.

It's wrong to tell hardworking families who are earning less and paying more in taxes that we can't do anything to help them buy their own home or send their kids to college or care for them when they're sick. And it's right to expect that if you're willing to work hard in this country of American Dreamers, the sky is the limit on what you can achieve.

It's wrong to tell those brave men and women who are willing to fight and die for this country that when they come home, we may not have room for them at the VA hospitals or the benefits we promised them. And it's right to always provide the very best care for the very best of America.

My friends, we have not come this far as a people and a nation because we believe that we're better off simply fending for ourselves. We are here because we believe that all men are created equal, and that we are all connected to each other as one people. And we need to say that more. And say it again. And keep saying it.

And where will our courage come from to speak these truths? When we stand on our own Edmund Pettus Bridge, what hope will sustain us?

I believe it is the hope of knowing that people like John Lewis have stood on that same bridge and lived to cross it.

For me, this kind of hope often comes from a memory of a trip I took during the campaign. About a week after the primary, Dick Durbin and I embarked on a nineteen-city tour of Southern Illinois. And one of the towns we went to was a place called Cairo, which, as many of you might know, achieved a certain notoriety during the late sixties and early seventies as having one of the worst racial climates in the country. You had an active white citizen's council there, you had cross burnings, Jewish families were being harassed, you had segregated schools, race riots, you name it—it was going on in Cairo.

And we're riding down to Cairo and Dick Durbin turns to me and says, "Let me tell you about the first time I went to Cairo. It was about thirty years ago. I was twenty-three years old and Paul Simon, who was Lieutenant Governor at the time, sent me down there to investigate what could be done to improve the racial climate in Cairo."

And Dick tells me how he diligently goes down there and gets picked up by a local resident who takes him to his motel. And as Dick's getting out of the car, the driver says "excuse me, let me just give you a piece of advice. Don't use the phone in your motel room because the switchboard operator is a member of the white citizen's council, and they'll report on anything you do."

Well, this obviously makes Dick Durbin upset, but he's a brave young man, so he checks in to his room, unpacks his bags and a few minutes later he hears a knock on the door. He opens up the door and there's a guy standing there who just stares at Dick for a second, and then says, "What the hell are you doing here?" and walks away.

Well, now Dick is really feeling concerned and so am I because as he's telling me this story, we're pulling in to Cairo. So I'm wondering what kind of reception we're going to get. And we wind our way through the town and we go past the old courthouse, take a turn and suddenly we're in a big parking lot and about three hundred people are standing there. About a fourth of them are black and three fourths are white and they

religious teachings to justify his own agenda. At the same time, it stands as one of the most searching and comprehensive statements about religion's role in public life delivered by any progressive politician.

I APPRECIATE THE OPPORTUNITY to speak here at the Call to Renewal's Building a Covenant for a New America conference. I've had the opportunity to take a look at your Covenant for a New America. It is filled with outstanding policies and prescriptions for much of what ails this country. So I'd like to congratulate you all on the thoughtful presentations you've given so far about poverty and justice in America, and for putting fire under the feet of the political leadership here in Washington.

But today I'd like to talk about the connection between religion and politics and perhaps offer some thoughts about how we can sort through some of the often bitter arguments that we've been seeing over the last several years.

I do so because, as you all know, we can affirm the importance of poverty in the Bible; and we can raise up and pass out this Covenant for a New America. We can talk to the press, and we can discuss the religious call to address poverty and environmental stewardship all we want, but it won't have an impact unless we tackle head-on the mutual suspicion that sometimes exists between religious America and secular America.

I want to give you an example that I think illustrates this fact. As some of you know, during the 2004 U.S. Senate General Election I ran against a gentleman named Alan Keyes. Mr. Keyes is well-versed in the Jerry Falwell-Pat Robertson style of rhetoric that often labels progressives as both immoral and godless.

Indeed, Mr. Keyes announced towards the end of the campaign that, "Jesus Christ would not vote for Barack Obama. Christ would not vote for Barack Obama because Barack Obama has behaved in a way that it is inconceivable for Christ to have behaved."

Jesus Christ would not vote for Barack Obama.

Now, I was urged by some of my liberal supporters not to take this statement seriously, to essentially ignore it. To them, Mr. Keyes was an extremist, and his arguments not worth entertaining. And since at the time, I was up forty points in the polls, it probably wasn't a bad piece of strategic advice.

But what they didn't understand, however, was that I had to take Mr. Keyes seriously, for he claimed to speak for my religion, and my God. He claimed knowledge of certain truths.

Mr. Obama says he's a Christian, he was saying, and yet he supports a lifestyle that the Bible calls an abomination.

Mr. Obama says he's a Christian, but supports the destruction of innocent and sacred life.

And so what would my supporters have me say? How should I respond? Should I say that a literalist reading of the Bible was folly? Should I say that Mr. Keyes, who is a Roman Catholic, should ignore the teachings of the Pope?

Unwilling to go there, I answered with what has come to be the typically liberal response in such debates—namely, I said that we live in a pluralistic society, that I can't impose my own religious views on another, that I was running to be the U.S. Senator of Illinois and not the Minister of Illinois.

But Mr. Keyes's implicit accusation that I was not a true Christian nagged at me, and I was also aware that my answer did not adequately address the role my faith has in guiding my own values and my own beliefs.

Now, my dilemma was by no means unique. In a way, it reflected the broader debate we've been having in this country for the last thirty years over the role of religion in politics.

For some time now, there has been plenty of talk among pundits and pollsters that the political divide in this country has fallen sharply along religious lines. Indeed, the single biggest "gap" in party affiliation among white Americans today is not between men and women, or those who reside in so-called Red States and those who reside in Blue, but between those who attend church regularly and those who don't.

Conservative leaders have been all too happy to exploit this gap, consistently reminding evangelical Christians that Democrats disrespect their values and dislike their Church, while suggesting to the rest of the country that religious Americans care only about issues like abortion and gay marriage; school prayer and intelligent design.

Democrats, for the most part, have taken the bait. At best, we may try to avoid the conversation about religious values altogether, fearful of offending anyone and claiming that—regardless of our personal beliefs—constitutional principles tie our hands. At worst, there are some liberals who dismiss religion in the public square as inherently irrational or intolerant, insisting on a caricature of religious Americans that paints them as fanatical, or thinking that the very word "Christian" describes one's political opponents, not people of faith.

Now, such strategies of avoidance may work for progressives when our opponent is Alan Keyes. But over the long haul, I think we make a mistake when we fail to acknowledge the power of faith in people's lives—in the lives of the American people—and I think it's time that we join a serious debate about how to reconcile faith with our modern, pluralistic democracy.

And if we're going to do that then we first need to understand that Americans are a religious people. Ninety percent of us believe in God, 70 percent affiliate themselves with an organized religion, 38 percent call themselves committed Christians, and substantially more people in America believe in angels than they do in evolution.

This religious tendency is not simply the result of successful marketing by skilled preachers or the draw of popular megachurches. In fact, it speaks to a hunger that's deeper than that—a hunger that goes beyond any particular issue or cause.

Each day, it seems, thousands of Americans are going about their daily rounds—dropping off the kids at school, driving to the office, flying to a business meeting, shopping at the mall, trying to stay on their diets—and they're coming to the realization that something is missing. They are deciding that their work, their possessions, their diversions, their sheer busyness, is not enough.

They want a sense of purpose, a narrative arc to their lives. They're looking to relieve a chronic loneliness, a feeling supported by a recent study that shows Americans have fewer close friends and confidants than ever before. And so they need an assurance that somebody out there cares about them, is listening to them—that they are not just destined to travel down that long highway towards nothingness.

And I speak with some experience on this matter. I was not raised in a particularly religious household, as undoubtedly many in the audience were. My father, who returned to Kenya when I was just two, was born Muslim but as an adult became an atheist. My mother, whose parents were non-practicing Baptists and Methodists, was probably one of the most spiritual and kindest people I've ever known, but grew up with a healthy skepticism of organized religion herself. As a consequence, so did I.

It wasn't until after college, when I went to Chicago to work as a community organizer for a group of Christian churches, that I confronted my own spiritual dilemma.

I was working with churches, and the Christians who I worked with recognized themselves in me. They saw that I knew their Book and that I shared their values and sang their songs. But they sensed that a part of me remained detached and removed, that I was an observer in their midst.

And in time, I came to realize that something was missing as well—that without a vessel for my beliefs, without a commitment to a particular community of faith, at some level I would always remain apart, and alone.

And if it weren't for the particular attributes of the historically black church, I may have accepted this fate. But as the months passed in Chicago, I found myself drawn—not just to work with the church, but to be in the church.

For one thing, I believed and still believe in the power of the African American religious tradition to spur social change, a power made real by some of the leaders here today. Because of its past, the black church understands in an intimate way the Biblical call to feed the hungry and clothe the naked and challenge powers and principalities. And in its historical struggles for freedom and the rights of man, I was able to see faith as more than just a comfort to the weary or a hedge against death, but rather as an active, palpable agent in the world. As a source of hope.

And perhaps it was out of this intimate knowledge of hardship—the grounding of faith in struggle—that the church offered me a second insight, one that I think is important to emphasize today.

Faith doesn't mean that you don't have doubts.

You need to come to church in the first place precisely because you are first of this world, not apart from it. You need to embrace Christ precisely because you have sins to wash away—because you are human and need an ally in this difficult journey.

It was because of these newfound understandings that I was finally able to walk down the aisle of Trinity United Church of Christ on 95th Street in the Southside of Chicago one day and affirm my Christian faith. It came about as a choice, and not an epiphany. I didn't fall out in church. The questions I had didn't magically disappear. But kneeling beneath that cross on the South Side, I felt that I heard God's spirit beckoning me. I submitted myself to His will, and dedicated myself to discovering His truth.

That's a path that has been shared by millions upon millions of Americans—evangelicals, Catholics, Protestants, Jews and Muslims alike; some since birth, others at certain turning points in their lives. It is not something they set apart from the rest of their beliefs and values. In fact, it is often what drives their beliefs and their values.

And that is why, if we truly hope to speak to people where they're at—to communicate our hopes and values in a way that's relevant to their own—then as progressives, we cannot abandon the field of religious discourse.

Because when we ignore the debate about what it means to be a good Christian or Muslim or Jew; when we discuss religion only in the negative sense of where or how it should not be practiced, rather than in the positive sense of what it tells us about our obligations towards one another; when we shy away from religious venues and religious broadcasts because we assume that we will be unwelcome—others will fill the vacuum, those with the most insular views of faith, or those who cynically use religion to justify partisan ends.

In other words, if we don't reach out to evangelical Christians and other religious Americans and tell them what we stand for, then the Jerry Falwells and Pat Robertsons and Alan Keyeses will continue to hold sway.

More fundamentally, the discomfort of some progressives with any hint of religion has often prevented us from effectively addressing issues in moral terms. Some of the problem here is rhetorical—if we scrub language of all religious content, we forfeit the imagery and terminology through which millions of Americans understand both their personal morality and social justice. Imagine Lincoln's Second Inaugural Address without reference to "the judgments of the Lord." Or King's I Have a Dream speech without references to "all of God's children." Their summoning of a higher truth helped inspire what had seemed impossible, and move the nation to embrace a common destiny.

Our failure as progressives to tap into the moral underpinnings of the nation is not just rhetorical, though. Our fear of getting "preachy" may also lead us to discount the role that values and culture play in some of our most urgent social problems.

After all, the problems of poverty and racism, the uninsured and the unemployed, are not simply technical problems in search of the perfect ten point plan. They are rooted in both societal indifference and individual callousness—in the imperfections of man.

Solving these problems will require changes in government policy, but it will also require changes in hearts and a change in minds. I believe in keeping guns out of our inner cities, and that our leaders must say so in the face of the gun manufacturers' lobby—but I also believe that when a gang-banger shoots indiscriminately into a crowd because he feels somebody disrespected him, we've got a moral problem. There's a hole in that young man's heart—a hole that the government alone cannot fix.

I believe in vigorous enforcement of our non-discrimination laws. But I also believe that a transformation of conscience and a genuine commitment to diversity on the part of the nation's CEOs could bring about quicker results than a battalion of lawyers. They have more lawyers than us anyway.

I think that we should put more of our tax dollars into educating poor girls and boys. I think that the work that Marian Wright Edelman has done all her life is absolutely how we should prioritize our resources in the wealthiest nation on earth. I also think that we should give them the information about contraception that can prevent unwanted pregnancies, lower abortion rates, and help assure that every child is loved and cherished.

But, you know, my Bible tells me that if we train a child in the way he should go, when he is old he will not turn from it. So I think faith and guidance can help fortify a young woman's sense of self, a young man's sense of responsibility, and a sense of reverence that all young people should have for the act of sexual intimacy.

I am not suggesting that every progressive suddenly latch on to religious terminology—that can be dangerous. Nothing is more transparent than inauthentic expressions of faith. As Jim has mentioned, some politicians come and clap—off rhythm— to the choir. We don't need that.

In fact, because I do not believe that religious people have a monopoly on morality, I would rather have someone who is grounded in morality and ethics, and who is also secular, affirm their morality and ethics and values without pretending that they're something they're not. They don't need to do that. None of us need to do that.

But what I am suggesting is this—secularists are wrong when they ask believers to leave their religion at the door before entering into the public square. Frederick Douglass, Abraham Lincoln, Williams Jennings Bryan, Dorothy Day, Martin Luther King—indeed, the majority of great reformers in American history—were not only motivated by faith, but repeatedly used religious language to argue for their cause. So to say that men and women should not inject their "personal morality" into public policy debates is a practical absurdity. Our law is by definition a codification of morality, much of it grounded in the Judeo-Christian tradition.

Moreover, if we progressives shed some of these biases, we might recognize some overlapping values that both religious and secular people share when it comes to the moral and material direction of our country. We might recognize that the call to sacrifice on behalf of the next generation, the need to think in terms of "thou" and not just "I," resonates in religious congregations all across the country. And we might realize that we have the ability to reach out to the evangelical community and engage millions of religious Americans in the larger project of American renewal.

Some of this is already beginning to happen. Pastors, friends of mine like Rick Warren and T. D. Jakes are wielding their enormous influences to confront AIDS, Third World debt relief, and the genocide in Darfur. Religious thinkers and activists like our good friend Jim Wallis and Tony Campolo are lifting up the Biblical injunction to help the poor as a means of mobilizing Christians against budget cuts to social programs and growing inequality.

And by the way, we need Christians on Capitol Hill, Jews on Capitol Hill, and Muslims on Capitol Hill talking about the estate tax. When you've got an estate tax debate that proposes a trillion dollars being taken out of social programs to go to a handful of folks who don't need and weren't even asking for it, you know that we need an injection of morality in our political debate.

Across the country, individual churches like my own and your own are sponsoring day care programs, building senior centers, helping ex-offenders reclaim their lives, and rebuilding our gulf coast in the aftermath of Hurricane Katrina.

So the question is, how do we build on these still-tentative partnerships between religious and secular people of good will? It's going to take more work, a lot more work than we've done so far. The tensions and the suspicions on each side of the religious divide will have to be squarely addressed. And each side will need to accept some ground rules for collaboration.

While I've already laid out some of the work that progressive leaders need to do, I want to talk a little bit about what conservative leaders need to do—some truths they need to acknowledge.

For one, they need to understand the critical role that the separation of church and state has played in preserving not only our democracy, but the robustness of our religious practice. Folks tend to forget that during our founding, it wasn't the atheists or the civil libertarians who were the most effective champions of the First Amendment. It was the persecuted minorities, it was Baptists like John Leland who didn't want the established churches to impose their views on folks who were getting happy out in the fields and teaching the scripture to slaves. It was the forebearers of the evangelicals who were the most adamant about not mingling government with religion, because they did not want state-sponsored religion hindering their ability to practice their faith as they understood it.

Moreover, given the increasing diversity of America's population, the dangers of sectarianism have never been greater. Whatever we once were, we are no longer just a Christian nation; we are also a Jewish nation, a Muslim nation, a Buddhist nation, a Hindu nation, and a nation of nonbelievers.

And even if we did have only Christians in our midst, if we expelled every non-Christian from the United States of America, whose Christianity would we teach in the schools? Would we go with James Dobson's, or Al Sharpton's? Which passages of Scripture should guide our public policy? Should we go with Leviticus, which suggests slavery is ok and that eating shellfish is abomination? How about Deuteronomy, which suggests stoning your child if he strays from the faith? Or should we just stick to the Sermon on the Mount—a passage that is so radical that it's doubtful that our own Defense Department would survive its application? So before we get carried away, let's read our bibles. Folks haven't been reading their bibles.

This brings me to my second point. Democracy demands that the religiously motivated translate their concerns into universal, rather than religion-specific, values. It requires that their proposals be subject to argument, and amenable to reason. I may be opposed to abortion for religious reasons, but if I seek to pass a law banning the practice, I cannot simply point to the teachings of my church or evoke God's will. I have to explain why abortion violates some principle that is accessible to people of all faiths, including those with no faith at all.

Now this is going to be difficult for some who believe in the inerrancy of the Bible, as many evangelicals do. But in a pluralistic democracy, we have no choice. Politics depends on our ability to persuade each other of common aims based on a common reality. It involves the compromise, the art of what's possible. At some fundamental level, religion does not allow for compromise. It's the art of the impossible. If God has spoken, then followers are expected to live up to God's edicts, regardless of the consequences. To base one's life on such uncompromising commitments may be sublime, but to base our policy making on such commitments would be a dangerous thing. And if you doubt that, let me give you an example.

We all know the story of Abraham and Isaac. Abraham is

ordered by God to offer up his only son, and without argument, he takes Isaac to the mountaintop, binds him to an altar, and raises his knife, prepared to act as God has commanded.

Of course, in the end God sends down an angel to intercede at the very last minute, and Abraham passes God's test of devotion.

But it's fair to say that if any of us leaving this church saw Abraham on a roof of a building raising his knife, we would, at the very least, call the police and expect the Department of Children and Family Services to take Isaac away from Abraham. We would do so because we do not hear what Abraham hears, do not see what Abraham sees, true as those experiences may be. So the best we can do is act in accordance with those things that we all see, and that we all hear, be it common laws or basic reason.

Finally, any reconciliation between faith and democratic pluralism requires some sense of proportion.

This goes for both sides.

Even those who claim the Bible's inerrancy make distinctions between Scriptural edicts, sensing that some passages—the Ten Commandments, say, or a belief in Christ's divinity—are central to Christian faith, while others are more culturally specific and may be modified to accommodate modern life.

The American people intuitively understand this, which is why the majority of Catholics practice birth control and some of those opposed to gay marriage nevertheless are opposed to a Constitutional amendment to ban it. Religious leadership need not accept such wisdom in counseling their flocks, but they should recognize this wisdom in their politics.

But a sense of proportion should also guide those who police the boundaries between church and state. Not every mention of God in public is a breach to the wall of separation—context matters. It is doubtful that children reciting the Pledge of Allegiance feel oppressed or brainwashed as a consequence of muttering the phrase "under God." I didn't. Having voluntary student prayer groups use school property to meet should not be a threat, any more than its use by the high school Republicans should threaten Democrats. And one can envision certain faith-based programs—targeting ex-offenders or substance abusers—that offer a uniquely powerful way of solving problems.

So we all have some work to do here. But I am hopeful that we can bridge the gaps that exist and overcome the prejudices each of us bring to this debate. And I have faith that millions of believing Americans want that to happen. No matter how religious they may or may not be, people are tired of seeing faith used as a tool of attack. They don't want faith used to belittle or to divide. They're tired of hearing folks deliver more screed than sermon. Because in the end, that's not how they think about faith in their own lives.

So let me end with just one other interaction I had during my campaign. A few days after I won the Democratic nomination in my U.S. Senate race, I received an e-mail from a doctor at the University of Chicago Medical School that said the following:

"Congratulations on your overwhelming and inspiring primary win. I was happy to vote for you, and I will tell you that I am seriously considering voting for you in the general election. I write to express my concerns that may, in the end, prevent me from supporting you." The doctor described himself as a

Christian who understood his commitments to be "totalizing." His faith led him to a strong opposition to abortion and gay marriage, although he said that his faith also led him to question the idolatry of the free market and quick resort to militarism that seemed to characterize much of the Republican agenda.

But the reason the doctor was considering not voting for me was not simply my position on abortion. Rather, he had read an entry that my campaign had posted on my website, which suggested that I would fight "right-wing ideologues who want to take away a woman's right to choose." The doctor went on to write:

"I sense that you have a strong sense of justice . . . and I also sense that you are a fair minded person with a high regard for reason . . . Whatever your convictions, if you truly believe that those who oppose abortion are all ideologues driven by perverse desires to inflict suffering on women, then you, in my judgment, are not fair-minded . . . You know that we enter times that are fraught with possibilities for good and for harm, times when we are struggling to make sense of a common polity in the context of plurality, when we are unsure of what grounds we have for making any claims that involve others . . . I do not ask at this point that you oppose abortion, only that you speak about this issue in fair-minded words."

Fair-minded words.

So I looked at my website and found the offending words. In fairness to them, my staff had written them using standard Democratic boilerplate language to summarize my pro-choice position during the Democratic primary, at a time when some of my opponents were questioning my commitment to protect *Roe v. Wade.*

Rereading the doctor's letter, though, I felt a pang of shame. It is people like him who are looking for a deeper, fuller conversation about religion in this country. They may not change their positions, but they are willing to listen and learn from those who are willing to speak in fair-minded words. Those who know of the central and awesome place that God holds in the lives of so many, and who refuse to treat faith as simply another political issue with which to score points.

So I wrote back to the doctor, and I thanked him for his advice. The next day, I circulated the e-mail to my staff and changed the language on my website to state in clear but simple terms my pro-choice position. And that night, before I went to bed, I said a prayer of my own—a prayer that I might extend the same presumption of good faith to others that the doctor had extended to me.

And that night, before I went to bed I said a prayer of my own. It's a prayer I think I share with a lot of Americans. A hope that we can live with one another in a way that reconciles the beliefs of each with the good of all. It's a prayer worth praying, and a conversation worth having in this country in the months and years to come.

"WHAT'S NEXT FOR AMERICA?"

Speech at the Jefferson–Jackson Dinner

DES MOINES, IOWA, NOVEMBER 10, 2007

A relative newcomer to the national political stage, Obama faced two major primary opponents in 2008: Hillary Clinton, the heavy favorite, and John Edwards, whose talk of "two Americas" captured populist imaginations. How Obama fared in Iowa, the first competition in the primary season, would send a signal about the viability of his bid for the party nomination and the presidency. The Obama team recognized that he needed to use the Jefferson-Jackson Dinner, a regular pre-primary Democratic fundraising event held in Des Moines, as a hinge moment for his campaign. As Obama committed his address to memory per dinner rules, his organizing team worked to ensure that his partisans would dominate the audience. Ultimately, of the estimated nine thousand people that attended, the Obama campaign claimed three thousand as its own supporters. The combination of the stirring speech and the raucous crowd was electrifying; as Mark Halperin and John Heilemann wrote in their

account of the 2008 election: "That Obama won the
night dramatically was apparent even to Clinton's
staunchest allies." This new and fierier side of
Obama paid off in January when he handily won
the caucus with 37.6 percent of the elected delegates
on an astonishingly high turnout.

THANK YOU SO much. To the great Governor of Iowa
and Lieutenant Governor of Iowa. To my dear friend Tom
Harkin for the outstanding work that he does. To the congressional delegation of Iowa that is doing outstanding work and to
Nancy Pelosi, Madam Speaker, thank you all for the wonderful
welcome and the wonderful hospitality.

[*Responding to audience*] I love you back.

A little less than one year from today, you will go into the
voting booth and you will select the president of the United
States of America. Now, here's the good news—the name
George W. Bush will not be on the ballot. The name of my
cousin Dick Cheney will not be on the ballot. We've been
trying to hide that for a long time. Everybody has a black sheep
in the family. The era of Scooter Libby justice, and Brownie
incompetence, and Karl Rove politics will finally be over.

But the question you're going to have to ask yourself when
you caucus in January and you vote in November is, "What's
next for America?" We are in a defining moment in our history.
Our nation is at war. The planet is in peril. The dream that so
many generations fought for feels as if it's slowly slipping away.
We are working harder for less. We've never paid more for
health care or for college. It's harder to save and it's harder to

retire. And most of all we've lost faith that our leaders can or will do anything about it.

We were promised compassionate conservatism and all we got was Katrina and wiretaps. We were promised a uniter, and we got a president who could not even lead the half of the country that voted for him. We were promised a more ethical and more efficient government, and instead we have a town called Washington that is more corrupt and more wasteful than it was before. And the only mission that was ever accomplished is to use fear and falsehood to take this country to a war that should have never been authorized and should have never been waged.

It is because of these failures that America is listening, intently, to what we say here today—not just Democrats, but Republicans and Independents who've lost trust in their government, but want to believe again.

And it is because of these failures that we not only have a moment of great challenge, but also a moment of great opportunity. We have a chance to bring the country together in a new majority—to finally tackle problems that George Bush made far worse, but that had festered long before George Bush ever took office—problems that we've talked about year after year after year after year.

And that is why the same old Washington textbook campaigns just won't do in this election. That's why not answering questions 'cause we are afraid our answers won't be popular just won't do. That's why telling the American people what we think they want to hear instead of telling the American people what they need to hear just won't do. Triangulating and poll-driven positions because we're worried about what Mitt or

Rudy might say about us just won't do. If we are really serious about winning this election Democrats, we can't live in fear of losing it.

This party—the party of Jefferson and Jackson; of Roosevelt and Kennedy—has always made the biggest difference in the lives of the American people when we led, not by polls, but by principle; not by calculation, but by conviction; when we summoned the entire nation to a common purpose—a higher purpose. And I run for the presidency of the United States of America because that's the party America needs us to be right now.

A party that offers not just a difference in policies, but a difference in leadership.

A party that doesn't just focus on how to win but why we should. A party that doesn't just offer change as a slogan, but real, meaningful change—change that America can believe in. That's why I'm in this race. That's why I am running for the presidency of the United States of America—to offer change that we can believe in.

I am in this race to tell the corporate lobbyists that their days of setting the agenda in Washington are over. I have done more than any other candidate in this race to take on lobbyists—and won. They have not funded my campaign, they will not get a job in my White House, and they will not drown out the voices of the American people when I am president. I'm in this race to take those tax breaks away from companies that are moving jobs overseas and put them in the pockets of hard working Americans who deserve it. And I won't raise the minimum wage every ten years—I will raise it to keep pace so that workers don't fall behind.

That is why I am in it. To protect the American worker. To fight for the American worker.

I'm in this race because I want to stop talking about the outrage of forty-seven million Americans without health care and start actually doing something about it. I expanded health care in Illinois by bringing Democrats and Republicans together. By taking on the insurance industry. And that is how I will make certain that every single American in this country has health care they can count on and I won't do it twenty years from now, I won't do it ten years from now, I will do it by the end of my first term as president of the United States of America.

I run for president to make sure that every American child has the best education that we have to offer—from the day they are born to the day they graduate from college. And I won't just talk about how great teachers are—as president I will reward them for their greatness—by raising salaries and giving them more support. That's why I'm in this race.

I am running for president because I am sick and tired of Democrats thinking that the only way to look tough on national security is by talking, and acting, and voting like George Bush Republicans.

When I am this party's nominee, my opponent will not be able to say that I voted for the war in Iraq; or that I gave George Bush the benefit of the doubt on Iran; or that I supported Bush-Cheney policies of not talking to leaders that we don't like. And he will not be able to say that I wavered on something as fundamental as whether or not it is ok for America to torture— because it is never ok. That's why I am in it.

As president, I will end the war in Iraq. We will have our

troops home in sixteen months. I will close Guantánamo. I will restore habeas corpus. I will finish the fight against al Qaeda. And I will lead the world to combat the common threats of the twenty-first century—nuclear weapons and terrorism; climate change and poverty; genocide and disease. And I will send once more a message to those yearning faces beyond our shores that says, "You matter to us. Your future is our future. And our moment is now."

America, our moment is now.

Our moment is now.

I don't want to spend the next year or the next four years refighting the same fights that we had in the 1990s.

I don't want to pit Red America against Blue America, I want to be the president of the United States of America.

And if those Republicans come at me with the same fear-mongering and swift-boating that they usually do, then I will take them head on. Because I believe the American people are tired of fear and tired of distractions and tired of diversions. We can make this election not about fear, but about the future. And that won't just be a Democratic victory; that will be an American victory.

And that is a victory America needs right now.

I am not in this race to fulfill some long-held ambitions or because I believe it's somehow owed to me. I never expected to be here, I always knew this journey was improbable. I've never been on a journey that wasn't.

I am running in this race because of what Dr. King called "the fierce urgency of now." Because I believe that there's such a thing as being too late. And that hour is almost upon us.

I don't want to wake up four years from now and find out

that millions of Americans still lack health care because we couldn't take on the insurance industry.

I don't want to see that the oceans have risen a few more inches. The planet has reached a point of no return because we couldn't find a way to stop buying oil from dictators.

I don't want to see more American lives put at risk because no one had the judgment or the courage to stand up against a misguided war before we sent our troops into fight.

I don't want to see homeless veterans on the streets. I don't want to send another generation of American children to failing schools. I don't want that future for my daughters. I don't want that future for your sons. I do not want that future for America.

I'm in this race for the same reason that I fought for jobs for the jobless and hope for the hopeless on the streets of Chicago; for the same reason I fought for justice and equality as a civil rights lawyer; for the same reason that I fought for Illinois families for over a decade.

Because I will never forget that the only reason that I'm standing here today is because somebody, somewhere stood up for me when it was risky. Stood up when it was hard. Stood up when it wasn't popular. And because that somebody stood up, a few more stood up. And then a few thousand stood up. And then a few million stood up. And standing up, with courage and clear purpose, they somehow managed to change the world.

That's why I'm running, Iowa—to give our children and grandchildren the same chances somebody gave me.

That's why I'm running, Democrats—to keep the American Dream alive for those who still hunger for opportunity, who still thirst for equality.

That's why I'm asking you to stand with me, that's why I'm asking you to caucus for me, that's why I am asking you to stop settling for what the cynics say we have to accept. In this election—in this moment—let us reach for what we know is possible. A nation healed. A world repaired. An America that believes again.

"YES, WE CAN"

New Hampshire Primary Concession Speech
NASHUA, NEW HAMPSHIRE, JANUARY 8, 2008

Of all of Barack Obama's speeches, perhaps none has produced a more iconic turn of phrase than the remarks he delivered in Nashua, New Hampshire, on the night of January 8, 2008—not in victory, but in defeat. The closing stanza of the speech, in which he speaks of America's endless waves of dreamers, from the nation's imperfect founding to the present day, injected a breath of hope into his campaign. And the speech's signature phrase—"Yes, we can," first used in Massachusetts Governor Deval Patrick's successful 2006 campaign—became a cultural phenomenon, supplanting the campaign's official slogan, "Change We Can Believe In." It was later rendered in song by pop music icon Will.I.Am.

THANK YOU, NEW Hampshire. I love you back. Thank you. Thank you.

Well, thank you so much. I am still fired up and ready to go. Thank you. Thank you.

Well, first of all, I want to congratulate Senator Clinton on a hard-fought victory here in New Hampshire. She did an outstanding job. Give her a big round of applause.

You know, a few weeks ago, no one imagined that we'd have accomplished what we did here tonight in New Hampshire. No one could have imagined it.

For most of this campaign, we were far behind. We always knew our climb would be steep. But in record numbers, you came out, and you spoke up for change.

And with your voices and your votes, you made it clear that at this moment, in this election, there is something happening in America.

There is something happening when men and women in Des Moines and Davenport, in Lebanon and Concord, come out in the snows of January to wait in lines that stretch block after block because they believe in what this country can be.

There is something happening. There's something happening when Americans who are young in age and in spirit, who've never participated in politics before, turn out in numbers we have never seen because they know in their hearts that this time must be different.

There's something happening when people vote not just for the party that they belong to, but the hopes that they hold in common.

And whether we are rich or poor, black or white, Latino or Asian, whether we hail from Iowa or New Hampshire, Nevada or South Carolina, we are ready to take this country in a fundamentally new direction.

That's what's happening in America right now; change is what's happening in America.

You, all of you who are here tonight, all who put so much

heart and soul and work into this campaign, you can be the new majority who can lead this nation out of a long political darkness.

Democrats, independents, and Republicans who are tired of the division and distraction that has clouded Washington, who know that we can disagree without being disagreeable, who understand that, if we mobilize our voices to challenge the money and influence that stood in our way and challenge ourselves to reach for something better, there is no problem we cannot solve, there is no destiny that we cannot fulfill. Our new American majority can end the outrage of unaffordable, unavailable health care in our time. We can bring doctors and patients, workers and businesses, Democrats and Republicans together, and we can tell the drug and insurance industry that, while they get a seat at the table, they don't get to buy every chair, not this time, not now.

Our new majority can end the tax breaks for corporations that ship our jobs overseas and put a middle-class tax cut in the pockets of working Americans who deserve it.

We can stop sending our children to schools with corridors of shame and start putting them on a pathway to success.

We can stop talking about how great teachers are and start rewarding them for their greatness by giving them more pay and more support. We can do this with our new majority.

We can harness the ingenuity of farmers and scientists, citizens and entrepreneurs to free this nation from the tyranny of oil and save our planet from a point of no return.

And when I am president of the United States, we will end this war in Iraq and bring our troops home.

We will end this war in Iraq. We will bring our troops

home. We will finish the job—we will finish the job against al Qaeda in Afghanistan. We will care for our veterans. We will restore our moral standing in the world.

And we will never use 9/11 as a way to scare up votes, because it is not a tactic to win an election. It is a challenge that should unite America and the world against the common threats of the twenty-first century: terrorism and nuclear weapons, climate change and poverty, genocide and disease.

All of the candidates in this race share these goals. All of the candidates in this race have good ideas and all are patriots who serve this country honorably.

But the reason our campaign has always been different, the reason we began this improbable journey almost a year ago is because it's not just about what I will do as president. It is also about what you, the people who love this country, the citizens of the United States of America, can do to change it.

That's what this election is all about.

That's why tonight belongs to you. It belongs to the organizers, and the volunteers, and the staff who believed in this journey and rallied so many others to join the cause.

We know the battle ahead will be long. But always remember that, no matter what obstacles stand in our way, nothing can stand in the way of the power of millions of voices calling for change.

We have been told we cannot do this by a chorus of cynics. And they will only grow louder and more dissonant in the weeks and months to come.

We've been asked to pause for a reality check. We've been warned against offering the people of this nation false hope. But in the unlikely story that is America, there has never been anything false about hope.

For when we have faced down impossible odds, when we've been told we're not ready or that we shouldn't try or that we can't, generations of Americans have responded with a simple creed that sums up the spirit of a people: Yes, we can. Yes, we can. Yes, we can.

It was a creed written into the founding documents that declared the destiny of a nation: Yes, we can.

It was whispered by slaves and abolitionists as they blazed a trail towards freedom through the darkest of nights: Yes, we can.

It was sung by immigrants as they struck out from distant shores and pioneers who pushed westward against an unforgiving wilderness: Yes, we can.

It was the call of workers who organized, women who reached for the ballot, a president who chose the moon as our new frontier, and a king who took us to the mountaintop and pointed the way to the promised land: Yes, we can, to justice and equality.

Yes, we can, to opportunity and prosperity. Yes, we can heal this nation. Yes, we can repair this world. Yes, we can.

And so, tomorrow, as we take the campaign south and west, as we learn that the struggles of the textile workers in Spartanburg are not so different than the plight of the dishwasher in Las Vegas, that the hopes of the little girl who goes to the crumbling school in Dillon are the same as the dreams of the boy who learns on the streets of L.A., we will remember that there is something happening in America, that we are not as divided as our politics suggest, that we are one people, we are one nation.

And, together, we will begin the next great chapter in the American story, with three words that will ring from coast to coast, from sea to shining sea: Yes, we can.

"A MORE PERFECT UNION"

Speech at the National Constitution Center

PHILADELPHIA, PENNSYLVANIA, MARCH 18, 2008

Obama the historian shines through in many of his speeches, as he walks the listener through the hills and valleys of American history. But it is Obama the sociologist—the man of two worlds—who stepped forward to defend his ties to his and Michelle's longtime Chicago pastor, Jeremiah Wright, in March of 2008. The media firestorm over a selection of Wright's sermons threatened to derail Obama's insurgent campaign. In response, he delivered a dissertation on race that touched not just on black pain, but also on white fear of economic and cultural displacement. And he did so with a compassion and nuanced understanding that few Americans— black or white—have publicly put into words, before or since. The speech was the first instance of what became an Obama habit: using a lengthy, detailed address to solve a political problem and quell a crisis.

LET ME BEGIN by thanking Harris Wofford for his contributions to this country in so many different ways. He exemplifies what we mean by the word "citizen." And so we are very grateful to him for all the work he has done, and I'm thankful for the gracious and thoughtful introduction.

"We the people, in order to form a more perfect union."

Two hundred and twenty one years ago, in a hall that still stands across the street, a group of men gathered and, with these simple words, launched America's improbable experiment in democracy.

Farmers and scholars; statesmen and patriots who had traveled across the ocean to escape tyranny and persecution finally made real their declaration of independence at a Philadelphia convention that lasted through the spring of 1787.

The document they produced was eventually signed but ultimately unfinished. It was stained by this nation's original sin of slavery, a question that divided the colonies and brought the convention to a stalemate until the founders chose to allow the slave trade to continue for at least twenty more years, and to leave any final resolution to future generations.

Of course, the answer to the slavery question was already embedded within our Constitution—a Constitution that had at its very core the ideal of equal citizenship under the law; a Constitution that promised its people liberty and justice, and a union that could be and should be perfected over time.

And yet words on a parchment would not be enough to deliver slaves from bondage, or provide men and women of every color and creed their full rights and obligations as citizens of the United States.

What would be needed were Americans in successive generations who were willing to do their part—through protests and struggle, on the streets and in the courts, through a civil war and civil disobedience, and always at great risk—to narrow that gap between the promise of our ideals and the reality of their time.

This was one of the tasks we set forth at the beginning of this presidential campaign—to continue the long march of those who came before us, a march for a more just, more equal, more free, more caring and more prosperous America.

I chose to run for president at this moment in history because I believe deeply that we cannot solve the challenges of our time unless we solve them together, unless we perfect our union by understanding that we may have different stories, but we hold common hopes; that we may not look the same and may not have come from the same place, but we all want to move in the same direction: toward a better future for our children and our grandchildren.

And this belief comes from my unyielding faith in the decency and generosity of the American people. But it also comes from my own story. I am the son of a black man from Kenya and a white woman from Kansas. I was raised with the help of a white grandfather who survived a Depression to serve in Patton's army during World War II and a white grandmother who worked on a bomber assembly line at Fort Leavenworth while he was overseas.

I've gone to some of the best schools in America and I've lived in one of the world's poorest nations. I am married to a black American who carries within her the blood of slaves and slave owners, an inheritance we pass on to our two precious daughters.

I have brothers, sisters, nieces, nephews, uncles, and cousins of every race and every hue scattered across three continents.

And for as long as I live, I will never forget that in no other country on earth is my story even possible.

It's a story that hasn't made me the most conventional of candidates. But it is a story that has seared into my genetic makeup the idea that this nation is more than the sum of its parts—that out of many, we are truly one.

Throughout the first year of this campaign, against all predictions to the contrary, we saw how hungry the American people were for this message of unity. Despite the temptation to view my candidacy through a purely racial lens, we won commanding victories in states with some of the whitest populations in the country. In South Carolina, where the Confederate flag still flies, we built a powerful coalition of African Americans and white Americans.

This is not to say that race has not been an issue in this campaign. At various stages in the campaign, some commentators have deemed me either "too black" or "not black enough." We saw racial tensions bubble to the surface during the week before the South Carolina primary. The press has scoured every single exit poll for the latest evidence of racial polarization, not just in terms of white and black, but black and brown as well.

And yet, it's only been in the last couple of weeks that the discussion of race in this campaign has taken a particularly divisive turn.

On one end of the spectrum, we've heard the implication that my candidacy is somehow an exercise in affirmative action; that it's based solely on the desire of wild- and wide-eyed liberals to purchase racial reconciliation on the cheap.

On the other end, we've heard my former pastor, Jeremiah

Wright, use incendiary language to express views that have the potential not only to widen the racial divide, but views that denigrate both the greatness and the goodness of our nation and that rightly offend white and black alike.

I have already condemned, in unequivocal terms, the statements of Reverend Wright that have caused such controversy, and in some cases, pain.

For some, nagging questions remain: Did I know him to be an occasionally fierce critic of American domestic and foreign policy? Of course. Did I ever hear him make remarks that could be considered controversial while I sat in the church? Yes. Did I strongly disagree with many of his political views? Absolutely, just as I'm sure many of you have heard remarks from your pastors, priests, or rabbis with which you strongly disagree.

But the remarks that have caused this recent firestorm weren't simply controversial. They weren't simply a religious leader's effort to speak out against perceived injustice. Instead, they expressed a profoundly distorted view of this country, a view that sees white racism as endemic and that elevates what is wrong with America above all that we know is right with America; a view that sees the conflicts in the Middle East as rooted primarily in the actions of stalwart allies like Israel instead of emanating from the perverse and hateful ideologies of radical Islam.

As such, Reverend Wright's comments were not only wrong but divisive, divisive at a time when we need unity; racially charged at a time when we need to come together to solve a set of monumental problems—two wars, a terrorist threat, a falling economy, a chronic health care crisis, and potentially devastating climate change, problems that are neither black or white or Latino or Asian, but rather problems that confront us all.

Given my background, my politics, and my professed values and ideals, there will no doubt be those for whom my statements of condemnation are not enough.

Why associate myself with Reverend Wright in the first place, they may ask? Why not join another church? And I confess that if all that I knew of Reverend Wright were the snippets of those sermons that have run in an endless loop on the television sets and YouTube, if Trinity United Church of Christ conformed to the caricatures being peddled by some commentators, there is no doubt that I would react in much the same way.

But the truth is, that isn't all that I know of the man. The man I met more than twenty years ago is a man who helped introduce me to my Christian faith, a man who spoke to me about our obligations to love one another; to care for the sick and lift up the poor.

He is a man who served his country as a U.S. Marine, and who has studied and lectured at some of the finest universities and seminaries in the country, and who over thirty years has led a church that serves the community by doing God's work here on Earth—by housing the homeless, ministering to the needy, providing day care services and scholarships and prison ministries, and reaching out to those suffering from HIV/AIDS.

In my first book, *Dreams from My Father*, I described the experience of my first service at Trinity, and it goes as follows: "People began to shout, to rise from their seats and clap and cry out, a forceful wind carrying the reverend's voice up into the rafters.

"And in that single note—hope—I heard something else; at the foot of that cross, inside the thousands of churches across the city, I imagined the stories of ordinary black people merging with the stories of David and Goliath, Moses and Pharaoh, the Christians in the lion's den, Ezekiel's field of dry bones.

"Those stories of survival and freedom and hope became our story, my story. The blood that spilled was our blood; the tears our tears; until this black church, on this bright day, seemed once more a vessel carrying the story of a people into future generations and into a larger world.

"Our trials and triumphs became at once unique and universal, black and more than black. In chronicling our journey, the stories and songs gave us a meaning to reclaim memories that we didn't need to feel shame about—memories that all people might study and cherish and with which we could start to rebuild."

That has been my experience at Trinity. Like other predominantly black churches across the country, Trinity embodies the black community in its entirety—the doctor and the welfare mom, the model student and the former gangbanger.

Like other black churches, Trinity's services are full of raucous laughter and sometimes bawdy humor. They are full of dancing and clapping and screaming and shouting that may seem jarring to the untrained ear.

The church contains in full the kindness and cruelty, the fierce intelligence and the shocking ignorance, the struggles and successes, the love and, yes, the bitterness and biases that make up the black experience in America.

And this helps explain, perhaps, my relationship with Reverend Wright. As imperfect as he may be, he has been like family to me. He strengthened my faith, officiated my wedding, and baptized my children.

Not once in my conversations with him have I heard him talk about any ethnic group in derogatory terms or treat whites with whom he interacted with anything but courtesy and respect.

He contains within him the contradictions—the good and the bad—of the community that he has served diligently for so many years.

I can no more disown him than I can disown the black community. I can no more disown him than I can disown my white grandmother, a woman who helped raise me, a woman who sacrificed again and again for me, a woman who loves me as much as she loves anything in this world, but a woman who once confessed her fear of black men who passed her by on the street, and who on more than one occasion has uttered racial or ethnic stereotypes that made me cringe.

These people are a part of me. And they are part of America, this country that I love.

Now, some will see this as an attempt to justify or excuse comments that are simply inexcusable. I can assure you it is not.

And I suppose the politically safe thing to do would be to move on from this episode and just hope that it fades into the woodwork. We can dismiss Reverend Wright as a crank or a demagogue, just as some have dismissed Geraldine Ferraro in the aftermath of her recent statements as harboring some deep-seated bias.

But race is an issue that I believe this nation cannot afford to ignore right now. We would be making the same mistake that Reverend Wright made in his offending sermons about America: to simplify and stereotype and amplify the negative to the point that it distorts reality.

The fact is that the comments that have been made and the issues that have surfaced over the last few weeks reflect the complexities of race in this country that we've never really worked through, a part of our union that we have not yet made perfect.

And if we walk away now, if we simply retreat into our respective corners we will never be able to come together and solve challenges like health care or education or the need to find good jobs for every American.

Understanding this reality requires a reminder of how we arrived at this point. As William Faulkner once wrote, "The past isn't dead and buried. In fact, it isn't even past."

We do not need to recite here the history of racial injustice in this country.

But we do need to remind ourselves that so many of the disparities that exist between the African American community and the larger American community today can be traced directly to inequalities passed on from an earlier generation that suffered under the brutal legacy of slavery and Jim Crow.

Segregated schools were, and are, inferior schools. We still haven't fixed them, fifty years after *Brown v. Board of Education.*

And the inferior education they provided, then and now, helps explain the pervasive achievement gap between today's black and white students.

Legalized discrimination, where blacks were prevented, often through violence, from owning property, or loans were not granted to African American business owners, or black homeowners could not access FHA mortgages, or blacks were excluded from unions, or the police force, or fire department meant that black families could not amass any meaningful wealth to bequeath to future generations.

That history helps explain the wealth and income gap between blacks and whites and the concentrated pockets of poverty that persist in so many of today's urban and rural communities.

A lack of economic opportunity among black men and the shame and frustration that came from not being able to provide for one's family contributed to the erosion of black families, a problem that welfare policies for many years may have worsened.

And the lack of basic services in so many urban black neighborhoods—parks for kids to play in, police walking the beat, regular garbage pick-up, building code enforcement—all help create a cycle of violence, blight, and neglect that continues to haunt us.

This is the reality in which Reverend Wright and other African Americans of his generation grew up. They came of age in the late fifties and early sixties, a time when segregation was still the law of the land and opportunity was systematically constricted.

What's remarkable is not how many failed in the face of discrimination, but how many men and women overcame the odds; how many were able to make a way out of no way for those like me who would come after them.

But for all those who scratched and clawed their way to get a piece of the American Dream, there were many who didn't make it—those who were ultimately defeated, in one way or another, by discrimination. That legacy of defeat was passed on to future generations—those young men and increasingly young women who we see standing on street corners or languishing in our prisons, without hope or prospects for the future.

Even for those blacks who did make it, questions of race, and racism, continue to define their world view in fundamental ways. For the men and women of Reverend Wright's generation, the memories of humiliation and doubt and fear have not gone away; nor has the anger and the bitterness of those years.

That anger may not get expressed in public, in front of white co-workers or white friends. But it does find voice in the barbershop or the beauty shop or around the kitchen table. At times, that anger is exploited by politicians to gin up votes along racial lines or to make up for a politician's own failings.

And occasionally it finds voice in the church on Sunday morning, in the pulpit and in the pews.

That anger is not always productive. Indeed, all too often it distracts attention from solving real problems. It keeps us from squarely facing our own complicity within the African American community in our condition, it prevents the African American community from forging the alliances it needs to bring about real change.

But the anger is real, it is powerful, and to simply wish it away, to condemn it without understanding its roots only serves to widen the chasm of misunderstanding that exists between the races.

In fact, a similar anger exists within segments of the white community. Most working- and middle-class white Americans don't feel that they have been particularly privileged by their race.

Their experience is the immigrant experience. As far as they're concerned, no one handed them anything, they built it from scratch. They've worked hard all their lives, many times only to see their jobs shipped overseas or their pensions dumped after a lifetime of labor. They are anxious about their futures, and they feel their dreams slipping away. And in an era of stagnant wages and global competition, opportunity comes to be seen as a zero sum game, in which your dreams come at my expense.

So when they are told to bus their children to a school across town, when they hear that an African American is getting an advantage in landing a good job or a spot in a good college because of an injustice that they themselves never committed, when they're told that their fears about crime in urban neighborhoods are somehow prejudice, resentment builds over time.

Like the anger within the black community, these resentments aren't always expressed in polite company. But they have helped shape the political landscape for at least a generation.

Anger over welfare and affirmative action helped forge the Reagan Coalition. Politicians routinely exploited fears of crime for their own electoral ends.

Talk show hosts and conservative commentators built entire careers unmasking bogus claims of racism while dismissing legitimate discussions of racial injustice and inequality as mere political correctness or reverse racism.

And just as black anger often proved counterproductive, so have these white resentments distracted attention from the real culprits of the middle class squeeze: a corporate culture rife with inside dealing and questionable accounting practices and short-term greed; a Washington dominated by lobbyists and special interests; economic policies that favor the few over the many.

And yet, to wish away the resentments of white Americans, to label them as misguided or even racist without recognizing they are grounded in legitimate concerns, this, too, widens the racial divide and blocks the path to understanding.

This is where we are right now. It's a racial stalemate we've been stuck in for years. And contrary to the claims of some of my critics, black and white, I have never been so naïve as to believe that we can get beyond our racial divisions in a single election cycle or with a single candidate, particularly a candidacy as imperfect as my own.

But I have asserted a firm conviction, a conviction rooted in my faith in God and my faith in the American people, that, working together, we can move beyond some of our old racial wounds and that, in fact, we have no choice—we have no choice if we are to continue on the path of a more perfect union.

For the African American community, that path means embracing the burdens of our past without becoming victims of our past. It means continuing to insist on a full measure of justice in every aspect of American life.

But it also means binding our particular grievances, for better health care and better schools and better jobs, to the larger aspirations of all Americans—the white woman struggling to break the glass ceiling, the white man who's been laid off, the immigrant trying to feed his family.

And it means also taking full responsibility for our own

lives—by demanding more from our fathers, and spending more time with our children, and reading to them, and teaching them that while they may face challenges and discrimination in their own lives, they must never succumb to despair or cynicism; they must always believe that they can write their own destiny.

Ironically, this quintessentially American—and, yes, conservative—notion of self-help found frequent expression in Reverend Wright's sermons. But what my former pastor too often failed to understand is that embarking on a program of self-help also requires a belief that society can change.

The profound mistake of Reverend Wright's sermons is not that he spoke about racism in our society. It's that he spoke as if our society was static; as if no progress had been made; as if this country—a country that has made it possible for one of his own members to run for the highest office in the land and build a coalition of white and black, Latino, Asian, rich, poor, young and old—is still irrevocably bound to a tragic past.

What we know—what we have seen—is that America can change.

That is the true genius of this nation. What we have already achieved gives us hope—the audacity to hope—for what we can and must achieve tomorrow.

Now, in the white community, the path to a more perfect union means acknowledging that what ails the African American community does not just exist in the minds of black people; that the legacy of discrimination—and current incidents of discrimination, while less overt than in the past—that these things are real and must be addressed.

Not just with words, but with deeds—by investing in our

schools and our communities; by enforcing our civil rights laws and ensuring fairness in our criminal justice system; by providing this generation with ladders of opportunity that were unavailable for previous generations.

It requires all Americans to realize that your dreams do not have to come at the expense of my dreams, that investing in the health, welfare, and education of black and brown and white children will ultimately help all of America prosper.

In the end, then, what is called for is nothing more and nothing less than what all the world's great religions demand: that we do unto others as we would have them do unto us.

Let us be our brother's keeper, Scripture tells us. Let us be our sister's keeper. Let us find that common stake we all have in one another, and let our politics reflect that spirit as well.

For we have a choice in this country. We can accept a politics that breeds division and conflict and cynicism. We can tackle race only as spectacle, as we did in the OJ trial; or in the wake of tragedy, as we did in the aftermath of Katrina; or as fodder for the nightly news.

We can play Reverend Wright's sermons on every channel every day and talk about them from now until the election, and make the only question in this campaign whether or not the American people think that I somehow believe or sympathize with his most offensive words.

We can pounce on some gaffe by a Hillary supporter as evidence that she's playing the race card or we can speculate on whether white men will all flock to John McCain in the general election regardless of his policies.

We can do that. But if we do, I can tell you that in the next election, we'll be talking about some other distraction, and then another one, and then another one. And nothing will change.

That is one option.

Or, at this moment, in this election, we can come together and say, "Not this time."

This time we want to talk about the crumbling schools that are stealing the future of black children and white children and Asian children and Hispanic children and Native-American children.

This time we want to reject the cynicism that tells us that these kids can't learn; that those kids who don't look like us are somebody else's problem.

The children of America are not those kids; they are our kids, and we will not let them fall behind in a twenty-first-century economy. Not this time.

This time we want to talk about how the lines in the emergency room are filled with whites and blacks and Hispanics who do not have health care, who don't have the power on their own to overcome the special interests in Washington, but who can take them on if we do it together.

This time we want to talk about the shuttered mills that once provided a decent life for men and women of every race, and the homes for sale that once belonged to Americans from every religion, every region, every walk of life.

This time we want to talk about the fact that the real problem is not that someone who doesn't look like you might take your job; it's that the corporation you work for will ship it overseas for nothing more than a profit.

This time we want to talk about the men and women of every color and creed who serve together, and fight together, and bleed together under the same proud flag. We want to talk about how to bring them home from a war that should've never been authorized and should've never been waged.

And we want to talk about how we'll show our patriotism by caring for them, and their families, and giving them the benefits that they have earned.

I would not be running for president if I didn't believe with all my heart that this is what the vast majority of Americans want for this country. This union may never be perfect, but generation after generation has shown that it can always be perfected.

And today, whenever I find myself feeling doubtful or cynical about this possibility, what gives me the most hope is the next generation—the young people whose attitudes and beliefs and openness to change have already made history in this election.

There's one story in particular that I'd like to leave you with today, a story I told when I had the great honor of speaking on Dr. King's birthday at his home church, Ebenezer Baptist, in Atlanta.

There is a young, twenty-three-year-old woman, a white woman named Ashley Baia, who organized for our campaign in Florence, South Carolina.

She'd been working to organize a mostly African American community since the beginning of this campaign, and one day she was at a roundtable discussion where everyone went around telling their story and why they were there.

And Ashley said that when she was nine years old, her mother got cancer. And because she had to miss days of work, she was let go and lost her health care. They had to file for bankruptcy, and that's when Ashley decided that she had to do something to help her mom.

She knew that food was one of their most expensive costs, and so Ashley convinced her mother that what she really liked and really wanted to eat more than anything else was mustard and relish sandwiches. Because that was the cheapest way to eat. That's the mind of a nine-year-old.

She did this for a year until her mom got better. And so Ashley told everyone at the roundtable that the reason she had joined our campaign was so that she could help the millions of other children in the country who want and need to help their parents too.

Now, Ashley might have made a different choice. Perhaps somebody told her along the way that the source of her mother's problems were blacks who were on welfare and too lazy to work, or Hispanics who were coming into the country illegally. But she didn't. She sought out allies in her fight against injustice.

Anyway, Ashley finishes her story and then goes around the room and asks everyone else why they're supporting the campaign.

They all have different stories and different reasons. Many bring up a specific issue.

And finally they come to this elderly black man who's been sitting there quietly the entire time. And Ashley asks him why he's there.

And he doesn't bring up a specific issue. He does not say health care or the economy. He does not say education or the war. He does not say that he was there because of Barack Obama.

He simply says to everyone in the room, "I am here because of Ashley."

"I'm here because of Ashley."

Now, by itself, that single moment of recognition between that young white girl and that old black man is not enough. It is not enough to give health care to the sick, or jobs to the jobless, or education to our children. But it is where we start. It is where our union grows stronger.

And as so many generations have come to realize over the course of the 221 years since a band of patriots signed that document right here in Philadelphia, that is where perfection begins.

"CHANGE HAPPENS"

Acceptance Speech at the 2008 Democratic National Convention

DENVER, COLORADO, AUGUST 28, 2008

Barack Obama's acceptance of the Democratic Party nomination for president came on a date of great historical significance: August 28, 2008—forty-five years to the day after the March on Washington, and fifty-three years after the disappearance and lynching of Emmett Till, which the March had commemorated. Obama drew some criticism for too few nods to that history in the speech—he spoke of "a preacher from Georgia," but didn't mention King by name— and for his rhetoric, which was seen as un-Obama-like in that it contrasted with his normal mellifluous style. Far more, it was a bare-knuckles political broadside against his soon-to-be opponent, Senator John McCain, and the Bush years.

THANK YOU SO much.
Thank you very much.
Thank you, everybody.
To Chairman Dean and my great friend Dick Durbin, and to

all my fellow citizens of this great nation, with profound gratitude and great humility, I accept your nomination for presidency
of the United States.

Let me express my thanks to the historic slate of candidates
who accompanied me on this journey, and especially the one
who traveled the farthest, a champion for working Americans
and an inspiration to my daughters and to yours, Hillary
Rodham Clinton.

To President Clinton, to President Bill Clinton, who made
last night the case for change as only he can make it, to Ted
Kennedy, who embodies the spirit of service, and to the next
vice president of the United States, Joe Biden, I thank you.

I am grateful to finish this journey with one of the finest
statesmen of our time, a man at ease with everyone from world
leaders to the conductors on the Amtrak train he still takes
home every night.

To the love of my life, our next first lady, Michelle Obama,
and to Malia and Sasha, I love you so much, and I am so proud
of you.

Four years ago, I stood before you and told you my story, of
the brief union between a young man from Kenya and a young
woman from Kansas who weren't well-off or well-known, but
shared a belief that in America their son could achieve whatever
he put his mind to.

It is that promise that's always set this country apart, that
through hard work and sacrifice each of us can pursue our individual dreams, but still come together as one American family,
to ensure that the next generation can pursue their dreams, as
well. That's why I stand here tonight. Because for 232 years, at
each moment when that promise was in jeopardy, ordinary

men and women—students and soldiers, farmers and teachers, nurses and janitors—found the courage to keep it alive.

We meet at one of those defining moments, a moment when our nation is at war, our economy is in turmoil, and the American promise has been threatened once more.

Tonight, more Americans are out of work and more are working harder for less. More of you have lost your homes and even more are watching your home values plummet. More of you have cars you can't afford to drive, credit cards, bills you can't afford to pay, and tuition that's beyond your reach.

These challenges are not all of government's making. But the failure to respond is a direct result of a broken politics in Washington and the failed policies of George W. Bush.

America, we are better than these last eight years. We are a better country than this.

This country is more decent than one where a woman in Ohio, on the brink of retirement, finds herself one illness away from disaster after a lifetime of hard work.

We're a better country than one where a man in Indiana has to pack up the equipment that he's worked on for twenty years and watch as it's shipped off to China, and then chokes up as he explains how he felt like a failure when he went home to tell his family the news.

We are more compassionate than a government that lets veterans sleep on our streets and families slide into poverty, that sits on its hands while a major American city drowns before our eyes.

Tonight, I say to the people of America, to Democrats and Republicans and independents across this great land: Enough. This moment, this moment, this moment, this election is our chance to keep, in the twenty-first century, the American promise alive.

Because next week, in Minnesota, the same party that brought you two terms of George Bush and Dick Cheney will ask this country for a third.

And we are here because we love this country too much to let the next four years look just like the last eight.

On November fourth, we must stand up and say: Eight is enough.

Now, now, let me—let there be no doubt. The Republican nominee, John McCain, has worn the uniform of our country with bravery and distinction, and for that we owe him our gratitude and our respect.

And next week, we'll also hear about those occasions when he's broken with his party as evidence that he can deliver the change that we need.

But the record's clear: John McCain has voted with George Bush 90 percent of the time.

Senator McCain likes to talk about judgment, but, really, what does it say about your judgment when you think George Bush has been right more than 90 percent of the time?

I don't know about you, but I am not ready to take a 10 percent chance on change.

The truth is, on issue after issue that would make a difference in your lives—on health care, and education, and the economy—Senator McCain has been anything but independent.

He said that our economy has made great progress under this president. He said that the fundamentals of the economy are strong.

And when one of his chief advisers, the man who wrote his economic plan, was talking about the anxieties that Americans are feeling, he said that we were just suffering from a mental recession and that we've become, and I quote, "a nation of whiners."

A nation of whiners? Tell that to the proud auto workers at a Michigan plant who, after they found out it was closing, kept showing up every day and working as hard as ever, because they knew there were people who counted on the brakes that they made.

Tell that to the military families who shoulder their burdens silently as they watch their loved ones leave for their third, or fourth, or fifth tour of duty.

These are not whiners. They work hard, and they give back, and they keep going without complaint. These are the Americans I know.

Now, I don't believe that Senator McCain doesn't care what's going on in the lives of Americans; I just think he doesn't know.

Why else would he define middle-class as someone making under five million dollars a year? How else could he propose hundreds of billions in tax breaks for big corporations and oil companies, but not one penny of tax relief to more than one hundred million Americans?

How else could he offer a health care plan that would actually tax people's benefits, or an education plan that would do nothing to help families pay for college, or a plan that would privatize Social Security and gamble your retirement?

It's not because John McCain doesn't care; it's because John McCain doesn't get it.

For over two decades he's subscribed to that old, discredited Republican philosophy: Give more and more to those with the most and hope that prosperity trickles down to everyone else.

In Washington, they call this the "Ownership Society," but what it really means is that you're on your own. Out of work? Tough luck, you're on your own. No health care? The market will fix it. You're on your own. Born into poverty? Pull yourself up by your own bootstraps, even if you don't have boots. You are on your own.

Well, it's time for them to own their failure. It's time for us to change America. And that's why I'm running for president of the United States.

You see, we Democrats have a very different measure of what constitutes progress in this country.

We measure progress by how many people can find a job that pays the mortgage, whether you can put a little extra money away at the end of each month so you can someday watch your child receive her college diploma.

We measure progress in the twenty-three million new jobs that were created when Bill Clinton was president, when the average American family saw its income go up $7,500 instead of go down $2,000, like it has under George Bush.

We measure the strength of our economy not by the number of billionaires we have or the profits of the Fortune 500, but by whether someone with a good idea can take a risk and start a new business, or whether the waitress who lives on tips can take a day off and look after a sick kid without losing her job, an economy that honors the dignity of work.

The fundamentals we use to measure economic strength are

whether we are living up to that fundamental promise that has made this country great, a promise that is the only reason I am standing here tonight.

Because, in the faces of those young veterans who come back from Iraq and Afghanistan, I see my grandfather, who signed up after Pearl Harbor, marched in Patton's army, and was rewarded by a grateful nation with the chance to go to college on the GI Bill.

In the face of that young student, who sleeps just three hours before working the night shift, I think about my mom, who raised my sister and me on her own while she worked and earned her degree, who once turned to food stamps, but was still able to send us to the best schools in the country with the help of student loans and scholarships.

When I listen to another worker tell me that his factory has shut down, I remember all those men and women on the South Side of Chicago who I stood by and fought for two decades ago after the local steel plant closed.

And when I hear a woman talk about the difficulties of starting her own business or making her way in the world, I think about my grandmother, who worked her way up from the secretarial pool to middle management, despite years of being passed over for promotions because she was a woman.

She's the one who taught me about hard work. She's the one who put off buying a new car or a new dress for herself so that I could have a better life. She poured everything she had into me. And although she can no longer travel, I know that she's watching tonight and that tonight is her night, as well.

Now, I don't know what kind of lives John McCain thinks that celebrities lead, but this has been mine.

These are my heroes; theirs are the stories that shaped my life. And it is on behalf of them that I intend to win this election and keep our promise alive as president of the United States.

What is that American promise? It's a promise that says each of us has the freedom to make of our own lives what we will, but that we also have obligations to treat each other with dignity and respect.

It's a promise that says the market should reward drive and innovation and generate growth, but that businesses should live up to their responsibilities to create American jobs, to look out for American workers, and play by the rules of the road.

Ours is a promise that says government cannot solve all our problems, but what it should do is that which we cannot do for ourselves: protect us from harm and provide every child a decent education; keep our water clean and our toys safe; invest in new schools, and new roads, and science, and technology.

Our government should work for us, not against us. It should help us, not hurt us. It should ensure opportunity not just for those with the most money and influence, but for every American who's willing to work.

That's the promise of America, the idea that we are responsible for ourselves, but that we also rise or fall as one nation, the fundamental belief that I am my brother's keeper, I am my sister's keeper.

That's the promise we need to keep. That's the change we need right now.

So let me spell out exactly what that change would mean if I am president.

Change means a tax code that doesn't reward the lobbyists who wrote it, but the American workers and small businesses who deserve it.

You know, unlike John McCain, I will stop giving tax breaks to companies that ship jobs overseas, and I will start giving them to companies that create good jobs right here in America.

I'll eliminate capital gains taxes for the small businesses and start-ups that will create the high-wage, high-tech jobs of tomorrow.

I will—listen now—I will cut taxes—cut taxes—for 95 percent of all working families, because, in an economy like this, the last thing we should do is raise taxes on the middle class.

And for the sake of our economy, our security, and the future of our planet, I will set a clear goal as president: In ten years, we will finally end our dependence on oil from the Middle East.

We will do this. Washington has been talking about our oil addiction for the last thirty years. And, by the way, John McCain has been there for twenty-six of them.

And in that time, he has said no to higher fuel-efficiency standards for cars, no to investments in renewable energy, no to renewable fuels. And today, we import triple the amount of oil than we had on the day that Senator McCain took office.

Now is the time to end this addiction and to understand that drilling is a stop-gap measure, not a long-term solution, not even close.

As president, I will tap our natural gas reserves, invest in clean coal technology, and find ways to safely harness nuclear power. I'll help our auto companies retool, so that the fuel-efficient cars of the future are built right here in America.

I'll make it easier for the American people to afford these new cars.

And I'll invest $150 billion over the next decade in affordable, renewable sources of energy—wind power, and solar power, and the next generation of biofuels—an investment that will lead to new industries and five million new jobs that pay well and can't be outsourced.

America, now is not the time for small plans. Now is the time to finally meet our moral obligation to provide every child a world-class education, because it will take nothing less to compete in the global economy.

You know, Michelle and I are only here tonight because we were given a chance at an education. And I will not settle for an America where some kids don't have that chance.

I'll invest in early childhood education. I'll recruit an army of new teachers, and pay them higher salaries, and give them more support. And in exchange, I'll ask for higher standards and more accountability.

And we will keep our promise to every young American: If you commit to serving your community or our country, we will make sure you can afford a college education.

Now is the time to finally keep the promise of affordable, accessible health care for every single American.

If you have health care, my plan will lower your premiums. If you don't, you'll be able to get the same kind of coverage that members of Congress give themselves.

And as someone who watched my mother argue with insurance companies while she lay in bed dying of cancer, I will make certain those companies stop discriminating against those who are sick and need care the most.

Now is the time to help families with paid sick days and better family leave, because nobody in America should have to choose between keeping their job and caring for a sick child or an ailing parent.

Now is the time to change our bankruptcy laws, so that your pensions are protected ahead of CEO bonuses, and the time to protect Social Security for future generations.

And now is the time to keep the promise of equal pay for an equal day's work, because I want my daughters to have the exact same opportunities as your sons.

Now, many of these plans will cost money, which is why I've laid out how I'll pay for every dime: by closing corporate loopholes and tax havens that don't help America grow.

But I will also go through the federal budget line by line, eliminating programs that no longer work and making the ones we do need work better and cost less, because we cannot meet twenty-first-century challenges with a twentieth-century bureaucracy.

And, Democrats, we must also admit that fulfilling America's promise will require more than just money. It will require a renewed sense of responsibility from each of us to recover what John F. Kennedy called our intellectual and moral strength.

Yes, government must lead on energy independence, but each of us must do our part to make our homes and businesses more efficient.

Yes, we must provide more ladders to success for young men who fall into lives of crime and despair. But we must also admit that programs alone can't replace parents, that government can't turn off the television and make a child do her homework, that fathers must take more responsibility to provide love and guidance to their children.

Individual responsibility and mutual responsibility, that's the essence of America's promise. And just as we keep our promise to the next generation here at home, so must we keep America's promise abroad.

If John McCain wants to have a debate about who has the temperament and judgment to serve as the next commander in chief, that's a debate I'm ready to have.

For while Senator McCain was turning his sights to Iraq just days after 9/11, I stood up and opposed this war, knowing that it would distract us from the real threats that we face.

When John McCain said we could just muddle through in Afghanistan, I argued for more resources and more troops to finish the fight against the terrorists who actually attacked us on 9/11, and made clear that we must take out Osama bin Laden and his lieutenants if we have them in our sights.

You know, John McCain likes to say that he'll follow bin Laden to the gates of Hell, but he won't even follow him to the cave where he lives.

And today, as my call for a timeframe to remove our troops from Iraq has been echoed by the Iraqi government and even the Bush administration, even after we learned that Iraq has $79 billion in surplus while we are wallowing in deficit, John McCain stands alone in his stubborn refusal to end a misguided war.

That's not the judgment we need; that won't keep America safe. We need a president who can face the threats of the future, not keep grasping at the ideas of the past.

You don't defeat a terrorist network that operates in eighty countries by occupying Iraq. You don't protect Israel and deter Iran just by talking tough in Washington. You can't truly stand up for Georgia when you've strained our oldest alliances.

If John McCain wants to follow George Bush with more tough talk and bad strategy, that is his choice, but that is not the change that America needs.

We are the party of Roosevelt. We are the party of Kennedy. So don't tell me that Democrats won't defend this country. Don't tell me that Democrats won't keep us safe.

The Bush-McCain foreign policy has squandered the legacy that generations of Americans, Democrats and Republicans, have built, and we are here to restore that legacy.

As commander in chief, I will never hesitate to defend this nation, but I will only send our troops into harm's way with a clear mission and a sacred commitment to give them the equipment they need in battle and the care and benefits they deserve when they come home.

I will end this war in Iraq responsibly and finish the fight against al Qaeda and the Taliban in Afghanistan. I will rebuild our military to meet future conflicts, but I will also renew the tough, direct diplomacy that can prevent Iran from obtaining nuclear weapons and curb Russian aggression.

I will build new partnerships to defeat the threats of the twenty-first century: terrorism and nuclear proliferation, poverty and genocide, climate change and disease.

And I will restore our moral standing so that America is once again that last, best hope for all who are called to the cause of freedom, who long for lives of peace, and who yearn for a better future.

These are the policies I will pursue. And in the weeks ahead, I look forward to debating them with John McCain.

But what I will not do is suggest that the senator takes his positions for political purposes, because one of the things that we have to change in our politics is the idea that people cannot disagree without challenging each other's character and each other's patriotism.

The times are too serious, the stakes are too high for this same partisan playbook. So let us agree that patriotism has no party. I love this country, and so do you, and so does John McCain.

The men and women who serve in our battlefields may be Democrats and Republicans and independents, but they have fought together, and bled together, and some died together under the same proud flag. They have not served a red America or a blue America; they have served the United States of America.

So I've got news for you, John McCain: We all put our country first.

America, our work will not be easy. The challenges we face require tough choices. And Democrats, as well as Republicans, will need to cast off the worn-out ideas and politics of the past, for part of what has been lost these past eight years can't just be measured by lost wages or bigger trade deficits. What has also been lost is our sense of common purpose, and that's what we have to restore.

We may not agree on abortion, but surely we can agree on reducing the number of unwanted pregnancies in this country.

The reality of gun ownership may be different for hunters in rural Ohio than they are for those plagued by gang violence in Cleveland, but don't tell me we can't uphold the Second Amendment while keeping AK-47s out of the hands of criminals.

I know there are differences on same-sex marriage, but surely we can agree that our gay and lesbian brothers and sisters deserve to visit the person they love in a hospital and to live lives free of discrimination.

You know, passions may fly on immigration, but I don't know anyone who benefits when a mother is separated from her infant child or an employer undercuts American wages by hiring illegal workers.

But this, too, is part of America's promise, the promise of a democracy where we can find the strength and grace to bridge divides and unite in common effort.

I know there are those who dismiss such beliefs as happy talk. They claim that our insistence on something larger, something firmer, and more honest in our public life is just a Trojan horse for higher taxes and the abandonment of traditional values.

And that's to be expected, because if you don't have any fresh ideas, then you use stale tactics to scare voters.

If you don't have a record to run on, then you paint your opponent as someone people should run from. You make a big election about small things.

And you know what? It's worked before, because it feeds into the cynicism we all have about government. When Washington doesn't work, all its promises seem empty. If your hopes have been dashed again and again, then it's best to stop hoping and settle for what you already know.

I get it. I realize that I am not the likeliest candidate for this office. I don't fit the typical pedigree, and I haven't spent my career in the halls of Washington.

But I stand before you tonight because all across America something is stirring. What the naysayers don't understand is that this election has never been about me; it's about you.

It's about you.

For eighteen long months, you have stood up, one by one, and said, "Enough," to the politics of the past. You understand that, in this election, the greatest risk we can take is to try the same, old politics with the same, old players and expect a different result.

You have shown what history teaches us, that at defining moments like this one, the change we need doesn't come from Washington. Change comes to Washington.

Change happens—change happens because the American people demand it, because they rise up and insist on new ideas and new leadership, a new politics for a new time.

America, this is one of those moments.

I believe that, as hard as it will be, the change we need is coming, because I've seen it, because I've lived it.

Because I've seen it in Illinois, when we provided health care to more children and moved more families from welfare to work.

I've seen it in Washington, where we worked across party lines to open up government and hold lobbyists more accountable, to give better care for our veterans, and keep nuclear weapons out of the hands of terrorists.

And I've seen it in this campaign, in the young people who voted for the first time and the young at heart, those who got involved again after a very long time; in the Republicans who never thought they'd pick up a Democratic ballot, but did.

I've seen it in the workers who would rather cut their hours back a day, even though they can't afford it, than see their friends lose their jobs; in the soldiers who reenlist after losing a limb; in the good neighbors who take a stranger in when a hurricane strikes and the floodwaters rise.

You know, this country of ours has more wealth than any nation, but that's not what makes us rich. We have the most powerful military on Earth, but that's not what makes us strong. Our universities and our culture are the envy of the world, but that's not what keeps the world coming to our shores.

Instead, it is that American spirit, that American promise, that pushes us forward even when the path is uncertain; that binds us together in spite of our differences; that makes us fix our eye not on what is seen, but what is unseen, that better place around the bend.

That promise is our greatest inheritance. It's a promise I make to my daughters when I tuck them in at night and a promise that you make to yours, a promise that has led immigrants to cross oceans and pioneers to travel west, a promise that led workers to picket lines and women to reach for the ballot.

And it is that promise that, forty-five years ago today, brought Americans from every corner of this land to stand together on a Mall in Washington, before Lincoln's Memorial, and hear a young preacher from Georgia speak of his dream.

The men and women who gathered there could've heard many things. They could've heard words of anger and discord. They could've been told to succumb to the fear and frustrations of so many dreams deferred.

But what the people heard instead—people of every creed

and color, from every walk of life—is that, in America, our destiny is inextricably linked, that together our dreams can be one.

"We cannot walk alone," the preacher cried. "And as we walk, we must make the pledge that we shall always march ahead. We cannot turn back."

America, we cannot turn back—not with so much work to be done; not with so many children to educate, and so many veterans to care for; not with an economy to fix, and cities to rebuild, and farms to save; not with so many families to protect and so many lives to mend.

America, we cannot turn back. We cannot walk alone.

At this moment, in this election, we must pledge once more to march into the future. Let us keep that promise, that American promise, and in the words of scripture hold firmly, without wavering, to the hope that we confess.

Thank you. God bless you. And God bless the United States of America.

"THIS IS YOUR VICTORY"

Election Night Victory Speech
CHICAGO, ILLINOIS, NOVEMBER 4, 2008

On November 4, 2008, Barack Obama defeated Arizona senator John McCain to become the forty-fourth president of the United States. The victory was decisive—Obama received 52.9 percent of the popular vote and 365 electoral votes to McCain's 45.7 percent and 173 electoral votes. That night, Obama delivered his victory speech in Grant Park in his hometown of Chicago, Illinois. Although only 70,000 people received tickets for the event, an estimated 240,000 showed up, the vast majority watching the historic moment via Jumbotron from blocks away. Millions more across the country tuned into the address from home. The theme of the speech, "This is your victory," conveyed that Americans had forcefully chosen to break with the previous eight years of Republican control of the White House and put their faith in the belief "that America can change." In his very first sentence, Obama obliquely yet plainly called attention to the remarkable national achievement that the election of the first African American president represented.

H ELLO, CHICAGO.

If there is anyone out there who still doubts that America is a place where all things are possible, who still wonders if the dream of our founders is alive in our time, who still questions the power of our democracy, tonight is your answer.

It's the answer told by lines that stretched around schools and churches in numbers this nation has never seen, by people who waited three hours and four hours, many for the first time in their lives, because they believed that this time must be different, that their voices could be that difference.

It's the answer spoken by young and old, rich and poor, Democrat and Republican, black, white, Hispanic, Asian, Native American, gay, straight, disabled and not disabled. Americans who sent a message to the world that we have never been just a collection of individuals or a collection of red states and blue states.

We are, and always will be, the United States of America.

It's the answer that led those who've been told for so long by so many to be cynical and fearful and doubtful about what we can achieve to put their hands on the arc of history and bend it once more toward the hope of a better day.

It's been a long time coming, but tonight, because of what we did on this date in this election at this defining moment change has come to America.

A little bit earlier this evening, I received an extraordinarily gracious call from Senator McCain.

Senator McCain fought long and hard in this campaign. And he's fought even longer and harder for the country that he loves. He has endured sacrifices for America that most of us cannot begin to imagine. We are better off for the service rendered by this brave and selfless leader.

I congratulate him; I congratulate Governor Palin for all that they've achieved. And I look forward to working with them to renew this nation's promise in the months ahead.

I want to thank my partner in this journey, a man who campaigned from his heart, and spoke for the men and women he grew up with on the streets of Scranton and rode with on the train home to Delaware, the vice president-elect of the United States, Joe Biden.

And I would not be standing here tonight without the unyielding support of my best friend for the last sixteen years, the rock of our family, the love of my life, the nation's next first lady, Michelle Obama.

Sasha and Malia, I love you both more than you can imagine. And you have earned the new puppy that's coming with us to the new White House.

And while she's no longer with us, I know my grandmother's watching, along with the family that made me who I am. I miss them tonight. I know that my debt to them is beyond measure.

To my sister Maya, my sister Alma, all my other brothers and sisters, thank you so much for all the support that you've given me. I am grateful to them.

And to my campaign manager, David Plouffe, the unsung hero of this campaign, who built the best political campaign, I think, in the history of the United States of America.

To my chief strategist David Axelrod who's been a partner with me every step of the way.

To the best campaign team ever assembled in the history of

politics, you made this happen, and I am forever grateful for what you've sacrificed to get it done.

But above all, I will never forget who this victory truly belongs to. It belongs to you. It belongs to you.

I was never the likeliest candidate for this office. We didn't start with much money or many endorsements. Our campaign was not hatched in the halls of Washington. It began in the backyards of Des Moines and the living rooms of Concord and the front porches of Charleston. It was built by working men and women who dug into what little savings they had to give five dollars and ten dollars and twenty dollars to the cause.

It grew strength from the young people who rejected the myth of their generation's apathy, who left their homes and their families for jobs that offered little pay and less sleep.

It drew strength from the not-so-young people who braved the bitter cold and scorching heat to knock on doors of perfect strangers, and from the millions of Americans who volunteered and organized and proved that more than two centuries later a government of the people, by the people, and for the people has not perished from the Earth.

This is your victory.

And I know you didn't do this just to win an election. And I know you didn't do it for me.

You did it because you understand the enormity of the task that lies ahead. For even as we celebrate tonight, we know the challenges that tomorrow will bring are the greatest of our lifetime—two wars, a planet in peril, the worst financial crisis in a century.

Even as we stand here tonight, we know there are brave

Americans waking up in the deserts of Iraq and the mountains of Afghanistan to risk their lives for us.

There are mothers and fathers who will lie awake after the children fall asleep and wonder how they'll make the mortgage or pay their doctors' bills or save enough for their child's college education.

There's new energy to harness, new jobs to be created, new schools to build, and threats to meet, alliances to repair.

The road ahead will be long. Our climb will be steep. We may not get there in one year or even in one term. But, America, I have never been more hopeful than I am tonight that we will get there.

I promise you, we as a people will get there.

There will be setbacks and false starts. There are many who won't agree with every decision or policy I make as president. And we know the government can't solve every problem.

But I will always be honest with you about the challenges we face. I will listen to you, especially when we disagree. And, above all, I will ask you to join in the work of remaking this nation, the only way it's been done in America for 221 years— block by block, brick by brick, calloused hand by calloused hand.

What began 21 months ago in the depths of winter cannot end on this autumn night.

This victory alone is not the change we seek. It is only the chance for us to make that change. And that cannot happen if we go back to the way things were.

It can't happen without you, without a new spirit of service, a new spirit of sacrifice.

So let us summon a new spirit of patriotism, of responsibility, where each of us resolves to pitch in and work harder and look after not only ourselves but each other.

Let us remember that, if this financial crisis taught us anything, it's that we cannot have a thriving Wall Street while Main Street suffers.

In this country, we rise or fall as one nation, as one people. Let's resist the temptation to fall back on the same partisanship and pettiness and immaturity that has poisoned our politics for so long.

Let's remember that it was a man from this state who first carried the banner of the Republican Party to the White House, a party founded on the values of self-reliance and individual liberty and national unity.

Those are values that we all share. And while the Democratic Party has won a great victory tonight, we do so with a measure of humility and determination to heal the divides that have held back our progress.

As Lincoln said to a nation far more divided than ours, we are not enemies but friends. Though passion may have strained, it must not break our bonds of affection.

And to those Americans whose support I have yet to earn, I may not have won your vote tonight, but I hear your voices. I need your help. And I will be your president, too.

And to all those watching tonight from beyond our shores, from parliaments and palaces, to those who are huddled around radios in the forgotten corners of the world, our stories are singular, but our destiny is shared, and a new dawn of American leadership is at hand.

To those who would tear the world down: We will defeat you. To those who seek peace and security: We support you. And to all those who have wondered if America's beacon still burns as bright: Tonight we proved once more that the true strength of our nation comes not from the might of our arms or the scale of our wealth, but from the enduring power of our ideals: democracy, liberty, opportunity, and unyielding hope.

That's the true genius of America: that America can change. Our union can be perfected. What we've already achieved gives us hope for what we can and must achieve tomorrow.

This election had many firsts and many stories that will be told for generations. But one that's on my mind tonight's about a woman who cast her ballot in Atlanta. She's a lot like the millions of others who stood in line to make their voice heard in this election except for one thing: Ann Nixon Cooper is 106 years old.

She was born just a generation past slavery; a time when there were no cars on the road or planes in the sky; when someone like her couldn't vote for two reasons—because she was a woman and because of the color of her skin.

And tonight, I think about all that she's seen throughout her century in America—the heartache and the hope; the struggle and the progress; the times we were told that we can't, and the people who pressed on with that American creed: Yes, we can.

At a time when women's voices were silenced and their hopes dismissed, she lived to see them stand up and speak out and reach for the ballot. Yes, we can.

When there was despair in the dust bowl and depression across the land, she saw a nation conquer fear itself with a New Deal, new jobs, a new sense of common purpose. Yes, we can.

When the bombs fell on our harbor and tyranny threatened the world, she was there to witness a generation rise to greatness and a democracy was saved. Yes, we can.

She was there for the buses in Montgomery, the hoses in Birmingham, a bridge in Selma, and a preacher from Atlanta who told a people that "we shall overcome." Yes, we can.

A man touched down on the moon, a wall came down in Berlin, a world was connected by our own science and imagination.

And this year, in this election, she touched her finger to a screen, and cast her vote, because after 106 years in America, through the best of times and the darkest of hours, she knows how America can change.

Yes, we can.

America, we have come so far. We have seen so much. But there is so much more to do. So tonight, let us ask ourselves—if our children should live to see the next century; if my daughters should be so lucky to live as long as Ann Nixon Cooper, what change will they see? What progress will we have made?

This is our chance to answer that call. This is our moment.

This is our time, to put our people back to work and open doors of opportunity for our kids; to restore prosperity and promote the cause of peace; to reclaim the American dream and reaffirm that fundamental truth, that, out of many, we are one; that while we breathe, we hope. And where we are met with cynicism and doubts and those who tell us that we can't, we will respond with that timeless creed that sums up the spirit of a people: Yes, we can.

Thank you. God bless you. And may God bless the United States of America.

"A NEW ERA OF RESPONSIBILITY"

First Inaugural Address

WASHINGTON, D.C., JANUARY 20, 2009

*January 20, 2009, had the makings of a historic day.
Although Obama had clinched the election more than
two months earlier, it was not until that freezing
Wednesday afternoon in January that he formally
became the forty-fourth president of the United
States. The inauguration of the first African
American president in a city that had been largely
built by black slaves and had been racially segregated
for decades suggested that hope remained for racial
reconciliation and national unity. Some 1.6 million
people packed the National Mall to catch a glimpse of
the new president. Obama's twenty-minute address
was inspired by the oratory of Lincoln and Kennedy.
He adopted a conciliatory, nonpartisan tone—one
that contrasted sharply with some of his more aggressive rhetoric during the campaign—and focused
primarily on the two pressing issues of the moment:
the sputtering economy and national security. Critics
saw the speech as less inspiring than his victory speech
and argued he did less than he could have to prepare*

the country for the long period of economic stagnation it faced. But it did reflect classic Obama themes, notably in its call on citizens to take responsibility for the nation's revival.

MY FELLOW CITIZENS: I stand here today humbled by the task before us, grateful for the trust you've bestowed, mindful of the sacrifices borne by our ancestors.

I thank President Bush for his service to our nation—as well as the generosity and cooperation he has shown throughout this transition.

Forty-four Americans have now taken the presidential oath. The words have been spoken during rising tides of prosperity and the still waters of peace. Yet, every so often, the oath is taken amidst gathering clouds and raging storms. At these moments, America has carried on not simply because of the skill or vision of those in high office, but because we, the people, have remained faithful to the ideals of our forebears and true to our founding documents.

So it has been; so it must be with this generation of Americans.

That we are in the midst of crisis is now well understood. Our nation is at war against a far-reaching network of violence and hatred. Our economy is badly weakened, a consequence of greed and irresponsibility on the part of some, but also our collective failure to make hard choices and prepare the nation for a new age. Homes have been lost, jobs shed, businesses shuttered. Our health care is too costly, our schools fail too many—and each day brings further evidence that the ways we use energy strengthen our adversaries and threaten our planet.

These are the indicators of crisis, subject to data and statistics. Less measurable, but no less profound, is a sapping of confidence across our land; a nagging fear that America's decline is inevitable, that the next generation must lower its sights.

Today I say to you that the challenges we face are real. They are serious and they are many. They will not be met easily or in a short span of time. But know this America: They will be met.

On this day, we gather because we have chosen hope over fear, unity of purpose over conflict and discord. On this day, we come to proclaim an end to the petty grievances and false promises, the recriminations and worn-out dogmas that for far too long have strangled our politics. We remain a young nation. But in the words of Scripture, the time has come to set aside childish things. The time has come to reaffirm our enduring spirit; to choose our better history; to carry forward that precious gift, that noble idea passed on from generation to generation: the God-given promise that all are equal, all are free, and all deserve a chance to pursue their full measure of happiness.

In reaffirming the greatness of our nation we understand that greatness is never a given. It must be earned. Our journey has never been one of short-cuts or settling for less. It has not been the path for the faint-hearted, for those that prefer leisure over work, or seek only the pleasures of riches and fame. Rather, it has been the risk-takers, the doers, the makers of things—some celebrated, but more often men and women obscure in their labor—who have carried us up the long rugged path towards prosperity and freedom.

For us, they packed up their few worldly possessions and traveled across oceans in search of a new life. For us, they toiled in sweatshops, and settled the West, endured the lash of the whip, and plowed the hard earth. For us, they fought and died in places like Concord and Gettysburg, Normandy and Khe Sahn.

Time and again these men and women struggled and sacrificed and worked till their hands were raw so that we might live a better life. They saw America as bigger than the sum of our individual ambitions, greater than all the differences of birth or wealth or faction.

This is the journey we continue today. We remain the most prosperous, powerful nation on Earth. Our workers are no less productive than when this crisis began. Our minds are no less inventive, our goods and services no less needed than they were last week, or last month, or last year. Our capacity remains undiminished. But our time of standing pat, of protecting narrow interests and putting off unpleasant decisions—that time has surely passed. Starting today, we must pick ourselves up, dust ourselves off, and begin again the work of remaking America.

For everywhere we look, there is work to be done. The state of our economy calls for action, bold and swift. And we will act, not only to create new jobs, but to lay a new foundation for growth. We will build the roads and bridges, the electric grids and digital lines that feed our commerce and bind us together. We'll restore science to its rightful place, and wield technology's wonders to raise health care's quality and lower its cost.

We will harness the sun and the winds and the soil to fuel our cars and run our factories. And we will transform our schools and colleges and universities to meet the demands of a new age. All this we can do. All this we will do.

Now, there are some who question the scale of our ambitions, who suggest that our system cannot tolerate too many big plans. Their memories are short, for they have forgotten what this country has already done, what free men and women can achieve when imagination is joined to common purpose, and necessity to courage. What the cynics fail to understand is that the ground has shifted beneath them, that the stale political arguments that have consumed us for so long no longer apply.

The question we ask today is not whether our government is too big or too small, but whether it works—whether it helps families find jobs at a decent wage, care they can afford, a retirement that is dignified. Where the answer is yes, we intend to move forward. Where the answer is no, programs will end. And those of us who manage the public's dollars will be held to account, to spend wisely, reform bad habits, and do our business in the light of day, because only then can we restore the vital trust between a people and their government.

Nor is the question before us whether the market is a force for good or ill. Its power to generate wealth and expand freedom is unmatched. But this crisis has reminded us that without a watchful eye, the market can spin out of control. The nation cannot prosper long when it favors only the prosperous. The success of our economy has always depended not just on the size of our gross domestic product, but on the reach of our prosperity, on the ability to extend opportunity to every willing heart—not out of charity, but because it is the surest route to our common good.

As for our common defense, we reject as false the choice between our safety and our ideals. Our Founding Fathers, faced with perils that we can scarcely imagine, drafted a charter to assure the rule of law and the rights of man— a charter expanded by the blood of generations. Those ideals still light the world, and we will not give them up for expedience sake.

And so, to all the other peoples and governments who are watching today, from the grandest capitals to the small village where my father was born, know that America is a friend of each nation, and every man, woman, and child who seeks a future of peace and dignity. And we are ready to lead once more.

Recall that earlier generations faced down fascism and communism not just with missiles and tanks, but with the sturdy alliances and enduring convictions. They understood that our power alone cannot protect us, nor does it entitle us to do as we please. Instead they knew that our power grows through its prudent use; our security emanates from the justness of our cause, the force of our example, the tempering qualities of humility and restraint.

We are the keepers of this legacy. Guided by these principles once more we can meet those new threats that demand even greater effort, even greater cooperation and understanding between nations. We will begin to responsibly leave Iraq to its people and forge a hard-earned peace in Afghanistan. With old friends and former foes, we'll work tirelessly to lessen the nuclear threat, and roll back the specter of a warming planet.

We will not apologize for our way of life, nor will we waver in its defense. And for those who seek to advance their aims by inducing terror and slaughtering innocents, we say to you now that our spirit is stronger and cannot be broken—you cannot outlast us, and we will defeat you.

For we know that our patchwork heritage is a strength, not a weakness. We are a nation of Christians and Muslims, Jews and Hindus, and non-believers. We are shaped by every language and culture, drawn from every end of this Earth; and because we have tasted the bitter swill of civil war and segregation, and emerged from that dark chapter stronger and more united, we cannot help but believe that the old hatreds shall someday pass; that the lines of tribe shall soon dissolve; that as the world grows smaller, our common humanity shall reveal itself; and that America must play its role in ushering in a new era of peace.

To the Muslim world, we seek a new way forward, based on mutual interest and mutual respect. To those leaders around the globe who seek to sow conflict, or blame their society's ills on the West, know that your people will judge you on what you can build, not what you destroy.

To those who cling to power through corruption and deceit and the silencing of dissent, know that you are on the wrong side of history, but that we will extend a hand if you are willing to unclench your fist.

To the people of poor nations, we pledge to work alongside you to make your farms flourish and let clean waters flow; to nourish starved bodies and feed hungry minds. And to those nations like ours that enjoy relative plenty, we say we can no longer afford indifference to the suffering outside our borders, nor can we consume the world's resources without regard to effect. For the world has changed, and we must change with it.

As we consider the role that unfolds before us, we remember with humble gratitude those brave Americans who at this very hour patrol far-off deserts and distant mountains. They have something to tell us, just as the fallen heroes who lie in Arlington whisper through the ages.

We honor them not only because they are the guardians of our liberty, but because they embody the spirit of service— a willingness to find meaning in something greater than themselves.

And yet at this moment, a moment that will define a generation, it is precisely this spirit that must inhabit us all. For as much as government can do, and must do, it is ultimately the faith and determination of the American people upon which this nation relies. It is the kindness to take in a stranger when the levees break, the selflessness of workers who would rather cut their hours than see a friend lose their job which sees us through our darkest hours. It is the firefighter's courage to storm a stairway filled with smoke, but also a parent's willingness to nurture a child that finally decides our fate.

Our challenges may be new. The instruments with which we meet them may be new. But those values upon which our success depends—honesty and hard work, courage and fair play, tolerance and curiosity, loyalty and patriotism—these things are old. These things are true. They have been the quiet force of progress throughout our history.

What is demanded, then, is a return to these truths. What is required of us now is a new era of responsibility—a recognition on the part of every American that we have duties to ourselves, our nation and the world; duties that we do not grudgingly accept, but rather seize gladly, firm in the knowledge that there is nothing so satisfying to the spirit, so defining of our character than giving our all to a difficult task.

This is the price and the promise of citizenship. This is the source of our confidence—the knowledge that God calls on us to shape an uncertain destiny. This is the meaning of our liberty and our creed, why men and women and children of every race and every faith can join in celebration across this magnificent mall; and why a man whose father less than sixty years ago might not have been served in a local restaurant can now stand before you to take a most sacred oath.

So let us mark this day with remembrance of who we are and how far we have traveled. In the year of America's birth, in the coldest of months, a small band of patriots huddled by dying campfires on the shores of an icy river. The capital was abandoned. The enemy was advancing. The snow was stained with blood. At the moment when the outcome of our revolution was most in doubt, the father of our nation ordered these words to be read to the people:

"Let it be told to the future world, that in the depth of winter, when nothing but hope and virtue could survive, that the city and the country, alarmed at one common danger, came forth to meet [it]."

America: In the face of our common dangers, in this winter of our hardship, let us remember these timeless words. With hope and virtue, let us brave once more the icy currents, and endure what storms may come. Let it be said by our children's children that when we were tested we refused to let this journey end, that we did not turn back nor did we falter; and with eyes fixed on the horizon and God's grace upon us, we carried forth that great gift of freedom and delivered it safely to future generations.

Thank you. God bless you. And God bless the United States of America.

"OPEN HEARTS. OPEN MINDS. FAIR-MINDED WORDS."

Remarks at Notre Dame Commencement

SOUTH BEND, INDIANA, MAY 17, 2009

When the University of Notre Dame invited President Obama to deliver the commencement address and receive an honorary degree in law in 2009, the university faced an angry storm of criticism from conservative Catholics, including some of the Church's leading prelates. Although he won a comfortable 54 percent of the Catholic vote in 2008, Obama had campaigned as pro-choice and was supportive of embryonic stem cell research. During his speech, Obama chose not to ignore the elephant in the room (or the protestors outside), instead tackling the issue of abortion head-on. He talked about the importance of recognizing the common humanity shared by people on both sides of the debate, and encouraged the graduates to approach difficult conversations with "open hearts," "open minds," and "fair-minded words." He also spoke of his own indebtedness to the Catholic social tradition, his deep respect for the late Chicago Archbishop, Cardinal Joseph Bernardin, and the fact

that his first work as a community organizer was
sponsored by the Church.

WELL, FIRST OF all, congratulations, Class of 2009. Congratulations to all the parents, the cousins, the aunts, the uncles—all the people who helped to bring you to the point that you are here today. Thank you so much to Father Jenkins for that extraordinary introduction, even though you said what I want to say much more elegantly. You are doing an extraordinary job as president of this extraordinary institution. Your continued and courageous—and contagious—commitment to honest, thoughtful dialogue is an inspiration to us all.

Good afternoon. To Father Hesburgh, to Notre Dame trustees, to faculty, to family: I am honored to be here today. And I am grateful to all of you for allowing me to be a part of your graduation.

And I also want to thank you for the honorary degree that I received. I know it has not been without controversy. I don't know if you're aware of this, but these honorary degrees are apparently pretty hard to come by. So far I'm only one for two as president. Father Hesburgh is 150 for 150. I guess that's better. So, Father Ted, after the ceremony, maybe you can give me some pointers to boost my average.

I also want to congratulate the Class of 2009 for all your accomplishments. And since this is Notre Dame—

AUDIENCE MEMBER: Abortion is murder! Stop killing children!

AUDIENCE: Booo!

PRESIDENT: That's all right. And since—

AUDIENCE: We are ND! We are ND!

AUDIENCE: Yes, we can! Yes, we can!

PRESIDENT: We're fine, everybody. We're following Brennan's adage that we don't do things easily. We're not going to shy away from things that are uncomfortable sometimes.

Now, since this is Notre Dame I think we should talk not only about your accomplishments in the classroom, but also in the competitive arena. No, don't worry, I'm not going to talk about that. We all know about this university's proud and storied football team, but I also hear that Notre Dame holds the largest outdoor five-on-five basketball tournament in the world—Bookstore Basketball.

Now this excites me. I want to congratulate the winners of this year's tournament, a team by the name of Hallelujah Holla Back. Congratulations. Well done. Though I have to say, I am personally disappointed that the Barack O'Ballers did not pull it out this year. So next year, if you need a 6´2˝ forward with a decent jumper, you know where I live.

Every one of you should be proud of what you have achieved at this institution. One hundred and sixty-three classes of Notre Dame graduates have sat where you sit today. Some were here during years that simply rolled into the next without much notice or fanfare—periods of relative peace and prosperity that required little by way of sacrifice or struggle.

You, however, are not getting off that easy. You have a different deal. Your class has come of age at a moment of great consequence for our nation and for the world—a rare inflection point in history where the size and scope of the challenges before us require that we remake our world to renew its promise; that we align our deepest values and commitments to the demands of a new age. It's a privilege and a responsibility afforded to few generations—and a task that you're now called to fulfill.

This generation, your generation is the one that must find a path back to prosperity and decide how we respond to a global economy that left millions behind even before the most recent crisis hit—an economy where greed and short-term thinking were too often rewarded at the expense of fairness, and diligence, and an honest day's work.

Your generation must decide how to save God's creation from a changing climate that threatens to destroy it. Your generation must seek peace at a time when there are those who will stop at nothing to do us harm, and when weapons in the hands of a few can destroy the many. And we must find a way to reconcile our ever-shrinking world with its ever-growing diversity—diversity of thought, diversity of culture, and diversity of belief.

In short, we must find a way to live together as one human family.

And it's this last challenge that I'd like to talk about today, despite the fact that Father John stole all my best lines. For the major threats we face in the twenty-first century—whether it's global recession or violent extremism; the spread of nuclear weapons or pandemic disease—these things do not discriminate. They do not recognize borders. They do not see color. They do not target specific ethnic groups.

Moreover, no one person, or religion, or nation can meet these challenges alone. Our very survival has never required greater cooperation and greater understanding among all people from all places than at this moment in history.

Unfortunately, finding that common ground—recognizing that our fates are tied up, as Dr. King said, in a "single garment of destiny"—is not easy. And part of the problem, of course, lies in the imperfections of man—our selfishness, our pride, our stubbornness, our acquisitiveness, our insecurities, our egos; all the cruelties large and small that those of us in the Christian tradition understand to be rooted in original sin. We too often seek advantage over others. We cling to outworn prejudice and fear those who are unfamiliar. Too many of us view life only through the lens of immediate self-interest and crass materialism; in which the world is necessarily a zero-sum game. The strong too often dominate the weak, and too many of those with wealth and with power find all manner of justification for their own privilege in the face of poverty and injustice. And so, for all our technology and scientific advances, we see here in this country and around the globe violence and want and strife that would seem sadly familiar to those in ancient times.

We know these things; and hopefully one of the benefits of the wonderful education that you've received here at Notre Dame is that you've had time to consider these wrongs in the world; perhaps recognized impulses in yourself that you want to leave behind. You've grown determined, each in your own way, to right them. And yet, one of the vexing things for those of us interested in promoting greater understanding and cooperation among people is the discovery that even bringing together persons of good will, bringing together men and women of principle and purpose—even accomplishing that can be difficult.

The soldier and the lawyer may both love this country with

equal passion, and yet reach very different conclusions on the specific steps needed to protect us from harm. The gay activist and the evangelical pastor may both deplore the ravages of HIV/AIDS, but find themselves unable to bridge the cultural divide that might unite their efforts. Those who speak out against stem cell research may be rooted in an admirable conviction about the sacredness of life, but so are the parents of a child with juvenile diabetes who are convinced that their son's or daughter's hardships can be relieved.

The question, then, is how do we work through these conflicts? Is it possible for us to join hands in common effort? As citizens of a vibrant and varied democracy, how do we engage in vigorous debate? How does each of us remain firm in our principles, and fight for what we consider right, without, as Father John said, demonetizing those with just as strongly held convictions on the other side?

And of course, nowhere do these questions come up more powerfully than on the issue of abortion.

As I considered the controversy surrounding my visit here, I was reminded of an encounter I had during my Senate campaign, one that I describe in a book I wrote called *The Audacity of Hope*. A few days after I won the Democratic nomination, I received an e-mail from a doctor who told me that while he voted for me in the Illinois primary, he had a serious concern that might prevent him from voting for me in the general election. He described himself as a Christian who was strongly pro-life—but that was not what was preventing him potentially from voting for me.

What bothered the doctor was an entry that my campaign staff had posted on my website—an entry that said I would fight "right-wing ideologues who want to take away a woman's right to choose." The doctor said he had assumed I was a reasonable person, he supported my policy initiatives to help the poor and to lift up our educational system, but that if I truly believed that every pro-life individual was simply an ideologue who wanted to inflict suffering on women, then I was not very reasonable. He wrote, "I do not ask at this point that you oppose abortion, only that you speak about this issue in fair-minded words." Fair-minded words.

After I read the doctor's letter, I wrote back to him and I thanked him. And I didn't change my underlying position, but I did tell my staff to change the words on my website. And I said a prayer that night that I might extend the same presumption of good faith to others that the doctor had extended to me. Because when we do that—when we open up our hearts and our minds to those who may not think precisely like we do or believe precisely what we believe— that's when we discover at least the possibility of common ground.

That's when we begin to say, "Maybe we won't agree on abortion, but we can still agree that this heart-wrenching deci-sion for any woman is not made casually, it has both moral and spiritual dimensions."

So let us work together to reduce the number of women seeking abortions, let's reduce unintended pregnancies. Let's make adoption more available. Let's provide care and support for women who do carry their children to term. Let's honor the conscience of those who disagree with abortion, and draft a sensible conscience clause, and make sure that all of our health care policies are grounded not only in sound science, but also in clear ethics, as well as respect for the equality of women. Those are things we can do.

Now, understand, Class of 2009, I do not suggest that the debate surrounding abortion can or should go away. Because no matter how much we may want to fudge it—indeed, while we know that the views of most Americans on the subject are complex and even contradictory—the fact is that at some level, the views of the two camps are irreconcilable. Each side will continue to make its case to the public with passion and conviction. But surely we can do so without reducing those with differing views to caricature.

Open hearts. Open minds. Fair-minded words. It's a way of life that has always been the Notre Dame tradition. Father Hesburgh has long spoken of this institution as both a lighthouse and a crossroads. A lighthouse that stands apart, shining with the wisdom of the Catholic tradition, while the crossroads is where "differences of culture and religion and conviction can co-exist with friendship, civility, hospitality, and especially love." And I want to join him and Father John in saying how inspired I am by the maturity and responsibility with which this class has approached the debate surrounding today's ceremony. You are an example of what Notre Dame is about.

This tradition of cooperation and understanding is one that I learned in my own life many years ago—also with the help of the Catholic Church.

You see, I was not raised in a particularly religious household, but my mother instilled in me a sense of service and empathy that eventually led me to become a community organizer after I graduated college. And a group of Catholic churches in Chicago helped fund an organization known as the

Developing Communities Project, and we worked to lift up South Side neighborhoods that had been devastated when the local steel plant closed.

And it was quite an eclectic crew—Catholic and Protestant churches, Jewish and African American organizers, working-class black, white, and Hispanic residents—all of us with different experiences, all of us with different beliefs. But all of us learned to work side by side because all of us saw in these neighborhoods other human beings who needed our help—to find jobs and improve schools. We were bound together in the service of others.

And something else happened during the time I spent in these neighborhoods—perhaps because the church folks I worked with were so welcoming and understanding; perhaps because they invited me to their services and sang with me from their hymnals; perhaps because I was really broke and they fed me. Perhaps because I witnessed all of the good works their faith inspired them to perform, I found myself drawn not just to the work with the church; I was drawn to be in the church. It was through this service that I was brought to Christ.

And at the time, Cardinal Joseph Bernardin was the Archbishop of Chicago. For those of you too young to have known him or known of him, he was a kind and good and wise man. A saintly man. I can still remember him speaking at one of the first organizing meetings I attended on the South Side. He stood as both a lighthouse and a crossroads—unafraid to speak his mind on moral issues ranging from poverty and AIDS and abortion to the death penalty and nuclear war. And yet, he was congenial and gentle in his persuasion, always trying to bring people together, always trying to find common ground. Just before he died, a reporter asked Cardinal Bernardin about this approach to his ministry. And he said, "You can't really get on with preaching the Gospel until you've touched hearts and minds."

My heart and mind were touched by him. They were touched by the words and deeds of the men and women I worked alongside in parishes across Chicago. And I'd like to think that we touched the hearts and minds of the neighborhood families whose lives we helped change. For this, I believe, is our highest calling.

Now, you, Class of 2009, are about to enter the next phase of your life at a time of great uncertainty. You'll be called to help restore a free market that's also fair to all who are willing to work. You'll be called to seek new sources of energy that can save our planet; to give future generations the same chance that you had to receive an extraordinary education. And whether as a person drawn to public service, or simply someone who insists on being an active citizen, you will be exposed to more opinions and ideas broadcast through more means of communication than ever existed before. You'll hear talking heads scream on cable, and you'll read blogs that claim definitive knowledge, and you will watch politicians pretend they know what they're talking about. Occasionally, you may have the great fortune of actually seeing important issues debated by people who do know what they're talking about—by well-intentioned people with brilliant minds and mastery of the facts. In fact, I suspect that some of you will be among those brightest stars.

And in this world of competing claims about what is right

and what is true, have confidence in the values with which you've been raised and educated. Be unafraid to speak your mind when those values are at stake. Hold firm to your faith and allow it to guide you on your journey. In other words, stand as a lighthouse.

But remember, too, that you can be a crossroads. Remember, too, that the ultimate irony of faith is that it necessarily admits doubt. It's the belief in things not seen. It's beyond our capacity as human beings to know with certainty what God has planned for us or what He asks of us. And those of us who believe must trust that His wisdom is greater than our own.

And this doubt should not push away our faith. But it should humble us. It should temper our passions, cause us to be wary of too much self-righteousness. It should compel us to remain open and curious and eager to continue the spiritual and moral debate that began for so many of you within the walls of Notre Dame. And within our vast democracy, this doubt should remind us even as we cling to our faith to persuade through reason, through an appeal whenever we can to universal rather than parochial principles, and most of all through an abiding example of good works and charity and kindness and service that moves hearts and minds.

For if there is one law that we can be most certain of, it is the law that binds people of all faiths and no faith together. It's no coincidence that it exists in Christianity and Judaism; in Islam and Hinduism; in Buddhism and humanism. It is, of course, the Golden Rule—the call to treat one another as we wish to be treated. The call to love. The call to serve. To do what we can to make a difference in the lives of those with whom we share the same brief moment on this Earth.

So many of you at Notre Dame—by the last count, upwards of 80 percent—have lived this law of love through the service you've performed at schools and hospitals; international relief agencies and local charities. Brennan is just one example of what your class has accomplished. That's incredibly impressive, a powerful testament to this institution.

Now you must carry the tradition forward. Make it a way of life. Because when you serve, it doesn't just improve your community, it makes you a part of your community. It breaks down walls. It fosters cooperation. And when that happens—when people set aside their differences, even for a moment, to work in common effort toward a common goal; when they struggle together, and sacrifice together, and learn from one another—then all things are possible.

After all, I stand here today, as president and as an African American, on the fifty-fifth anniversary of the day that the Supreme Court handed down the decision in *Brown v. Board of Education*. Now, Brown was of course the first major step in dismantling the "separate but equal" doctrine, but it would take a number of years and a nationwide movement to fully realize the dream of civil rights for all of God's children. There were freedom rides and lunch counters and Billy clubs, and there was also a Civil Rights Commission appointed by President Eisenhower. It was the twelve resolutions recommended by this commission that would ultimately become law in the Civil Rights Act of 1964.

There were six members of this commission. It included five whites and one African American; Democrats and Republicans;

two Southern governors, the dean of a Southern law school, a Midwestern university president, and your own Father Ted Hesburgh, president of Notre Dame. So they worked for two years, and at times, President Eisenhower had to intervene personally since no hotel or restaurant in the South would serve the black and white members of the commission together. And finally, when they reached an impasse in Louisiana, Father Ted flew them all to Notre Dame's retreat in Land O'Lakes, Wisconsin—where they eventually overcame their differences and hammered out a final deal.

And years later, President Eisenhower asked Father Ted how on Earth he was able to broker an agreement between men of such different backgrounds and beliefs. And Father Ted simply said that during their first dinner in Wisconsin, they discovered they were all fishermen. And so he quickly readied a boat for a twilight trip out on the lake. They fished, and they talked, and they changed the course of history.

I will not pretend that the challenges we face will be easy, or that the answers will come quickly, or that all our differences and divisions will fade happily away—because life is not that simple. It never has been.

But as you leave here today, remember the lessons of Cardinal Bernardin, of Father Hesburgh, of movements for change both large and small. Remember that each of us, endowed with the dignity possessed by all children of God, has the grace to recognize ourselves in one another; to understand that we all seek the same love of family, the same fulfillment of a life well lived. Remember that in the end, in some way we are all fishermen.

If nothing else, that knowledge should give us faith that

through our collective labor, and God's providence, and our willingness to shoulder each other's burdens, America will continue on its precious journey towards that more perfect union. Congratulations, Class of 2009. May God bless you, and may God bless the United States of America.

"A NEW BEGINNING"

Remarks at Cairo University

CAIRO, EGYPT, JUNE 4, 2009

In the midst of a national fight over healthcare in the summer of 2009, President Obama flew to Cairo, Egypt, to deliver a speech challenging the Muslim world to accept the "outstretched hand" of his America. He spoke blunt truths about America's past treatment of Middle Eastern countries, and about the need for reform within Arab and Muslim societies. And he spoke of his father's Muslim faith for the first time in an extended fashion, further stoking the ire of his most vociferous and suspicious critics back home. The results of Obama's outreach to the Muslim world have been uneven, upended by the Arab Spring, which some analysts believe was given fuel by the warm words delivered in Cairo by this new, and very different, American president.

I AM HONORED TO be in the timeless city of Cairo, and to be hosted by two remarkable institutions. For over a thousand years, Al-Azhar has stood as a beacon of Islamic learning;

and for over a century, Cairo University has been a source of Egypt's advancement. And together, you represent the harmony between tradition and progress. I'm grateful for your hospitality, and the hospitality of the people of Egypt. And I'm also proud to carry with me the goodwill of the American people, and a greeting of peace from Muslim communities in my country: *Assalaamu alaykum.*

We meet at a time of great tension between the United States and Muslims around the world—tension rooted in historical forces that go beyond any current policy debate. The relationship between Islam and the West includes centuries of coexistence and cooperation, but also conflict and religious wars. More recently, tension has been fed by colonialism that denied rights and opportunities to many Muslims, and a Cold War in which Muslim-majority countries were too often treated as proxies without regard to their own aspirations. Moreover, the sweeping change brought by modernity and globalization led many Muslims to view the West as hostile to the traditions of Islam.

Violent extremists have exploited these tensions in a small but potent minority of Muslims. The attacks of September 11, 2001, and the continued efforts of these extremists to engage in violence against civilians has led some in my country to view Islam as inevitably hostile not only to America and Western countries, but also to human rights. All this has bred more fear and more mistrust.

So long as our relationship is defined by our differences, we will empower those who sow hatred rather than peace, those who promote conflict rather than the cooperation that can help all of our people achieve justice and prosperity. And this cycle of suspicion and discord must end.

I've come here to Cairo to seek a new beginning between the United States and Muslims around the world, one based on mutual interest and mutual respect, and one based upon the truth that America and Islam are not exclusive and need not be in competition. Instead, they overlap, and share common principles—principles of justice and progress; tolerance and the dignity of all human beings.

I do so recognizing that change cannot happen overnight. I know there's been a lot of publicity about this speech, but no single speech can eradicate years of mistrust, nor can I answer in the time that I have this afternoon all the complex questions that brought us to this point. But I am convinced that in order to move forward, we must say openly to each other the things we hold in our hearts and that too often are said only behind closed doors. There must be a sustained effort to listen to each other; to learn from each other; to respect one another; and to seek common ground. As the Holy Koran tells us, "Be conscious of God and speak always the truth." That is what I will try to do today—to speak the truth as best I can, humbled by the task before us, and firm in my belief that the interests we share as human beings are far more powerful than the forces that drive us apart.

Now part of this conviction is rooted in my own experience. I'm a Christian, but my father came from a Kenyan family that includes generations of Muslims. As a boy, I spent several years in Indonesia and heard the call of the *azaan* at the break of dawn and at the fall of dusk. As a young man, I worked in Chicago communities where many found dignity and peace in their Muslim faith.

As a student of history, I also know civilization's debt to

Islam. It was Islam—at places like Al-Azhar—that carried the light of learning through so many centuries, paving the way for Europe's Renaissance and Enlightenment. It was innovation in Muslim communities that developed the order of algebra; our magnetic compass and tools of navigation; our mastery of pens and printing; our understanding of how disease spreads and how it can be healed. Islamic culture has given us majestic arches and soaring spires; timeless poetry and cherished music; elegant calligraphy and places of peaceful contemplation. And throughout history, Islam has demonstrated through words and deeds the possibilities of religious tolerance and racial equality.

I also know that Islam has always been a part of America's story. The first nation to recognize my country was Morocco. In signing the Treaty of Tripoli in 1796, our second president, John Adams, wrote, "The United States has in itself no character of enmity against the laws, religion or tranquility of Muslims." And since our founding, American Muslims have enriched the United States. They have fought in our wars, they have served in our government, they have stood for civil rights, they have started businesses, they have taught at our universities, they've excelled in our sports arenas, they've won Nobel Prizes, built our tallest building, and lit the Olympic Torch. And when the first Muslim American was recently elected to Congress, he took the oath to defend our Constitution using the same Holy Koran that one of our Founding Fathers—Thomas Jefferson—kept in his personal library.

So I have known Islam on three continents before coming to the region where it was first revealed. That experience guides my conviction that partnership between America and Islam must be based on what Islam is, not what it isn't. And I consider it part of my responsibility as president of the United States to fight against negative stereotypes of Islam wherever they appear.

But that same principle must apply to Muslim perceptions of America. Just as Muslims do not fit a crude stereotype, America is not the crude stereotype of a self-interested empire. The United States has been one of the greatest sources of progress that the world has ever known. We were born out of revolution against an empire. We were founded upon the ideal that all are created equal, and we have shed blood and struggled for centuries to give meaning to those words—within our borders, and around the world. We are shaped by every culture, drawn from every end of the Earth, and dedicated to a simple concept: *E pluribus unum*—"Out of many, one."

Now, much has been made of the fact that an African American with the name Barack Hussein Obama could be elected president. But my personal story is not so unique. The dream of opportunity for all people has not come true for everyone in America, but its promise exists for all who come to our shores—and that includes nearly seven million American Muslims in our country today who, by the way, enjoy incomes and educational levels that are higher than the American average.

Moreover, freedom in America is indivisible from the freedom to practice one's religion. That is why there is a mosque in every state in our union, and over 1,200 mosques within our borders. That's why the United States government has gone to court to protect the right of women and girls to wear the hijab and to punish those who would deny it.

So let there be no doubt: Islam is a part of America. And I believe that America holds within her the truth that regardless of race, religion, or station in life, all of us share common aspirations—to live in peace and security; to get an education and to work with dignity; to love our families, our communities, and our God. These things we share. This is the hope of all humanity.

Of course, recognizing our common humanity is only the beginning of our task. Words alone cannot meet the needs of our people. These needs will be met only if we act boldly in the years ahead; and if we understand that the challenges we face are shared, and our failure to meet them will hurt us all.

For we have learned from recent experience that when a financial system weakens in one country, prosperity is hurt everywhere. When a new flu infects one human being, all are at risk. When one nation pursues a nuclear weapon, the risk of nuclear attack rises for all nations. When violent extremists operate in one stretch of mountains, people are endangered across an ocean. When innocents in Bosnia and Darfur are slaughtered, that is a stain on our collective conscience. That is what it means to share this world in the twenty-first century. That is the responsibility we have to one another as human beings.

And this is a difficult responsibility to embrace. For human history has often been a record of nations and tribes—and, yes, religions—subjugating one another in pursuit of their own interests. Yet in this new age, such attitudes are self-defeating. Given our interdependence, any world order that elevates one nation or group of people over another will inevitably fail. So whatever we think of the past, we must not be prisoners to it.

Our problems must be dealt with through partnership; our progress must be shared.

Now, that does not mean we should ignore sources of tension. Indeed, it suggests the opposite: We must face these tensions squarely. And so in that spirit, let me speak as clearly and as plainly as I can about some specific issues that I believe we must finally confront together.

The first issue that we have to confront is violent extremism in all of its forms.

In Ankara, I made clear that America is not—and never will be—at war with Islam. We will, however, relentlessly confront violent extremists who pose a grave threat to our security— because we reject the same thing that people of all faiths reject: the killing of innocent men, women, and children. And it is my first duty as president to protect the American people.

The situation in Afghanistan demonstrates America's goals, and our need to work together. Over seven years ago, the United States pursued al Qaeda and the Taliban with broad international support. We did not go by choice; we went because of necessity. I'm aware that there's still some who would question or even justify the events of 9/11. But let us be clear: Al Qaeda killed nearly three thousand people on that day. The victims were innocent men, women, and children from America and many other nations who had done nothing to harm anybody. And yet al Qaeda chose to ruthlessly murder these people, claimed credit for the attack, and even now states their determination to kill on a massive scale. They have affiliates in many countries and are trying to expand their reach. These are not opinions to be debated; these are facts to be dealt with.

Now, make no mistake: We do not want to keep our troops in Afghanistan. We see no military bases there. It is agonizing for America to lose our young men and women. It is costly and politically difficult to continue this conflict. We would gladly bring every single one of our troops home if we could be confident that there were not violent extremists in Afghanistan and now Pakistan determined to kill as many Americans as they possibly can. But that is not yet the case.

And that's why we're partnering with a coalition of forty-six countries. And despite the costs involved, America's commitment will not weaken. Indeed, none of us should tolerate these extremists. They have killed in many countries. They have killed people of different faiths—but more than any other, they have killed Muslims. Their actions are irreconcilable with the rights of human beings, the progress of nations, and with Islam. The Holy Koran teaches that whoever kills an innocent, it is as if he has killed all mankind. And the Holy Koran also says whoever saves a person, it is as if he has saved all mankind. The enduring faith of over a billion people is so much bigger than the narrow hatred of a few. Islam is not part of the problem in combating violent extremism—it is an important part of promoting peace.

Now, we also know that military power alone is not going to solve the problems in Afghanistan and Pakistan. That's why we plan to invest $1.5 billion each year over the next five years to partner with Pakistanis to build schools and hospitals, roads and businesses, and hundreds of millions to help those who've been displaced. That's why we are providing more than $2.8 billion to help Afghans develop their economy and deliver services that people depend on.

Let me also address the issue of Iraq. Unlike Afghanistan, Iraq was a war of choice that provoked strong differences in my country and around the world. Although I believe that the Iraqi people are ultimately better off without the tyranny of Saddam Hussein, I also believe that events in Iraq have reminded America of the need to use diplomacy and build international consensus to resolve our problems whenever possible. Indeed, we can recall the words of Thomas Jefferson, who said: "I hope that our wisdom will grow with our power, and teach us that the less we use our power the greater it will be."

Today, America has a dual responsibility: to help Iraq forge a better future—and to leave Iraq to Iraqis. And I have made it clear to the Iraqi people that we pursue no bases, and no claim on their territory or resources. Iraq's sovereignty is its own. And that's why I ordered the removal of our combat brigades by next August. That is why we will honor our agreement with Iraq's democratically elected government to remove combat troops from Iraqi cities by July, and to remove all of our troops from Iraq by 2012. We will help Iraq train its security forces and develop its economy. But we will support a secure and united Iraq as a partner, and never as a patron.

And finally, just as America can never tolerate violence by extremists, we must never alter or forget our principles. Nine-eleven was an enormous trauma to our country. The fear and anger that it provoked was understandable, but in some cases, it led us to act contrary to our traditions and our ideals. We are taking concrete actions to change course. I have unequivocally prohibited the use of torture by the United States, and

I have ordered the prison at Guantánamo Bay closed by early next year.

So America will defend itself, respectful of the sovereignty of nations and the rule of law. And we will do so in partnership with Muslim communities which are also threatened. The sooner the extremists are isolated and unwelcome in Muslim communities, the sooner we will all be safer.

The second major source of tension that we need to discuss is the situation between Israelis, Palestinians, and the Arab world.

America's strong bonds with Israel are well known. This bond is unbreakable. It is based upon cultural and historical ties, and the recognition that the aspiration for a Jewish home-land is rooted in a tragic history that cannot be denied.

Around the world, the Jewish people were persecuted for centuries, and anti-Semitism in Europe culminated in an unprecedented Holocaust. Tomorrow, I will visit Buchenwald, which was part of a network of camps where Jews were enslaved, tortured, shot, and gassed to death by the Third Reich. Six million Jews were killed—more than the entire Jewish population of Israel today. Denying that fact is baseless, it is ignorant, and it is hateful. Threatening Israel with destruction—or repeating vile stereotypes about Jews—is deeply wrong, and only serves to evoke in the minds of Israelis this most painful of memories while preventing the peace that the people of this region deserve.

On the other hand, it is also undeniable that the Palestinian people—Muslims and Christians—have suffered in pursuit of a homeland. For more than sixty years they've endured the pain of dislocation. Many wait in refugee camps in the West Bank,

Gaza, and neighboring lands for a life of peace and security that they have never been able to lead. They endure the daily humiliations—large and small—that come with occupation. So let there be no doubt: The situation for the Palestinian people is intolerable. And America will not turn our backs on the legitimate Palestinian aspiration for dignity, opportunity, and a state of their own.

For decades then, there has been a stalemate: two peoples with legitimate aspirations, each with a painful history that makes compromise elusive. It's easy to point fingers—for Palestinians to point to the displacement brought about by Israel's founding, and for Israelis to point to the constant hostility and attacks throughout its history from within its borders as well as beyond. But if we see this conflict only from one side or the other, then we will be blind to the truth: The only resolution is for the aspirations of both sides to be met through two states, where Israelis and Palestinians each live in peace and security.

That is in Israel's interest, Palestine's interest, America's interest, and the world's interest. And that is why I intend to personally pursue this outcome with all the patience and dedication that the task requires. The obligations that the parties have agreed to under the road map are clear. For peace to come, it is time for them—and all of us—to live up to our responsibilities.

Palestinians must abandon violence. Resistance through violence and killing is wrong and it does not succeed. For centuries, black people in America suffered the lash of the whip as slaves and the humiliation of segregation. But it was not violence that won full and equal rights. It was a peaceful and determined insistence upon the ideals at the center of America's founding. This same story can be told by people from South Africa to South Asia; from Eastern Europe to Indonesia. It's a story with a simple truth: that violence is a dead end. It is a sign neither of courage nor power to shoot rockets at sleeping children, or to blow up old women on a bus. That's not how moral authority is claimed; that's how it is surrendered.

Now is the time for Palestinians to focus on what they can build. The Palestinian Authority must develop its capacity to govern, with institutions that serve the needs of its people. Hamas does have support among some Palestinians, but they also have to recognize they have responsibilities. To play a role in fulfilling Palestinian aspirations, to unify the Palestinian people, Hamas must put an end to violence, recognize past agreements, recognize Israel's right to exist.

At the same time, Israelis must acknowledge that just as Israel's right to exist cannot be denied, neither can Palestine's. The United States does not accept the legitimacy of continued Israeli settlements. This construction violates previous agreements and undermines efforts to achieve peace. It is time for these settlements to stop.

And Israel must also live up to its obligation to ensure that Palestinians can live and work and develop their society. Just as it devastates Palestinian families, the continuing humanitarian crisis in Gaza does not serve Israel's security; neither does the continuing lack of opportunity in the West Bank. Progress in the daily lives of the Palestinian people must be a critical part of a road to peace, and Israel must take concrete steps to enable such progress.

And finally, the Arab states must recognize that the Arab

Peace Initiative was an important beginning, but not the end of their responsibilities. The Arab-Israeli conflict should no longer be used to distract the people of Arab nations from other problems. Instead, it must be a cause for action to help the Palestinian people develop the institutions that will sustain their state, to recognize Israel's legitimacy, and to choose progress over a self-defeating focus on the past.

America will align our policies with those who pursue peace, and we will say in public what we say in private to Israelis and Palestinians and Arabs. We cannot impose peace. But privately, many Muslims recognize that Israel will not go away. Likewise, many Israelis recognize the need for a Palestinian state. It is time for us to act on what everyone knows to be true.

Too many tears have been shed. Too much blood has been shed. All of us have a responsibility to work for the day when the mothers of Israelis and Palestinians can see their children grow up without fear; when the Holy Land of the three great faiths is the place of peace that God intended it to be; when Jerusalem is a secure and lasting home for Jews and Christians and Muslims, and a place for all of the children of Abraham to mingle peacefully together as in the story of Isra, when Moses, Jesus, and Mohammed, peace be upon them, joined in prayer.

The third source of tension is our shared interest in the rights and responsibilities of nations on nuclear weapons.

This issue has been a source of tension between the United States and the Islamic Republic of Iran. For many years, Iran has defined itself in part by its opposition to my country, and there is in fact a tumultuous history between us. In the middle of the Cold War, the United States played a role in the overthrow of a democratically elected Iranian government. Since the Islamic Revolution, Iran has played a role in acts of hostage-taking and violence against U.S. troops and civilians. This history is well known. Rather than remain trapped in the past, I've made it clear to Iran's leaders and people that my country is prepared to move forward. The question now is not what Iran is against, but rather what future it wants to build.

I recognize it will be hard to overcome decades of mistrust, but we will proceed with courage, rectitude, and resolve. There will be many issues to discuss between our two countries, and we are willing to move forward without preconditions on the basis of mutual respect. But it is clear to all concerned that when it comes to nuclear weapons, we have reached a decisive point. This is not simply about America's interests. It's about preventing a nuclear arms race in the Middle East that could lead this region and the world down a hugely dangerous path.

I understand those who protest that some countries have weapons that others do not. No single nation should pick and choose which nation holds nuclear weapons. And that's why I strongly reaffirmed America's commitment to seek a world in which no nations hold nuclear weapons. And any nation—including Iran—should have the right to access peaceful nuclear power if it complies with its responsibilities under the nuclear Non-Proliferation Treaty. That commitment is at the core of the treaty, and it must be kept for all who fully abide by it. And I'm hopeful that all countries in the region can share in this goal.

The fourth issue that I will address is democracy.

I know there has been controversy about the promotion of democracy in recent years, and much of this controversy is connected to the war in Iraq. So let me be clear: No system of government can or should be imposed by one nation over any other.

That does not lessen my commitment, however, to governments that reflect the will of the people. Each nation gives life to this principle in its own way, grounded in the traditions of its own people. America does not presume to know what is best for everyone, just as we would not presume to pick the outcome of a peaceful election. But I do have an unyielding belief that all people yearn for certain things: the ability to speak your mind and have a say in how you are governed; confidence in the rule of law and the equal administration of justice; government that is transparent and doesn't steal from the people; the freedom to live as you choose. These are not just American ideas; they are human rights. And that is why we will support them everywhere.

Now, there is no straight line to realize this promise. But this much is clear: Governments that protect these rights are ultimately more stable, successful, and secure. Suppressing ideas never succeeds in making them go away. America respects the right of all peaceful and law-abiding voices to be heard around the world, even if we disagree with them. And we will welcome all elected, peaceful governments—provided they govern with respect for all their people.

This last point is important because there are some who advocate for democracy only when they're out of power; once in power, they are ruthless in suppressing the rights of others. So no matter where it takes hold, government of the people and by the people sets a single standard for all who would hold power: You must maintain your power through consent, not coercion; you must respect the rights of minorities, and participate with a spirit of tolerance and compromise; you must place the interests of your people and the legitimate workings of the political process above your party. Without these ingredients, elections alone do not make true democracy.

AUDIENCE MEMBER: Barack Obama, we love you!

PRESIDENT: Thank you. The fifth issue that we must address together is religious freedom.

Islam has a proud tradition of tolerance. We see it in the history of Andalusia and Cordoba during the Inquisition. I saw it firsthand as a child in Indonesia, where devout Christians worshiped freely in an overwhelmingly Muslim country. That is the spirit we need today. People in every country should be free to choose and live their faith based upon the persuasion of the mind and the heart and the soul. This tolerance is essential for religion to thrive, but it's being challenged in many different ways.

Among some Muslims, there's a disturbing tendency to measure one's own faith by the rejection of somebody else's faith. The richness of religious diversity must be upheld— whether it is for Maronites in Lebanon or the Copts in Egypt. And if we are being honest, fault lines must be closed among Muslims, as well, as the divisions between Sunni and Shia have led to tragic violence, particularly in Iraq.

Freedom of religion is central to the ability of peoples to live together. We must always examine the ways in which we protect it. For instance, in the United States, rules on charitable giving have made it harder for Muslims to fulfill their religious obligation. That's why I'm committed to working with American Muslims to ensure that they can fulfill zakat.

Likewise, it is important for Western countries to avoid impeding Muslim citizens from practicing religion as they see fit—for instance, by dictating what clothes a Muslim woman should wear. We can't disguise hostility towards any religion behind the pretence of liberalism.

In fact, faith should bring us together. And that's why we're forging service projects in America to bring together Christians, Muslims, and Jews. That's why we welcome efforts like Saudi Arabian King Abdullah's interfaith dialogue and Turkey's leadership in the Alliance of Civilizations. Around the world, we can turn dialogue into interfaith service, so bridges between peoples lead to action—whether it is combating malaria in Africa, or providing relief after a natural disaster.

The sixth issue that I want to address is women's rights. I know, and you can tell from this audience, that there is a healthy debate about this issue. I reject the view of some in the West that a woman who chooses to cover her hair is somehow less equal, but I do believe that a woman who is denied an education is denied equality. And it is no coincidence that countries where women are well educated are far more likely to be prosperous.

Now, let me be clear: Issues of women's equality are by no means simply an issue for Islam. In Turkey, Pakistan, Bangladesh, Indonesia, we've seen Muslim-majority countries elect a woman to lead. Meanwhile, the struggle for women's equality continues in many aspects of American life, and in countries around the world.

I am convinced that our daughters can contribute just as

much to society as our sons. Our common prosperity will be advanced by allowing all humanity—men and women—to reach their full potential. I do not believe that women must make the same choices as men in order to be equal, and I respect those women who choose to live their lives in traditional roles. But it should be their choice. And that is why the United States will partner with any Muslim-majority country to support expanded literacy for girls, and to help young women pursue employment through micro-financing that helps people live their dreams.

Finally, I want to discuss economic development and opportunity.

I know that for many, the face of globalization is contradictory. The Internet and television can bring knowledge and information, but also offensive sexuality and mindless violence into the home. Trade can bring new wealth and opportunities, but also huge disruptions and change in communities. In all nations—including America—this change can bring fear. Fear that because of modernity we lose control over our economic choices, our politics, and most importantly our identities—those things we most cherish about our communities, our families, our traditions, and our faith.

But I also know that human progress cannot be denied. There need not be contradictions between development and tradition. Countries like Japan and South Korea grew their economies enormously while maintaining distinct cultures. The same is true for the astonishing progress within Muslim-majority countries from Kuala Lumpur to Dubai. In ancient times and in our times, Muslim communities have been at the forefront of innovation and education.

And this is important because no development strategy can be based only upon what comes out of the ground, nor can it be sustained while young people are out of work. Many Gulf states have enjoyed great wealth as a consequence of oil, and some are beginning to focus it on broader development. But all of us must recognize that education and innovation will be the currency of the twenty-first century—and in too many Muslim communities, there remains underinvestment in these areas. I'm emphasizing such investment within my own country. And while America in the past has focused on oil and gas when it comes to this part of the world, we now seek a broader engagement.

On education, we will expand exchange programs, and increase scholarships, like the one that brought my father to America. At the same time, we will encourage more Americans to study in Muslim communities. And we will match promising Muslim students with internships in America; invest in online learning for teachers and children around the world; and create a new online network, so a young person in Kansas can communicate instantly with a young person in Cairo.

On economic development, we will create a new corps of business volunteers to partner with counterparts in Muslim-majority countries. And I will host a Summit on Entrepreneurship this year to identify how we can deepen ties between business leaders, foundations and social entrepreneurs in the United States and Muslim communities around the world.

On science and technology, we will launch a new fund to support technological development in Muslim-majority countries, and to help transfer ideas to the marketplace so they can create more jobs. We'll open centers of scientific excellence in Africa, the Middle East, and Southeast Asia, and appoint new science envoys to collaborate on programs that develop new sources of energy, create green jobs, digitize records, clean water, grow new crops. Today I'm announcing a new global effort with the Organization of the Islamic Conference to eradicate polio. And we will also expand partnerships with Muslim communities to promote child and maternal health.

All these things must be done in partnership. Americans are ready to join with citizens and governments; community organizations, religious leaders, and businesses in Muslim communities around the world to help our people pursue a better life.

The issues that I have described will not be easy to address. But we have a responsibility to join together on behalf of the world that we seek—a world where extremists no longer threaten our people, and American troops have come home; a world where Israelis and Palestinians are each secure in a state of their own, and nuclear energy is used for peaceful purposes; a world where governments serve their citizens, and the rights of all God's children are respected. Those are mutual interests. That is the world we seek. But we can only achieve it together.

I know there are many—Muslim and non-Muslim—who question whether we can forge this new beginning. Some are eager to stoke the flames of division, and to stand in the way of progress. Some suggest that it isn't worth the effort—that we are fated to disagree, and civilizations are doomed to clash. Many more are simply skeptical that real change can occur. There's so much fear, so much mistrust that has built up over the years. But if we choose to be bound by the past, we will never move forward. And I want to particularly say this to young people of every faith, in every country—you, more than anyone, have the ability to reimagine the world, to remake this world.

All of us share this world for but a brief moment in time. The question is whether we spend that time focused on what pushes us apart, or whether we commit ourselves to an effort— a sustained effort—to find common ground, to focus on the future we seek for our children, and to respect the dignity of all human beings.

It's easier to start wars than to end them. It's easier to blame others than to look inward. It's easier to see what is different about someone than to find the things we share. But we should choose the right path, not just the easy path. There's one rule that lies at the heart of every religion—that we do unto others as we would have them do unto us. This truth transcends nations and peoples—a belief that isn't new; that isn't black or white or brown; that isn't Christian or Muslim or Jew. It's a belief that pulsed in the cradle of civilization, and that still beats in the hearts of billions around the world. It's a faith in other people, and it's what brought me here today.

We have the power to make the world we seek, but only if we have the courage to make a new beginning, keeping in mind what has been written.

The Holy Koran tells us: "O mankind! We have created you male and a female; and we have made you into nations and tribes so that you may know one another."

The Talmud tells us: "The whole of the Torah is for the purpose of promoting peace."

The Holy Bible tells us: "Blessed are the peacemakers, for they shall be called sons of God."

The people of the world can live together in peace. We know that is God's vision. Now that must be our work here on Earth.

Thank you. And may God's peace be upon you.

"THE HAPPY WARRIOR"

Eulogy for Senator Edward M. "Ted" Kennedy

BOSTON, MASSACHUSETTS, AUGUST 29, 2009

Of all the endorsements Barack Obama—the young, upstart presidential candidate—received, the Kennedys' embrace may have mattered most of all. And Obama's clear admiration for Ted Kennedy and his family shone through in his tender eulogy for the Lion of the Senate, delivered during the "Tea Party" summer of 2009, as the debate over the establishment of universal access to health insurance—a premier cause of Senator Kennedy's life—roiled Washington.

MRS. KENNEDY, KARA, Edward, Patrick, Curran, Caroline, members of the Kennedy family, distinguished guests, and fellow citizens:

Today we say goodbye to the youngest child of Rose and Joseph Kennedy. The world will long remember their son Edward as the heir to a weighty legacy; a champion for those who had none; the soul of the Democratic Party; and the lion of the United States Senate—a man whose name graces nearly one thousand laws, and who penned more than three hundred laws himself.

But those of us who loved him, and ache with his passing, know Ted Kennedy by the other titles he held: Father. Brother. Husband. Uncle Teddy, or as he was often known to his younger nieces and nephews, "The Grand Fromage," or "The Big Cheese." I, like so many others in the city where he worked for nearly half a century, knew him as a colleague, a mentor, and above all, a friend.

Ted Kennedy was the baby of the family who became its patriarch; the restless dreamer who became its rock. He was the sunny, joyful child, who bore the brunt of his brothers' teasing, but learned quickly how to brush it off. When they tossed him off a boat because he didn't know what a jib was, six-year-old Teddy got back in and learned to sail. When a photographer asked the newly-elected Bobby to step back at a press conference because he was casting a shadow on his younger brother, Teddy quipped, "It'll be the same in Washington."

This spirit of resilience and good humor would see Ted Kennedy through more pain and tragedy than most of us will ever know. He lost two siblings by the age of sixteen. He saw two more taken violently from the country that loved them. He said goodbye to his beloved sister, Eunice, in the final days of his own life. He narrowly survived a plane crash, watched two children struggle with cancer, buried three nephews, and experienced personal failings and setbacks in the most public way possible.

It is a string of events that would have broken a lesser man. And it would have been easy for Teddy to let himself become bitter and hardened; to surrender to self-pity and regret; to retreat from public life and live out his years in peaceful quiet. No one would have blamed him for that.

But that was not Ted Kennedy. As he told us, "Individual faults and frailties are no excuse to give in—and no exemption from the common obligation to give of ourselves." Indeed, Ted was the "Happy Warrior" that the poet William Wordsworth spoke of when he wrote:

As tempted more; more able to endure,
As more exposed to suffering and distress;
Thence, also, more alive to tenderness.

Through his own suffering, Ted Kennedy became more alive to the plight and suffering of others—the sick child who could not see a doctor; the young soldier sent to battle without armor; the citizen denied her rights because of what she looks like or who she loves or where she comes from. The landmark laws that he championed—the Civil Rights Act, the Americans with Disabilities Act, immigration reform, children's health care, the Family and Medical Leave Act—all have a running thread. Ted Kennedy's life's work was not to champion those with wealth or power or special connections. It was to give a voice to those who were not heard; to add a rung to the ladder of opportunity; to make real the dream of our founding. He was given the gift of time that his brothers were not, and he used that gift to touch as many lives and right as many wrongs as the years would allow.

We can still hear his voice bellowing through the Senate chamber, face reddened, fist pounding the podium, a veritable force of nature, in support of health care or workers' rights or civil rights. And yet, while his causes became deeply personal, his disagreements never did. While he was seen by his fiercest critics as a partisan lightning rod, that is not the prism through which Ted Kennedy saw the world, nor was it the prism through which his colleagues saw Ted Kennedy. He was a product of an age when the joy and nobility of politics prevented differences of party and philosophy from becoming barriers to cooperation and mutual respect—a time when adversaries still saw each other as patriots.

And that's how Ted Kennedy became the greatest legislator of our time. He did it by hewing to principle, but also by seeking compromise and common cause—not through deal-making and horse-trading alone, but through friendship, and kindness, and humor. There was the time he courted Orrin Hatch's support for the Children's Health Insurance Program by having his Chief of Staff serenade the Senator with a song Orrin had written himself; the time he delivered shamrock cookies on a china plate to sweeten up a crusty Republican colleague; and the famous story of how he won the support of a Texas Committee Chairman on an immigration bill. Teddy walked into a meeting with a plain manila envelope, and showed only the Chairman that it was filled with the Texan's favorite cigars. When the negotiations were going well, he would inch the envelope closer to the Chairman. When they weren't, he would pull it back. Before long, the deal was done.

It was only a few years ago, on St. Patrick's Day, when Teddy buttonholed me on the floor of the Senate for my support on a certain piece of legislation that was coming up for vote. I gave him my pledge, but expressed my skepticism that it would pass. But when the roll call was over, the bill garnered the votes it needed, and then some. I looked at Teddy with astonishment and asked how he had done it. He just patted me on the back, and said "Luck of the Irish!"

Of course, luck had little to do with Ted Kennedy's legislative success, and he knew that. A few years ago, his father-in-law told him that he and Daniel Webster just might be the two greatest senators of all time. Without missing a beat, Teddy replied, "What did Webster do?"

But though it is Ted Kennedy's historic body of achievements that we will remember, it is his giving heart that we will miss. It was the friend and colleague who was always the first to pick up the phone and say, "I'm sorry for your loss," or "I hope you feel better," or "What can I do to help?" It was the boss who was so adored by his staff that over five hundred spanning five decades showed up for his seventy-fifth birthday party. It was the man who sent birthday wishes and thank you notes and even his own paintings to so many who never imagined that a U.S. Senator of such stature would take the time to think about someone like them. I have one of those paintings in my private study—a Cape Cod seascape that was a gift to a freshman legislator who had just arrived in Washington and happened to admire it when Ted Kennedy welcomed him into his office the first week he arrived in Washington; by the way, that's my second favorite gift from Teddy and Vicki after our dog Bo. And it seems like everyone has one of those stories—the ones that often start with "You wouldn't believe who called me today."

Ted Kennedy was the father who looked after not only his own three children, but John's and Bobby's as well. He took them camping and taught them to sail. He laughed and danced with them at birthdays and weddings; cried and mourned with them through hardship and tragedy; and passed on that same sense of service and selflessness that his parents had instilled in him. Shortly after Ted walked Caroline down the aisle and gave her away at the altar, he received a note from Jackie that read, "On you the carefree youngest brother fell a burden a hero would have begged to been spared. We are all going to make it because you were always there with your love."

Not only did the Kennedy family make it because of Ted's love—he made it because of theirs; and especially because of the love and the life he found in Vicki. After so much loss and so much sorrow, it could not have been easy for Ted to risk his heart again. That he did is a testament to how deeply he loved this remarkable woman from Louisiana. And she didn't just love him back. As Ted would often acknowledge, Vicki saved him. She gave him strength and purpose; joy and friendship; and stood by him always, especially in those last, hardest days.

We cannot know for certain how long we have here. We cannot foresee the trials or misfortunes that will test us along the way. We cannot know God's plan for us.

What we can do is to live out our lives as best we can with purpose, and love, and joy. We can use each day to show those who are closest to us how much we care about them, and treat others with the kindness and respect that we wish for ourselves. We can learn from our mistakes and grow from our failures. And we can strive at all costs to make a better world, so that someday, if we are blessed with the chance to look back on our time here, we can know that we spent it well; that we made a difference; that our fleeting presence had a lasting impact on the lives of other human beings.

This is how Ted Kennedy lived. This is his legacy. He once said of his brother Bobby that he need not be idealized or enlarged in death because of what he was in life, and I imagine he would say the same about himself. The greatest expectations were placed upon Ted Kennedy's shoulders because of who he was, but he surpassed them all because of who he became. We do not weep for him today because of the prestige attached to his name or his office. We weep because we loved this kind and tender hero who persevered through pain and tragedy—not for the sake of ambition or vanity; not for wealth or power; but only for the people and the country that he loved.

In the days after September 11th, Teddy made it a point to personally call each one of the 177 families of this state who lost a loved one in the attack. But he didn't stop there. He kept calling and checking up on them. He fought through red tape to get them assistance and grief counseling. He invited them sailing, played with their children, and would write each family a letter whenever the anniversary of that terrible day came along. To one widow, he wrote the following:

"As you know so well, the passage of time never really heals the tragic memory of such a great loss, but we carry on, because we have to, because our loved one would want us to, and because there is still light to guide us in the world from the love they gave us."

We carry on.

Ted Kennedy has gone home now, guided by his faith and by the light of those that he has loved and lost. At last he is with them once more, leaving those of us who grieve his passing with the memories he gave, the good that he did, the dream he kept alive, and a single, enduring image—the image of a man on a boat; white mane tousled; smiling broadly as he sails into the wind, ready for whatever storms may come, carrying on toward some new and wondrous place just beyond the horizon. May God bless Ted Kennedy, and may he rest in eternal peace.

"A JUST AND LASTING PEACE"

Nobel Peace Prize Lecture

OSLO, NORWAY, DECEMBER 10, 2009

When the news broke on October 9, 2009, that Obama had been awarded the Nobel Peace Prize, much of the world, and even the president himself, was surprised. While some praised the choice, many—even among Obama's supporters—found the award astonishingly premature. It seemed less a comment on his leadership than a reward to a man who had run against George W. Bush's foreign policy—and won. The remarks Obama would give at the Peace Prize Award Ceremony were seen as an opportunity to expand on his plan for renewed international engagement. However, on December 1, just days before traveling to Norway, Obama announced in a speech at West Point that he would be sending thirty thousand additional troops to Afghanistan. His address thus attempted to balance a broadly optimistic view of international relations with the harsh realities of continuing Bush's War on Terror. Strikingly for one receiving a peace prize, Obama stressed his belief in just war doctrine. It was a

realist's address offered in an idealistic idiom. And,
as he did at Notre Dame, he faced head-on the
controversy the award had created.

YOUR MAJESTIES, YOUR Royal Highnesses, distinguished members of the Norwegian Nobel Committee, citizens of America, and citizens of the world:

I receive this honor with deep gratitude and great humility. It is an award that speaks to our highest aspirations—that for all the cruelty and hardship of our world, we are not mere prisoners of fate. Our actions matter, and can bend history in the direction of justice.

And yet I would be remiss if I did not acknowledge the considerable controversy that your generous decision has generated. In part, this is because I am at the beginning, and not the end, of my labors on the world stage. Compared to some of the giants of history who've received this prize—Schweitzer and King; Marshall and Mandela—my accomplishments are slight. And then there are the men and women around the world who have been jailed and beaten in the pursuit of justice; those who toil in humanitarian organizations to relieve suffering; the unrecognized millions whose quiet acts of courage and compassion inspire even the most hardened cynics. I cannot argue with those who find these men and women—some known, some obscure to all but those they help—to be far more deserving of this honor than I.

But perhaps the most profound issue surrounding my receipt of this prize is the fact that I am the commander in chief of the military of a nation in the midst of two wars. One of these wars is winding down. The other is a conflict that America did not seek; one in which we are joined by forty-two other countries—including Norway—in an effort to defend ourselves and all nations from further attacks.

Still, we are at war, and I'm responsible for the deployment of thousands of young Americans to battle in a distant land. Some will kill, and some will be killed. And so I come here with an acute sense of the costs of armed conflict—filled with difficult questions about the relationship between war and peace, and our effort to replace one with the other.

Now these questions are not new. War, in one form or another, appeared with the first man. At the dawn of history, its morality was not questioned; it was simply a fact, like drought or disease—the manner in which tribes and then civilizations sought power and settled their differences.

And over time, as codes of law sought to control violence within groups, so did philosophers and clerics and statesmen seek to regulate the destructive power of war. The concept of a "just war" emerged, suggesting that war is justified only when certain conditions were met: if it is waged as a last resort or in self-defense; if the force used is proportional; and if, whenever possible, civilians are spared from violence.

Of course, we know that for most of history, this concept of "just war" was rarely observed. The capacity of human beings to think up new ways to kill one another proved inexhaustible, as did our capacity to exempt from mercy those who look different or pray to a different God. Wars between armies gave way to wars between nations—total wars in which the distinction between combatant and civilian became blurred. In the span of thirty years, such carnage would twice engulf this continent. And while it's hard to conceive of a cause more just than the defeat of the Third Reich and the Axis powers, World War II was a conflict in which the total number of civilians who died exceeded the number of soldiers who perished.

In the wake of such destruction, and with the advent of the nuclear age, it became clear to victor and vanquished alike that the world needed institutions to prevent another world war. And so, a quarter century after the United States Senate rejected the League of Nations—an idea for which Woodrow Wilson received this prize—America led the world in constructing an architecture to keep the peace: a Marshall Plan and a United Nations, mechanisms to govern the waging of war, treaties to protect human rights, prevent genocide, restrict the most dangerous weapons.

In many ways, these efforts succeeded. Yes, terrible wars have been fought, and atrocities committed. But there has been no Third World War. The Cold War ended with jubilant crowds dismantling a wall. Commerce has stitched much of the world together. Billions have been lifted from poverty. The ideals of liberty and self-determination, equality and the rule of law have haltingly advanced. We are the heirs of the fortitude and foresight of generations past, and it is a legacy for which my own country is rightfully proud.

And yet, a decade into a new century, this old architecture is buckling under the weight of new threats. The world may no longer shudder at the prospect of war between two nuclear superpowers, but proliferation may increase the risk of catastrophe. Terrorism has long been a tactic, but modern technology allows a few small men with outsized rage to murder innocents on a horrific scale.

Moreover, wars between nations have increasingly given way to wars within nations. The resurgence of ethnic or sectarian conflicts; the growth of secessionist movements, insurgencies, and failed states—all these things have increasingly trapped civilians in unending chaos. In today's wars, many more civilians are killed than soldiers; the seeds of future conflict are sown, economies are wrecked, civil societies torn asunder, refugees amassed, children scarred.

I do not bring with me today a definitive solution to the problems of war. What I do know is that meeting these challenges will require the same vision, hard work, and persistence of those men and women who acted so boldly decades ago. And it will require us to think in new ways about the notions of just war and the imperatives of a just peace.

We must begin by acknowledging the hard truth: We will not eradicate violent conflict in our lifetimes. There will be times when nations—acting individually or in concert—will find the use of force not only necessary but morally justified.

I make this statement mindful of what Martin Luther King Jr. said in this same ceremony years ago: "Violence never brings permanent peace. It solves no social problem: it merely creates new and more complicated ones." As someone who stands here as a direct consequence of Dr. King's life work, I am living testimony to the moral force of non-violence. I know there's nothing weak—nothing passive—nothing naïve—in the creed and lives of Gandhi and King.

But as a head of state sworn to protect and defend my nation, I cannot be guided by their examples alone. I face the world as it is, and cannot stand idle in the face of threats to the American people. For make no mistake: Evil does exist in the world. A non-violent movement could not have halted Hitler's armies. Negotiations cannot convince al Qaeda's leaders to lay down their arms. To say that force may sometimes be necessary is not a call to cynicism—it is a recognition of history; the imperfections of man and the limits of reason.

I raise this point, I begin with this point because in many countries there is a deep ambivalence about military action today, no matter what the cause. And at times, this is joined by a reflexive suspicion of America, the world's sole military superpower.

But the world must remember that it was not simply international institutions—not just treaties and declarations—that brought stability to a post–World War II world. Whatever mistakes we have made, the plain fact is this: The United States of America has helped underwrite global security for more than six decades with the blood of our citizens and the strength of our arms. The service and sacrifice of our men and women in uniform has promoted peace and prosperity from Germany to Korea, and enabled democracy to take hold in places like the Balkans. We have borne this burden not because we seek to impose our will. We have done so out of enlightened self-interest—because we seek a better future for our children and grandchildren, and we believe that their lives will be better if others' children and grandchildren can live in freedom and prosperity.

So yes, the instruments of war do have a role to play in preserving the peace. And yet this truth must coexist with another—that no matter how justified, war promises human tragedy. The soldier's courage and sacrifice is full of glory, expressing devotion to country, to cause, to comrades in arms.

But war itself is never glorious, and we must never trumpet it as such.

So part of our challenge is reconciling these two seemingly irreconcilable truths—that war is sometimes necessary, and war at some level is an expression of human folly. Concretely, we must direct our effort to the task that President Kennedy called for long ago. "Let us focus," he said, "on a more practical, more attainable peace, based not on a sudden revolution in human nature but on a gradual evolution in human institutions." A gradual evolution of human institutions.

What might this evolution look like? What might these practical steps be?

To begin with, I believe that all nations—strong and weak alike—must adhere to standards that govern the use of force. I—like any head of state—reserve the right to act unilaterally if necessary to defend my nation. Nevertheless, I am convinced that adhering to standards, international standards, strengthens those who do, and isolates and weakens those who don't.

The world rallied around America after the 9/11 attacks, and continues to support our efforts in Afghanistan, because of the horror of those senseless attacks and the recognized principle of self-defense. Likewise, the world recognized the need to confront Saddam Hussein when he invaded Kuwait— a consensus that sent a clear message to all about the cost of aggression.

Furthermore, America—in fact, no nation—can insist that others follow the rules of the road if we refuse to follow them ourselves. For when we don't, our actions appear arbitrary and undercut the legitimacy of future interventions, no matter how justified.

And this becomes particularly important when the purpose of military action extends beyond self-defense or the defense of one nation against an aggressor. More and more, we all confront difficult questions about how to prevent the slaughter of civilians by their own government, or to stop a civil war whose violence and suffering can engulf an entire region.

I believe that force can be justified on humanitarian grounds, as it was in the Balkans, or in other places that have been scarred by war. Inaction tears at our conscience and can lead to more costly intervention later. That's why all responsible nations must embrace the role that militaries with a clear mandate can play to keep the peace.

America's commitment to global security will never waver. But in a world in which threats are more diffuse, and missions more complex, America cannot act alone. America alone cannot secure the peace. This is true in Afghanistan. This is true in failed states like Somalia, where terrorism and piracy is joined by famine and human suffering. And sadly, it will continue to be true in unstable regions for years to come.

The leaders and soldiers of NATO countries, and other friends and allies, demonstrate this truth through the capacity and courage they've shown in Afghanistan. But in many countries, there is a disconnect between the efforts of those who serve and the ambivalence of the broader public. I understand why war is not popular, but I also know this: The belief that peace is desirable is rarely enough to achieve it. Peace requires responsibility. Peace entails sacrifice. That's why NATO continues to be indispensable. That's why we must strengthen UN and regional peacekeeping, and not leave the task to a few countries. That's why we honor those who return home from peacekeeping and training abroad to Oslo and Rome; to Ottawa and Sydney; to Dhaka and Kigali—we honor them not as makers of war, but as wagers of peace.

Let me make one final point about the use of force. Even as we make difficult decisions about going to war, we must also think clearly about how we fight it. The Nobel Committee recognized this truth in awarding its first prize for peace to Henry Dunant—the founder of the Red Cross, and a driving force behind the Geneva Conventions.

Where force is necessary, we have a moral and strategic interest in binding ourselves to certain rules of conduct. And even as we confront a vicious adversary that abides by no rules, I believe the United States of America must remain a standard bearer in the conduct of war. That is what makes us different from those whom we fight. That is a source of our strength. That is why I prohibited torture. That is why I ordered the prison at Guantánamo Bay closed. And that is why I have reaffirmed America's commitment to abide by the Geneva Conventions. We lose ourselves when we compromise the very ideals that we fight to defend. And we honor those ideals by upholding them not when it's easy, but when it is hard.

I have spoken at some length to the question that must weigh on our minds and our hearts as we choose to wage war. But let me now turn to our effort to avoid such tragic choices, and speak of three ways that we can build a just and lasting peace.

First, in dealing with those nations that break rules and laws, I believe that we must develop alternatives to violence that are tough enough to actually change behavior—for if we want a lasting peace, then the words of the international community must mean something. Those regimes that break the rules must be held accountable. Sanctions must exact a real price. Intransigence must be met with increased pressure—and such pressure exists only when the world stands together as one.

One urgent example is the effort to prevent the spread of nuclear weapons, and to seek a world without them. In the middle of the last century, nations agreed to be bound by a treaty whose bargain is clear: All will have access to peaceful nuclear power; those without nuclear weapons will forsake them; and those with nuclear weapons will work towards disarmament. I am committed to upholding this treaty. It is a centerpiece of my foreign policy. And I'm working with President Medvedev to reduce America's and Russia's nuclear stockpiles.

But it is also incumbent upon all of us to insist that nations like Iran and North Korea do not game the system. Those who claim to respect international law cannot avert their eyes when those laws are flouted. Those who care for their own security cannot ignore the danger of an arms race in the Middle East or East Asia. Those who seek peace cannot stand idly by as nations arm themselves for nuclear war.

The same principle applies to those who violate international laws by brutalizing their own people. When there is genocide in Darfur, systematic rape in Congo, repression in Burma—there must be consequences. Yes, there will be engagement; yes, there will be diplomacy—but there must be consequences when those things fail. And the closer we stand together, the less likely we will be faced with the choice between armed intervention and complicity in oppression.

This brings me to a second point—the nature of the peace that we seek. For peace is not merely the absence of visible conflict. Only a just peace based on the inherent rights and dignity of every individual can truly be lasting.

It was this insight that drove drafters of the Universal Declaration of Human Rights after the Second World War. In the wake of devastation, they recognized that if human rights are not protected, peace is a hollow promise.

And yet too often, these words are ignored. For some countries, the failure to uphold human rights is excused by the false suggestion that these are somehow Western principles, foreign to local cultures or stages of a nation's development. And within America, there has long been a tension between those who describe themselves as realists or idealists—a tension that suggests a stark choice between the narrow pursuit of interests or an endless campaign to impose our values around the world.

I reject these choices. I believe that peace is unstable where citizens are denied the right to speak freely or worship as they please; choose their own leaders or assemble without fear. Pent-up grievances fester, and the suppression of tribal and religious identity can lead to violence. We also know that the opposite is true. Only when Europe became free did it finally find peace. America has never fought a war against a democracy, and our closest friends are governments that protect the rights of their citizens. No matter how callously defined, neither America's interests—nor the world's—are served by the denial of human aspirations.

So even as we respect the unique culture and traditions of different countries, America will always be a voice for those aspirations that are universal. We will bear witness to the quiet dignity of reformers like Aung Sang Suu Kyi; to the bravery of Zimbabweans who cast their ballots in the face of beatings; to the hundreds of thousands who have marched silently through the streets of Iran. It is telling that the leaders of these governments fear the aspirations of their own people more than the power of any other nation. And it is the responsibility of all free people and free nations to make clear that these movements— these movements of hope and history—they have us on their side.

Let me also say this: The promotion of human rights cannot be about exhortation alone. At times, it must be coupled with painstaking diplomacy. I know that engagement with repressive regimes lacks the satisfying purity of indignation. But I also know that sanctions without outreach—condemnation without discussion—can carry forward only a crippling status quo. No repressive regime can move down a new path unless it has the choice of an open door.

In light of the Cultural Revolution's horrors, Nixon's meeting with Mao appeared inexcusable—and yet it surely helped set China on a path where millions of its citizens have been lifted from poverty and connected to open societies. Pope John Paul's engagement with Poland created space not just for the Catholic Church, but for labor leaders like Lech Walesa. Ronald Reagan's efforts on arms control and embrace of perestroika not only improved relations with the Soviet Union, but empowered dissidents throughout Eastern Europe. There's no simple formula here. But we must try as best we can to balance isolation and engagement, pressure and incentives, so that human rights and dignity are advanced over time.

Third, a just peace includes not only civil and political rights— it must encompass economic security and opportunity. For true peace is not just freedom from fear, but freedom from want.

It is undoubtedly true that development rarely takes root without security; it is also true that security does not exist where human beings do not have access to enough food, or clean water, or the medicine and shelter they need to survive. It does not exist where children can't aspire to a decent education or a job that supports a family. The absence of hope can rot a society from within.

And that's why helping farmers feed their own people—or nations educate their children and care for the sick—is not mere charity. It's also why the world must come together to confront climate change. There is little scientific dispute that if we do nothing, we will face more drought, more famine, more mass displacement—all of which will fuel more conflict for decades. For this reason, it is not merely scientists and environmental activists who call for swift and forceful action—it's military leaders in my own country and others who understand our common security hangs in the balance.

Agreements among nations. Strong institutions. Support for human rights. Investments in development. All these are vital ingredients in bringing about the evolution that President Kennedy spoke about. And yet, I do not believe that we will have the will, the determination, the staying power, to complete this work without something more—and that's the continued expansion of our moral imagination; an insistence that there's something irreducible that we all share.

As the world grows smaller, you might think it would be easier for human beings to recognize how similar we are; to understand that we're all basically seeking the same things; that we all hope for the chance to live out our lives with some measure of happiness and fulfillment for ourselves and our families.

And yet somehow, given the dizzying pace of globalization, the cultural leveling of modernity, it perhaps comes as no surprise that people fear the loss of what they cherish in their particular identities—their race, their tribe, and perhaps most powerfully their religion. In some places, this fear has led to conflict. At times, it even feels like we're moving backwards. We see it in the Middle East, as the conflict between Arabs and Jews seems to harden. We see it in nations that are torn asunder by tribal lines.

And most dangerously, we see it in the way that religion is used to justify the murder of innocents by those who have distorted and defiled the great religion of Islam, and who attacked my country from Afghanistan. These extremists are not the first to kill in the name of God; the cruelties of the Crusades are amply recorded. But they remind us that no Holy War can ever be a just war. For if you truly believe that you are carrying out divine will, then there is no need for restraint—no need to spare the pregnant mother, or the medic, or the Red Cross worker, or even a person of one's own faith. Such a warped view of religion is not just incompatible with the concept of peace, but I believe it's incompatible with the very purpose of faith—for the one rule that lies at the heart of every major religion is that we do unto others as we would have them do unto us.

Adhering to this law of love has always been the core struggle of human nature. For we are fallible. We make mistakes, and fall victim to the temptations of pride, and power, and sometimes evil. Even those of us with the best of intentions will at times fail to right the wrongs before us.

But we do not have to think that human nature is perfect for us to still believe that the human condition can be perfected. We do not have to live in an idealized world to still reach for those ideals that will make it a better place. The non-violence practiced by men like Gandhi and King may not have been practical or possible in every circumstance, but the love that they preached—their fundamental faith in human progress— that must always be the North Star that guides us on our journey.

For if we lose that faith—if we dismiss it as silly or naïve; if we divorce it from the decisions that we make on issues of war and peace—then we lose what's best about humanity. We lose our sense of possibility. We lose our moral compass.

Like generations have before us, we must reject that future. As Dr. King said at this occasion so many years ago, "I refuse to accept despair as the final response to the ambiguities of history. I refuse to accept the idea that the 'isness' of man's present condition makes him morally incapable of reaching up for the eternal 'oughtness' that forever confronts him."

Let us reach for the world that ought to be—that spark of the divine that still stirs within each of our souls.

Somewhere today, in the here and now, in the world as it is, a soldier sees he's outgunned, but stands firm to keep the peace. Somewhere today, in this world, a young protestor awaits the brutality of her government, but has the courage to march on. Somewhere today, a mother facing punishing poverty still takes the time to teach her child, scrapes together what few coins she has to send that child to school—because she believes that a cruel world still has a place for that child's dreams.

Let us live by their example. We can acknowledge that oppression will always be with us, and still strive for justice. We can admit the intractability of depravation, and still strive for dignity. Clear-eyed, we can understand that there will be war, and still strive for peace. We can do that—for that is the story of human progress; that's the hope of all the world; and at this moment of challenge, that must be our work here on Earth.

Thank you very much.

"JUSTICE HAS BEEN DONE"

Remarks on Osama bin Laden

WASHINGTON, D.C., MAY 2, 2011

Just after 11:30 P.M EDT on May 2, 2011, President Obama appeared on national television to announce that a U.S. military operation had killed Osama bin Laden earlier that day. Bin Laden, the leader of the terrorist organization al Qaeda, had played a major role in organizing the September 11 attacks and was viewed as the highest-value target in the country's struggle against global terrorism. The events of May 2 would later be recalled in the public imagination chiefly through a photograph that captured Obama and his advisors as they watched the operation unfold in the Situation Room, as well as through a successful Hollywood film that told the story of the years-long hunt for bin Laden. But on that night, the president's brief words—at once somber and celebratory— captivated the nation.

GOOD EVENING. TONIGHT, I can report to the American people and to the world that the United States has conducted an operation that killed Osama bin Laden, the leader of al Qaeda, and a terrorist who's responsible for the murder of thousands of innocent men, women, and children.

It was nearly ten years ago that a bright September day was darkened by the worst attack on the American people in our history. The images of 9/11 are seared into our national memory —hijacked planes cutting through a cloudless September sky; the Twin Towers collapsing to the ground; black smoke billowing up from the Pentagon; the wreckage of Flight 93 in Shanksville, Pennsylvania, where the actions of heroic citizens saved even more heartbreak and destruction.

And yet we know that the worst images are those that were unseen to the world. The empty seat at the dinner table. Children who were forced to grow up without their mother or their father. Parents who would never know the feeling of their child's embrace. Nearly three thousand citizens taken from us, leaving a gaping hole in our hearts.

On September 11, 2001, in our time of grief, the American people came together. We offered our neighbors a hand, and we offered the wounded our blood. We reaffirmed our ties to each other, and our love of community and country. On that day, no matter where we came from, what God we prayed to, or what race or ethnicity we were, we were united as one American family.

We were also united in our resolve to protect our nation and to bring those who committed this vicious attack to justice. We quickly learned that the 9/11 attacks were carried out by al Qaeda—an organization headed by Osama bin Laden, which had openly declared war on the United States and was committed to killing innocents in our country and around the globe. And so we went to war against al Qaeda to protect our citizens, our friends, and our allies.

Over the last ten years, thanks to the tireless and heroic work of our military and our counterterrorism professionals, we've made great strides in that effort. We've disrupted terrorist attacks and strengthened our homeland defense. In Afghanistan, we removed the Taliban government, which had given bin Laden and al Qaeda safe haven and support. And around the globe, we worked with our friends and allies to capture or kill scores of al Qaeda terrorists, including several who were a part of the 9/11 plot.

Yet Osama bin Laden avoided capture and escaped across the Afghan border into Pakistan. Meanwhile, al Qaeda continued to operate from along that border and operate through its affiliates across the world.

And so shortly after taking office, I directed Leon Panetta, the director of the CIA, to make the killing or capture of bin Laden the top priority of our war against al Qaeda, even as we continued our broader efforts to disrupt, dismantle, and defeat his network.

Then, last August, after years of painstaking work by our intelligence community, I was briefed on a possible lead to bin Laden. It was far from certain, and it took many months to run this thread to ground. I met repeatedly with my national security team as we developed more information about the possibility that we had located bin Laden hiding within a compound deep inside of Pakistan. And finally, last week, I determined that we had enough intelligence to take action, and authorized an operation to get Osama bin Laden and bring him to justice.

Today, at my direction, the United States launched a targeted operation against that compound in Abbottabad, Pakistan. A small team of Americans carried out the operation with extraordinary courage and capability. No Americans were harmed. They took care to avoid civilian casualties. After a firefight, they killed Osama bin Laden and took custody of his body.

For over two decades, bin Laden has been al Qaeda's leader and symbol, and has continued to plot attacks against our country and our friends and allies. The death of bin Laden marks the most significant achievement to date in our nation's effort to defeat al Qaeda.

Yet his death does not mark the end of our effort. There's no doubt that al Qaeda will continue to pursue attacks against us. We must—and we will—remain vigilant at home and abroad.

As we do, we must also reaffirm that the United States is not—and never will be—at war with Islam. I've made clear, just as President Bush did shortly after 9/11, that our war is not against Islam. Bin Laden was not a Muslim leader; he was a mass murderer of Muslims. Indeed, al Qaeda has slaughtered scores of Muslims in many countries, including our own. So his demise should be welcomed by all who believe in peace and human dignity.

Over the years, I've repeatedly made clear that we would take action within Pakistan if we knew where bin Laden was. That is what we've done. But it's important to note that our counterterrorism cooperation with Pakistan helped lead us to bin Laden and the compound where he was hiding. Indeed, bin Laden had declared war against Pakistan as well, and ordered attacks against the Pakistani people.

Tonight, I called President Zardari, and my team has also

spoken with their Pakistani counterparts. They agree that this is a good and historic day for both of our nations. And going forward, it is essential that Pakistan continue to join us in the fight against al Qaeda and its affiliates.

The American people did not choose this fight. It came to our shores, and started with the senseless slaughter of our citizens. After nearly ten years of service, struggle, and sacrifice, we know well the costs of war. These efforts weigh on me every time I, as commander in chief, have to sign a letter to a family that has lost a loved one, or look into the eyes of a service member who's been gravely wounded.

So Americans understand the costs of war. Yet as a country, we will never tolerate our security being threatened, nor stand idly by when our people have been killed. We will be relentless in defense of our citizens and our friends and allies. We will be true to the values that make us who we are. And on nights like this one, we can say to those families who have lost loved ones to al Qaeda's terror: Justice has been done.

Tonight, we give thanks to the countless intelligence and counterterrorism professionals who've worked tirelessly to achieve this outcome. The American people do not see their work, nor know their names. But tonight, they feel the satisfaction of their work and the result of their pursuit of justice.

We give thanks for the men who carried out this operation, for they exemplify the professionalism, patriotism, and unparalleled courage of those who serve our country. And they are part of a generation that has borne the heaviest share of the burden since that September day.

Finally, let me say to the families who lost loved ones on 9/11 that we have never forgotten your loss, nor wavered in our commitment to see that we do whatever it takes to prevent another attack on our shores.

And tonight, let us think back to the sense of unity that prevailed on 9/11. I know that it has, at times, frayed. Yet today's achievement is a testament to the greatness of our country and the determination of the American people.

The cause of securing our country is not complete. But tonight, we are once again reminded that America can do whatever we set our mind to. That is the story of our history, whether it's the pursuit of prosperity for our people, or the struggle for equality for all our citizens; our commitment to stand up for our values abroad, and our sacrifices to make the world a safer place.

Let us remember that we can do these things not just because of wealth or power, but because of who we are: one nation, under God, indivisible, with liberty and justice for all.

Thank you. May God bless you. And may God bless the United States of America.

"I AM HERE TO SAY THEY ARE WRONG"

Remarks on the Economy

OSAWATOMIE, KANSAS, DECEMBER 6, 2011

Early 2011 found Obama at one of the lowest points in his first term. Tea Party Republicans won big in the 2010 midterm elections, taking control of the House and narrowing the Democrats' Senate majority. They pushed conservative budget proposals to slash government spending at a time when unemployment still hovered around 9 percent. Many Democrats, meanwhile, were irate about what they saw as Obama's tendency to concede too much at the outset of negotiations. This dispute came to a head in the summer, as Obama circumvented his party and tried—unsuccessfully—to reach a deal on the debt ceiling with House Speaker John Boehner. Following that debacle, Obama's advisors recognized that, in order to win reelection, the embattled president needed to reset his approach and reemerge as a progressive champion. Obama delivered a speech on the economy in the small town of Osawatomie, Kansas, in December that reflected this new strategy and reminded his supporters of his ongoing progressive

commitments. Osawatomie was steeped in history—
it was there that Theodore Roosevelt had delivered
his famous "New Nationalism" speech 101 years
prior. At that time, Roosevelt had argued in favor of
government as a remedy for unbridled free-market
capitalism and the power of the wealthy. Obama
adapted Roosevelt's progressive ideas for a new
century and embraced the former Republican presi-
dent many times during his remarks.

W ELL, I WANT to start by thanking a few folks who've joined us today. We've got the mayor of Osawatomie, Phil Dudley is here. We have your superintendent Gary French in the house. And we have the principal of Osawatomie High, Doug Chisam. And I have brought your former governor, who is doing now an outstanding job as Secretary of Health and Human Services—Kathleen Sebelius is in the house. We love Kathleen.

Well, it is great to be back in the state of Tex—state of Kansas. I was giving Bill Self a hard time, he was here a while back. As many of you know, I have roots here. I'm sure you're all familiar with the Obamas of Osawatomie. Actually, I like to say that I got my name from my father, but I got my accent—and my values—from my mother. She was born in Wichita. Her mother grew up in Augusta. Her father was from El Dorado. So my Kansas roots run deep.

My grandparents served during World War II. He was a soldier in Patton's Army; she was a worker on a bomber assembly line. And together, they shared the optimism of a nation that triumphed over the Great Depression and over fascism. They believed in an America where hard work paid off, and responsibility was rewarded, and anyone could make it if they tried—no matter who you were, no matter where you came from, no matter how you started out.

And these values gave rise to the largest middle class and the strongest economy that the world has ever known. It was here in America that the most productive workers, the most innovative companies turned out the best products on Earth. And you know what? Every American shared in that pride and in that success—from those in the executive suites to those in middle management to those on the factory floor. So you could have some confidence that if you gave it your all, you'd take enough home to raise your family and send your kids to school and have your health care covered, put a little away for retirement.

Today, we're still home to the world's most productive workers. We're still home to the world's most innovative companies. But for most Americans, the basic bargain that made this country great has eroded. Long before the recession hit, hard work stopped paying off for too many people. Fewer and fewer of the folks who contributed to the success of our economy actually benefited from that success. Those at the very top grew wealthier from their incomes and their investments—wealthier than ever before. But everybody else struggled with costs that were growing and paychecks that weren't—and too many families found themselves racking up more and more debt just to keep up.

Now, for many years, credit cards and home equity loans papered over this harsh reality. But in 2008, the house of cards collapsed. We all know the story by now: Mortgages sold to people who couldn't afford them, or even sometimes understand them. Banks and investors allowed to keep packaging the risk and selling it off. Huge bets—and huge bonuses—made with other people's money on the line. Regulators who were supposed to warn us about the dangers of all this, but looked the other way or didn't have the authority to look at all.

It was wrong. It combined the breathtaking greed of a few with irresponsibility all across the system. And it plunged our economy and the world into a crisis from which we're still fighting to recover. It claimed the jobs and the homes and the basic security of millions of people—innocent, hardworking Americans who had met their responsibilities but were still left holding the bag.

And ever since, there's been a raging debate over the best way to restore growth and prosperity, restore balance, restore fairness. Throughout the country, it's sparked protests and political movements—from the tea party to the people who've been occupying the streets of New York and other cities. It's left Washington in a near-constant state of gridlock. It's been the topic of heated and sometimes colorful discussion among the men and women running for president.

But, Osawatomie, this is not just another political debate. This is the defining issue of our time. This is a make-or-break moment for the middle class, and for all those who are fighting to get into the middle class. Because what's at stake is whether this will be a country where working people can earn enough to raise a family, build a modest savings, own a home, secure their retirement.

Now, in the midst of this debate, there are some who seem

to be suffering from a kind of collective amnesia. After all that's happened, after the worst economic crisis, the worst financial crisis since the Great Depression, they want to return to the same practices that got us into this mess. In fact, they want to go back to the same policies that stacked the deck against middle-class Americans for way too many years. And their philosophy is simple: We are better off when everybody is left to fend for themselves and play by their own rules.

I am here to say they are wrong. I'm here in Kansas to reaffirm my deep conviction that we're greater together than we are on our own. I believe that this country succeeds when everyone gets a fair shot, when everyone does their fair share, when everyone plays by the same rules. These aren't Democratic values or Republican values. These aren't 1 percent values or 99 percent values. They're American values. And we have to reclaim them.

You see, this isn't the first time America has faced this choice. At the turn of the last century, when a nation of farmers was transitioning to become the world's industrial giant, we had to decide: Would we settle for a country where most of the new railroads and factories were being controlled by a few giant monopolies that kept prices high and wages low? Would we allow our citizens and even our children to work ungodly hours in conditions that were unsafe and unsanitary? Would we restrict education to the privileged few? Because there were people who thought massive inequality and exploitation of people was just the price you pay for progress.

Theodore Roosevelt disagreed. He was the Republican son of a wealthy family. He praised what the titans of industry had done to create jobs and grow the economy. He believed then what we know is true today, that the free market is the greatest force for economic progress in human history. It's led to a prosperity and a standard of living unmatched by the rest of the world.

But Roosevelt also knew that the free market has never been a free license to take whatever you can from whomever you can. He understood the free market only works when there are rules of the road that ensure competition is fair and open and honest. And so he busted up monopolies, forcing those companies to compete for consumers with better services and better prices. And today, they still must. He fought to make sure businesses couldn't profit by exploiting children or selling food or medicine that wasn't safe. And today, they still can't.

And in 1910, Teddy Roosevelt came here to Osawatomie and he laid out his vision for what he called a New Nationalism. "Our country," he said, "means nothing unless it means the triumph of a real democracy . . . of an economic system under which each man shall be guaranteed the opportunity to show the best that there is in him."

Now, for this, Roosevelt was called a radical. He was called a socialist—even a communist. But today, we are a richer nation and a stronger democracy because of what he fought for in his last campaign: an eight-hour work day and a minimum wage for women—insurance for the unemployed and for the elderly, and those with disabilities; political reform and a progressive income tax.

Today, over one hundred years later, our economy has gone through another transformation. Over the last few decades, huge advances in technology have allowed businesses to do more with less, and it's made it easier for them to set up shop and hire workers anywhere they want in the world. And many of you know firsthand the painful disruptions this has caused for a lot of Americans.

Factories where people thought they would retire suddenly picked up and went overseas, where workers were cheaper. Steel mills that needed one hundred—or one thousand—employees are now able to do the same work with one hundred employees, so layoffs too often became permanent, not just a temporary part of the business cycle. And these changes didn't just affect blue-collar workers. If you were a bank teller or a phone operator or a travel agent, you saw many in your profession replaced by ATMs and the Internet.

Today, even higher-skilled jobs, like accountants and middle management, can be outsourced to countries like China or India. And if you're somebody whose job can be done cheaper by a computer or someone in another country, you don't have a lot of leverage with your employer when it comes to asking for better wages or better benefits, especially since fewer Americans today are part of a union.

Now, just as there was in Teddy Roosevelt's time, there is a certain crowd in Washington who, for the last few decades, have said, let's respond to this economic challenge with the same old tune. "The market will take care of everything," they tell us. If we just cut more regulations and cut more taxes—especially for the wealthy—our economy will grow stronger. Sure, they say, there will be winners and losers. But if the winners do really well, then jobs and prosperity will eventually trickle down to everybody else. And, they argue, even if prosperity doesn't trickle down, well, that's the price of liberty.

Now, it's a simple theory. And we have to admit, it's one that speaks to our rugged individualism and our healthy skepticism of too much government. That's in America's DNA. And that theory fits well on a bumper sticker. But here's the problem: It doesn't work. It has never worked. It didn't work when it was tried in the decade before the Great Depression. It's not what led to the incredible postwar booms of the fifties and sixties. And it didn't work when we tried it during the last decade. I mean, understand, it's not as if we haven't tried this theory.

Remember in those years, in 2001 and 2003, Congress passed two of the most expensive tax cuts for the wealthy in history. And what did it get us? The slowest job growth in half a century. Massive deficits that have made it much harder to pay for the investments that built this country and provided the basic security that helped millions of Americans reach and stay in the middle class— things like education and infrastructure, science and technology, Medicare and Social Security.

Remember that in those same years, thanks to some of the same folks who are now running Congress, we had weak regulation, we had little oversight, and what did it get us? Insurance companies that jacked up people's premiums with impunity and denied care to patients who were sick, mortgage lenders that tricked families into buying homes they couldn't afford, a financial sector where irresponsibility and lack of basic oversight nearly destroyed our entire economy.

We simply cannot return to this brand of "you're on your own" economics if we're serious about rebuilding the middle class in this country. We know that it doesn't result in a strong economy. It results in an economy that invests too little in its

people and in its future. We know it doesn't result in a prosperity that trickles down. It results in a prosperity that's enjoyed
by fewer and fewer of our citizens.

Look at the statistics. In the last few decades, the average
income of the top 1 percent has gone up by more than 250
percent to $1.2 million per year. I'm not talking about million-
aires, people who have a million dollars. I'm saying people who
make a million dollars every single year. For the top one
hundredth of 1 percent, the average income is now $27 million
per year. The typical CEO who used to earn about thirty times
more than his or her worker now earns 110 times more. And
yet, over the last decade the incomes of most Americans have
actually fallen by about 6 percent.

Now, this kind of inequality—a level that we haven't seen
since the Great Depression—hurts us all. When middle-class
families can no longer afford to buy the goods and services that
businesses are selling, when people are slipping out of the
middle class, it drags down the entire economy from top
to bottom. America was built on the idea of broad-based
prosperity, of strong consumers all across the country. That's
why a CEO like Henry Ford made it his mission to pay
his workers enough so that they could buy the cars he made.
It's also why a recent study showed that countries with less
inequality tend to have stronger and steadier economic growth
over the long run.

Inequality also distorts our democracy. It gives an outsized
voice to the few who can afford high-priced lobbyists and
unlimited campaign contributions, and it runs the risk of selling
out our democracy to the highest bidder. It leaves everyone else
rightly suspicious that the system in Washington is rigged

against them, that our elected representatives aren't looking out for the interests of most Americans.

But there's an even more fundamental issue at stake. This kind of gaping inequality gives lie to the promise that's at the very heart of America: that this is a place where you can make it if you try. We tell people—we tell our kids—that in this country, even if you're born with nothing, work hard and you can get into the middle class. We tell them that your children will have a chance to do even better than you do. That's why immigrants from around the world historically have flocked to our shores.

And yet, over the last few decades, the rungs on the ladder of opportunity have grown farther and farther apart, and the middle class has shrunk. You know, a few years after World War II, a child who was born into poverty had a slightly better than fifty-fifty chance of becoming middle class as an adult. By 1980, that chance had fallen to around 40 percent. And if the trend of rising inequality over the last few decades continues, it's estimated that a child born today will only have a one-in-three chance of making it to the middle class— 33 percent.

It's heartbreaking enough that there are millions of working families in this country who are now forced to take their children to food banks for a decent meal. But the idea that those children might not have a chance to climb out of that situation and back into the middle class, no matter how hard they work? That's inexcusable. It is wrong. It flies in the face of everything that we stand for.

Now, fortunately, that's not a future that we have to accept, because there's another view about how we build a strong middle class in this country—a view that's truer to our history, a vision that's been embraced in the past by people of both parties for more than two hundred years.

It's not a view that we should somehow turn back technology or put up walls around America. It's not a view that says we should punish profit or success or pretend that government knows how to fix all of society's problems. It is a view that says in America we are greater together—when everyone engages in fair play and everybody gets a fair shot and everybody does their fair share.

So what does that mean for restoring middle-class security in today's economy? Well, it starts by making sure that everyone in America gets a fair shot at success. The truth is we'll never be able to compete with other countries when it comes to who's best at letting their businesses pay the lowest wages, who's best at busting unions, who's best at letting companies pollute as much as they want. That's a race to the bottom that we can't win, and we shouldn't want to win that race. Those countries don't have a strong middle class. They don't have our standard of living.

The race we want to win, the race we can win is a race to the top—the race for good jobs that pay well and offer middle-class security. Businesses will create those jobs in countries with the highest-skilled, highest-educated workers, the most advanced transportation and communication, the strongest commitment to research and technology.

The world is shifting to an innovation economy and nobody does innovation better than America. Nobody does it better. No one has better colleges. Nobody has better universities. Nobody has a greater diversity of talent and ingenuity. No one's workers or entrepreneurs are more driven or more daring. The things that have always been our strengths match up perfectly with the demands of the moment.

But we need to meet the moment. We've got to up our game. We need to remember that we can only do that together. It starts by making education a national mission. Government and businesses, parents and citizens. In this economy, a higher education is the surest route to the middle class. The unemployment rate for Americans with a college degree or more is about half the national average. And their incomes are twice as high as those who don't have a high school diploma. Which means we shouldn't be laying off good teachers right now—we should be hiring them. We shouldn't be expecting less of our schools—we should be demanding more. We shouldn't be making it harder to afford college—we should be a country where everyone has a chance to go and doesn't rack up one hundred thousand dollars of debt just because they went.

In today's innovation economy, we also need a world-class commitment to science and research, the next generation of high-tech manufacturing. Our factories and our workers shouldn't be idle. We should be giving people the chance to get new skills and training at community colleges so they can learn how to make wind turbines and semiconductors and high-powered batteries. And by the way, if we don't have an economy that's built on bubbles and financial speculation, our best and brightest won't all gravitate towards careers in banking and finance. Because if we want an economy that's built to last, we need more of those young people in science and engineering. This country should not be known for bad debt and phony profits. We should be known for creating and selling products all around the world that are stamped with three proud words: Made in America.

Today, manufacturers and other companies are setting up shop in the places with the best infrastructure to ship their products, move their workers, communicate with the rest of the world. And that's why the over 1 million construction workers who lost their jobs when the housing market collapsed, they shouldn't be sitting at home with nothing to do. They should be rebuilding our roads and our bridges, laying down faster railroads and broadband, modernizing our schools—all the things other countries are already doing to attract good jobs and businesses to their shores.

Yes, business, and not government, will always be the primary generator of good jobs with incomes that lift people into the middle class and keep them there. But as a nation, we've always come together, through our government, to help create the conditions where both workers and businesses can succeed. And historically, that hasn't been a partisan idea. Franklin Roosevelt worked with Democrats and Republicans to give veterans of World War II—including my grandfather, Stanley Dunham—the chance to go to college on the GI Bill. It was a Republican president, Dwight Eisenhower, a proud son of Kansas—who started the Interstate Highway System, and doubled down on science and research to stay ahead of the Soviets.

Of course, those productive investments cost money. They're not free. And so we've also paid for these investments by asking everybody to do their fair share. Look, if we had unlimited resources, no one would ever have to pay any taxes and we would never have to cut any spending. But we don't have unlimited resources. And so we have to set priorities. If we want a strong middle class, then our tax code must reflect our values. We have to make choices.

Today that choice is very clear. To reduce our deficit, I've already signed nearly one trillion dollars of spending cuts into law and I've proposed trillions more, including reforms that would lower the cost of Medicare and Medicaid.

But in order to structurally close the deficit, get our fiscal house in order, we have to decide what our priorities are. Now, most immediately, short term, we need to extend a payroll tax cut that's set to expire at the end of this month. If we don't do that, 160 million Americans, including most of the people here, will see their taxes go up by an average of one thousand dollars starting in January and it would badly weaken our recovery. That's the short term.

In the long term, we have to rethink our tax system more fundamentally. We have to ask ourselves: Do we want to make the investments we need in things like education and research and high-tech manufacturing—all those things that helped make us an economic superpower? Or do we want to keep in place the tax breaks for the wealthiest Americans in our country? Because we can't afford to do both. That is not politics. That's just math.

Now, so far, most of my Republican friends in Washington have refused under any circumstance to ask the wealthiest Americans to go to the same tax rate they were paying when Bill Clinton was president. So let's just do a trip down memory lane here.

Keep in mind, when President Clinton first proposed these

tax increases, folks in Congress predicted they would kill jobs and lead to another recession. Instead, our economy created nearly twenty-three million jobs and we eliminated the deficit. Today, the wealthiest Americans are paying the lowest taxes in over half a century. This isn't like in the early fifties, when the top tax rate was over 90 percent. This isn't even like the early eighties, when the top tax rate was about 70 percent. Under President Clinton, the top rate was only about 39 percent. Today, thanks to loopholes and shelters, a quarter of all million-aires now pay lower tax rates than millions of you, millions of middle-class families. Some billionaires have a tax rate as low as 1 percent. One percent.

That is the height of unfairness. It is wrong. It's wrong that in the United States of America, a teacher or a nurse or a construction worker, maybe earns fifty thousand dollars a year, should pay a higher tax rate than somebody raking in fifty million dollars. It's wrong for Warren Buffett's secretary to pay a higher tax rate than Warren Buffett. And by the way, Warren Buffett agrees with me. So do most Americans—Democrats, independents, and Republicans. And I know that many of our wealthiest citizens would agree to contribute a little more if it meant reducing the deficit and strengthening the economy that made their success possible.

This isn't about class warfare. This is about the nation's welfare. It's about making choices that benefit not just the people who've done fantastically well over the last few decades, but that benefits the middle class, and those fighting to get into the middle class, and the economy as a whole.

Finally, a strong middle class can only exist in an economy where everyone plays by the same rules, from Wall Street to

Main Street. As infuriating as it was for all of us, we rescued our major banks from collapse, not only because a full-blown financial meltdown would have sent us into a second Depression, but because we need a strong, healthy financial sector in this country.

But part of the deal was that we wouldn't go back to business as usual. And that's why last year we put in place new rules of the road that refocus the financial sector on what should be their core purpose: getting capital to the entrepreneurs with the best ideas, and financing millions of families who want to buy a home or send their kids to college.

Now, we're not all the way there yet, and the banks are fighting us every inch of the way. But already, some of these reforms are being implemented.

If you're a big bank or risky financial institution, you now have to write out a "living will" that details exactly how you'll pay the bills if you fail, so that taxpayers are never again on the hook for Wall Street's mistakes. There are also limits on the size of banks and new abilities for regulators to dismantle a firm that is going under. The new law bans banks from making risky bets with their customers' deposits, and it takes away big bonuses and paydays from failed CEOs, while giving shareholders a say on executive salaries.

This is the law that we passed. We are in the process of implementing it now. All of this is being put in place as we speak. Now, unless you're a financial institution whose business model is built on breaking the law, cheating consumers and making risky bets that could damage the entire economy, you should have nothing to fear from these new rules.

Some of you may know, my grandmother worked as a banker

for most of her life—worked her way up, started as a secretary, ended up being a vice president of a bank. And I know from her, and I know from all the people that I've come in contact with, that the vast majority of bankers and financial service professionals, they want to do right by their customers. They want to have rules in place that don't put them at a disadvantage for doing the right thing. And yet, Republicans in Congress are fighting as hard as they can to make sure that these rules aren't enforced.

I'll give you a specific example. For the first time in history, the reforms that we passed put in place a consumer watchdog who is charged with protecting everyday Americans from being taken advantage of by mortgage lenders or payday lenders or debt collectors. And the man we nominated for the post, Richard Cordray, is a former attorney general of Ohio who has the support of most attorney generals, both Democrat and Republican, throughout the country. Nobody claims he's not qualified.

But the Republicans in the Senate refuse to confirm him for the job; they refuse to let him do his job. Why? Does anybody here think that the problem that led to our financial crisis was too much oversight of mortgage lenders or debt collectors?

AUDIENCE: No!

PRESIDENT: Of course not. Every day we go without a consumer watchdog is another day when a student, or a senior citizen, or a member of our Armed Forces—because they are very vulnerable to some of this stuff—could be tricked into a loan that they can't afford—something that happens all the time. And the fact is that financial institutions have plenty of lobbyists looking out for their interests. Consumers deserve to have someone whose job it is to look out for them. And I intend to make sure they do. And I want you to hear me, Kansas: I will veto any effort to delay or defund or dismantle the new rules that we put in place.

We shouldn't be weakening oversight and accountability. We should be strengthening oversight and accountability. I'll give you another example. Too often, we've seen Wall Street firms violating major anti-fraud laws because the penalties are too weak and there's no price for being a repeat offender. No more. I'll be calling for legislation that makes those penalties count so that firms don't see punishment for breaking the law as just the price of doing business.

The fact is this crisis has left a huge deficit of trust between Main Street and Wall Street. And major banks that were rescued by the taxpayers have an obligation to go the extra mile in helping to close that deficit of trust. At minimum, they should be remedying past mortgage abuses that led to the financial crisis. They should be working to keep responsible homeowners in their home. We're going to keep pushing them to provide more time for unemployed homeowners to look for work without having to worry about immediately losing their house.

The big banks should increase access to refinancing opportunities to borrowers who haven't yet benefited from historically low interest rates. And the big banks should recognize that precisely because these steps are in the interest of middle-class families and the broader economy, it will also be in the banks' own long-term financial interest. What will be good for consumers over the long term will be good for the banks.

Investing in things like education that give everybody a chance to succeed. A tax code that makes sure everybody pays their fair share. And laws that make sure everybody follows the rules. That's what will transform our economy. That's what will grow our middle class again. In the end, rebuilding this economy based on fair play, a fair shot, and a fair share will require all of us to see that we have a stake in each other's success. And it will require all of us to take some responsibility.

It will require parents to get more involved in their children's education. It will require students to study harder. It will require some workers to start studying all over again. It will require greater responsibility from homeowners not to take out mortgages they can't afford. They need to remember that if something seems too good to be true, it probably is.

It will require those of us in public service to make government more efficient and more effective, more consumer-friendly, more responsive to people's needs. That's why we're cutting programs that we don't need to pay for those we do. That's why we've made hundreds of regulatory reforms that will save businesses billions of dollars. That's why we're not just throwing money at education, we're challenging schools to come up with the most innovative reforms and the best results.

And it will require American business leaders to understand that their obligations don't just end with their shareholders. Andy Grove, the legendary former CEO of Intel, put it best. He said, "There is another obligation I feel personally, given that everything I've achieved in my career, and a lot of what Intel has achieved . . . were made possible by a climate of democracy, an economic climate and investment climate provided by the United States."

This broader obligation can take many forms. At a time when the cost of hiring workers in China is rising rapidly, it should mean more CEOs deciding that it's time to bring jobs back to the United States—not just because it's good for business, but because it's good for the country that made their business and their personal success possible.

I think about the Big Three auto companies who, during recent negotiations, agreed to create more jobs and cars here in America, and then decided to give bonuses not just to their executives, but to all their employees, so that everyone was invested in the company's success.

I think about a company based in Warroad, Minnesota. It's called Marvin Windows and Doors. During the recession, Marvin's competitors closed dozens of plants, let hundreds of workers go. But Marvin's did not lay off a single one of their four thousand or so employees—not one. In fact, they've only laid off workers once in over a hundred years. Mr. Marvin's grandfather even kept his eight employees during the Great Depression.

Now, at Marvin's when times get tough, the workers agree to give up some perks and some pay, and so do the owners. As one owner said, "You can't grow if you're cutting your life-blood—and that's the skills and experience your workforce delivers." For the CEO of Marvin's, it's about the community. He said, "These are people we went to school with. We go to church with them. We see them in the same restaurants. Indeed, a lot of us have married local girls and boys. We could be anywhere, but we are in Warroad."

That's how America was built. That's why we're the greatest nation on Earth. That's what our greatest companies understand. Our success has never just been about survival of the fittest. It's about building a nation where we're all better off. We pull together. We pitch in. We do our part. We believe that hard work will pay off, that responsibility will be rewarded, and that our children will inherit a nation where those values live on.

And it is that belief that rallied thousands of Americans to Osawatomie—maybe even some of your ancestors—on a rain-soaked day more than a century ago. By train, by wagon, on buggy, bicycle, on foot, they came to hear the vision of a man who loved this country and was determined to perfect it.

"We are all Americans," Teddy Roosevelt told them that day. "Our common interests are as broad as the continent." In the final years of his life, Roosevelt took that same message all across this country, from tiny Osawatomie to the heart of New York City, believing that no matter where he went, no matter who he was talking to, everybody would benefit from a country in which everyone gets a fair chance.

And well into our third century as a nation, we have grown and we've changed in many ways since Roosevelt's time. The world is faster and the playing field is larger and the challenges are more complex. But what hasn't changed—what can never change—are the values that got us this far. We still have a stake in each other's success. We still believe that this should be a place where you can make it if you try. And we still believe, in the words of the man who called for a New Nationalism all those years ago, "The fundamental rule of our national life," he said, "the rule which underlies all others—is that, on the whole, and in the long run, we shall go up or down together." And I believe America is on the way up.

Thank you. God bless you. God bless the United States of America.

"NEWTOWN, YOU ARE NOT ALONE"

Remarks at Sandy Hook Interfaith Prayer Vigil

NEWTOWN, CONNECTICUT,

DECEMBER 16, 2012

On Friday, December 14, 2012, twenty-year-old Adam Lanza shot and killed his mother before traveling to Sandy Hook Elementary in Newtown, Connecticut, where he murdered twenty first-grade children and six staff members. When police arrived, he committed suicide. The massacre at Sandy Hook was one of the deadliest school shootings in U.S. history, and it sparked renewed debate in Washington and across the country about gun control and mental health reform. President Obama traveled to Newtown the weekend after the shooting to meet with the families of the victims and delivered these remarks at an interfaith prayer vigil held at the local high school. Just days later, Obama, who shied away from the gun issue before the election, announced his intention to pursue federal gun reform through executive and legislative action. His legislative goal would remain elusive for the remainder of his presidency.

THANK YOU, GOVERNOR. To all the families, first responders, to the community of Newtown, clergy, guests, scripture tells us, "Do not lose heart. Though outwardly we are wasting away, inwardly, we are being renewed day by day.

"For light and momentary troubles are achieving for us an eternal glory that far outweighs them all, so we fix our eyes not on what is seen, but on what is unseen, since what is seen is temporary, but what is unseen is eternal.

"For we know that if the earthly tent we live in is destroyed, we have a building from God, an eternal house in heaven not built by human hands."

We gather here in memory of twenty beautiful children and six remarkable adults. They lost their lives in a school that could have been any school in a quiet town full of good and decent people that could be any town in America.

Here in Newtown, I come to offer the love and prayers of a nation. I am very mindful that mere words cannot match the depths of your sorrow, nor can they heal your wounded hearts.

I can only hope it helps for you to know that you're not alone in your grief, that our world, too, has been torn apart, that all across this land of ours, we have wept with you. We've pulled our children tight.

And you must know that whatever measure of comfort we can provide, we will provide. Whatever portion of sadness that we can share with you to ease this heavy load, we will gladly bear it. Newtown, you are not alone.

As these difficult days have unfolded, you've also inspired us with stories of strength and resolve and sacrifice. We know that when danger arrived in the halls of Sandy Hook Elementary, the school's staff did not flinch. They did not hesitate.

Can we say that we're truly doing enough to give all the children of this country the chance they deserve to live out their lives in happiness and with purpose?

I've been reflecting on this the last few days, and if we're honest with ourselves, the answer's no. We're not doing enough. And we will have to change. Since I've been president, this is the fourth time we have come together to comfort a grieving community torn apart by mass shootings, fourth time we've hugged survivors, the fourth time we've consoled the families of victims.

And in between, there have been an endless series of deadly shootings across the country, almost daily reports of victims, many of them children, in small towns and in big cities all across America, victims whose—much of the time their only fault was being at the wrong place at the wrong time.

We can't tolerate this anymore. These tragedies must end. And to end them, we must change.

We will be told that the causes of such violence are complex, and that is true. No single law, no set of laws can eliminate evil from the world or prevent every senseless act of violence in our society, but that can't be an excuse for inaction. Surely we can do better than this.

If there's even one step we can take to save another child or another parent or another town from the grief that's visited Tucson and Aurora and Oak Creek and Newtown and communities from Columbine to Blacksburg before that, then surely we have an obligation to try.

In the coming weeks, I'll use whatever power this office holds to engage my fellow citizens, from law enforcement, to mental health professionals, to parents and educators, in an effort aimed at preventing more tragedies like this, because what choice do we have? We can't accept events like this as routine.

Are we really prepared to say that we're powerless in the face of such carnage, that the politics are too hard?

Are we prepared to say that such violence visited on our children year after year after year is somehow the price of our freedom?

You know, all the world's religions, so many of them represented here today, start with a simple question.

Why are we here? What gives our life meaning? What gives our acts purpose?

We know our time on this Earth is fleeting. We know that we will each have our share of pleasure and pain, that even after we chase after some earthly goal, whether it's wealth or power or fame or just simple comfort, we will, in some fashion, fall short of what we had hoped. We know that, no matter how good our intentions, we'll all stumble sometimes in some way.

We'll make mistakes, we'll experience hardships and even when we're trying to do the right thing, we know that much of our time will be spent groping through the darkness, so often unable to discern God's heavenly plans.

There's only one thing we can be sure of, and that is the love that we have for our children, for our families, for each other. The warmth of a small child's embrace, that is true.

The memories we have of them, the joy that they bring, the wonder we see through their eyes, that fierce and boundless love we feel for them, a love that takes us out of ourselves and binds us to something larger, we know that's what matters.

We know we're always doing right when we're taking care

of them, when we're teaching them well, when we're showing acts of kindness. We don't go wrong when we do that.

That's what we can be sure of, and that's what you, the people of Newtown, have reminded us. That's how you've inspired us. You remind us what matters. And that's what should drive us forward in everything we do for as long as God sees fit to keep us on this Earth.

"Let the little children come to me," Jesus said, "and do not hinder them, for to such belongs the kingdom of heaven."

Charlotte, Daniel, Olivia, Josephine, Ana, Dylan, Madeline, Catherine, Chase, Jesse, James, Grace, Emilie, Jack, Noah, Caroline, Jessica, Benjamin, Avielle, Allison, God has called them all home.

For those of us who remain, let us find the strength to carry on and make our country worthy of their memory. May God bless and keep those we've lost in His heavenly place. May He grace those we still have with His holy comfort, and may He bless and watch over this community and the United States of America.

"WE, THE PEOPLE . . ."

Second Inaugural Address
WASHINGTON, D.C., JANUARY 21, 2013

Perhaps no second inaugural address is more famous than President Abraham Lincoln's 1865 address, with its declaration of "malice toward none, and charity for all" in the call to "bind up the nation's wounds" after the Civil War. Obama, who is first and foremost a student of history, seems to have structured his second inaugural with a nod to Lincoln— it is a celebration of America's founding possibilities and enduring democracy, intriguing for a president often damned by his critics as insufficiently in love with the country. It also reflects the newly reelected president's hope that his second victory would convince Republicans to lay down their rhetorical arms and work with him. That, of course, was not meant to be.

VICE PRESIDENT BIDEN, Mr. Chief Justice, members of the United States Congress, distinguished guests, and fellow citizens:

Each time we gather to inaugurate a president we bear witness to the enduring strength of our Constitution. We affirm the promise of our democracy. We recall that what binds this nation together is not the colors of our skin or the tenets of our faith or the origins of our names. What makes us exceptional— what makes us American—is our allegiance to an idea articulated in a declaration made more than two centuries ago:

"We hold these truths to be self-evident, that all men are created equal; that they are endowed by their Creator with certain unalienable Rights; that among these are Life, Liberty, and the pursuit of Happiness."

Today we continue a never-ending journey to bridge the meaning of those words with the realities of our time. For history tells us that while these truths may be self-evident, they've never been self-executing; that while freedom is a gift from God, it must be secured by His people here on Earth. The patriots of 1776 did not fight to replace the tyranny of a king with the privileges of a few or the rule of a mob. They gave to us a republic, a government of, and by, and for the people, entrusting each generation to keep safe our founding creed.

And for more than two hundred years, we have.

Through blood drawn by lash and blood drawn by sword, we learned that no union founded on the principles of liberty and equality could survive half-slave and half-free. We made ourselves anew, and vowed to move forward together.

Together, we determined that a modern economy requires railroads and highways to speed travel and commerce, schools and colleges to train our workers.

Together, we discovered that a free market only thrives when there are rules to ensure competition and fair play.

Together, we resolved that a great nation must care for the vulnerable, and protect its people from life's worst hazards and misfortune.

Through it all, we have never relinquished our skepticism of central authority, nor have we succumbed to the fiction that all society's ills can be cured through government alone. Our celebration of initiative and enterprise, our insistence on hard work and personal responsibility, these are constants in our character.

But we have always understood that when times change, so must we; that fidelity to our founding principles requires new responses to new challenges; that preserving our individual freedoms ultimately requires collective action. For the American people can no more meet the demands of today's world by acting alone than American soldiers could have met the forces of fascism or communism with muskets and militias. No single person can train all the math and science teachers we'll need to equip our children for the future, or build the roads and networks and research labs that will bring new jobs and businesses to our shores. Now, more than ever, we must do these things together, as one nation and one people.

This generation of Americans has been tested by crises that steeled our resolve and proved our resilience. A decade of war is now ending. An economic recovery has begun. America's possibilities are limitless, for we possess all the qualities that this world without boundaries demands: youth and drive; diversity and openness; an endless capacity for risk and a gift for reinvention. My fellow Americans, we are made for this moment, and we will seize it—so long as we seize it together.

For we, the people, understand that our country cannot succeed when a shrinking few do very well and a growing many barely make it. We believe that America's prosperity must rest upon the broad shoulders of a rising middle class. We know that America thrives when every person can find independence and pride in their work; when the wages of honest labor liberate families from the brink of hardship. We are true to our creed when a little girl born into the bleakest poverty knows that she has the same chance to succeed as anybody else, because she is an American; she is free, and she is equal, not just in the eyes of God but also in our own.

We understand that outworn programs are inadequate to the needs of our time. So we must harness new ideas and technology to remake our government, revamp our tax code, reform our schools, and empower our citizens with the skills they need to work harder, learn more, reach higher. But while the means will change, our purpose endures: a nation that rewards the effort and determination of every single American. That is what this moment requires. That is what will give real meaning to our creed.

We, the people, still believe that every citizen deserves a basic measure of security and dignity. We must make the hard choices to reduce the cost of health care and the size of our deficit. But we reject the belief that America must choose between caring for the generation that built this country and investing in the generation that will build its future. For we remember the lessons of our past, when twilight years were spent in poverty and parents of a child with a disability had nowhere to turn.

We do not believe that in this country freedom is reserved for the lucky, or happiness for the few. We recognize that no matter how responsibly we live our lives, any one of us at any time may face a job loss, or a sudden illness, or a home swept away in a terrible storm. The commitments we make to each other through Medicare and Medicaid and Social Security, these things do not sap our initiative, they strengthen us. They do not make us a nation of takers; they free us to take the risks that make this country great.

We, the people, still believe that our obligations as Americans are not just to ourselves, but to all posterity. We will respond to the threat of climate change, knowing that the failure to do so would betray our children and future generations. Some may still deny the overwhelming judgment of science, but none can avoid the devastating impact of raging fires and crippling drought and more powerful storms.

The path towards sustainable energy sources will be long and sometimes difficult. But America cannot resist this transition, we must lead it. We cannot cede to other nations the technology that will power new jobs and new industries, we must claim its promise. That's how we will maintain our economic vitality and our national treasure—our forests and waterways, our crop lands and snow-capped peaks. That is how we will preserve our planet, commanded to our care by God. That's what will lend meaning to the creed our fathers once declared.

We, the people, still believe that enduring security and lasting peace do not require perpetual war. Our brave men and women in uniform, tempered by the flames of battle, are unmatched in skill and courage. Our citizens, seared by the memory of those we have lost, know too well the price that is paid for liberty. The knowledge of their sacrifice will keep us forever vigilant against those who would do us harm. But we are also heirs to those who won the peace and not just the war;

who turned sworn enemies into the surest of friends—and we must carry those lessons into this time as well.

We will defend our people and uphold our values through strength of arms and rule of law. We will show the courage to try and resolve our differences with other nations peacefully—not because we are naïve about the dangers we face, but because engagement can more durably lift suspicion and fear.

America will remain the anchor of strong alliances in every corner of the globe. And we will renew those institutions that extend our capacity to manage crisis abroad, for no one has a greater stake in a peaceful world than its most powerful nation. We will support democracy from Asia to Africa, from the Americas to the Middle East, because our interests and our conscience compel us to act on behalf of those who long for freedom. And we must be a source of hope to the poor, the sick, the marginalized, the victims of prejudice—not out of mere charity, but because peace in our time requires the constant advance of those principles that our common creed describes: tolerance and opportunity, human dignity and justice.

We, the people, declare today that the most evident of truths—that all of us are created equal—is the star that guides us still; just as it guided our forebears through Seneca Falls, and Selma, and Stonewall; just as it guided all those men and women, sung and unsung, who left footprints along this great Mall, to hear a preacher say that we cannot walk alone; to hear a King proclaim that our individual freedom is inextricably bound to the freedom of every soul on Earth.

It is now our generation's task to carry on what those pioneers began. For our journey is not complete until our wives, our mothers and daughters can earn a living equal to their efforts. Our journey is not complete until our gay brothers and sisters are treated like anyone else under the law—for if we are truly created equal, then surely the love we commit to one another must be equal as well. Our journey is not complete until no citizen is forced to wait for hours to exercise the right to vote. Our journey is not complete until we find a better way to welcome the striving, hopeful immigrants who still see America as a land of opportunity—until bright young students and engineers are enlisted in our workforce rather than expelled from our country. Our journey is not complete until all our children, from the streets of Detroit to the hills of Appalachia, to the quiet lanes of Newtown, know that they are cared for and cherished and always safe from harm.

That is our generation's task—to make these words, these rights, these values of life and liberty and the pursuit of happiness real for every American. Being true to our founding documents does not require us to agree on every contour of life. It does not mean we all define liberty in exactly the same way or follow the same precise path to happiness. Progress does not compel us to settle centuries-long debates about the role of government for all time, but it does require us to act in our time.

For now decisions are upon us and we cannot afford delay. We cannot mistake absolutism for principle, or substitute spectacle for politics, or treat name-calling as reasoned debate. We must act, knowing that our work will be imperfect. We must act, knowing that today's victories will be only partial and that it will be up to those who stand here in four years and forty years and four hundred years hence to advance the timeless spirit once conferred to us in a spare Philadelphia hall.

My fellow Americans, the oath I have sworn before you today, like the one recited by others who serve in this Capitol, was an oath to God and country, not party or faction. And we must faithfully execute that pledge during the duration of our service. But the words I spoke today are not so different from the oath that is taken each time a soldier signs up for duty or an immigrant realizes her dream. My oath is not so different from the pledge we all make to the flag that waves above and that fills our hearts with pride.

They are the words of citizens and they represent our greatest hope. You and I, as citizens, have the power to set this country's course. You and I, as citizens, have the obligation to shape the debates of our time—not only with the votes we cast, but with the voices we lift in defense of our most ancient values and enduring ideals.

Let us, each of us, now embrace with solemn duty and awesome joy what is our lasting birthright. With common effort and common purpose, with passion and dedication, let us answer the call of history and carry into an uncertain future that precious light of freedom.

Thank you. God bless you, and may He forever bless these United States of America.

"NOW WE NEED TO FINISH THE JOB"

2013 State of the Union Address
WASHINGTON, D.C., FEBRUARY 12, 2013

In his second inaugural address, Obama had made clear that the progressive message he developed during the 2012 campaign would not be abandoned in his second term. Although rhetorically sharp, his remarks on that occasion were relatively light on policy specifics. Those would come in his 2013 State of the Union address. The White House itself recognized the interconnectedness of the two speeches; Press Secretary Jay Carney referred to them as "two acts in the same play." Subsequent analysis largely focused on the more aggressive stance Obama adopted toward Republican obstructionism. Richard Stevenson of the New York Times *wrote that Obama "continued trying to define a twenty-first-century version of liberalism that could outlast his time in office and do for Democrats what Reagan did for Republicans." Obama had hoped that his reelection would "break the fever" in Washington. It didn't, leaving much of the ambitious agenda laid out here as work for a future president.*

Mr. speaker, mr. Vice President, members of Congress, fellow citizens:

Fifty-one years ago, John F. Kennedy declared to this chamber that "the Constitution makes us not rivals for power but partners for progress." "It is my task," he said, "to report the State of the Union—to improve it is the task of us all."

Tonight, thanks to the grit and determination of the American people, there is much progress to report. After a decade of grinding war, our brave men and women in uniform are coming home. After years of grueling recession, our businesses have created over six million new jobs. We buy more American cars than we have in five years, and less foreign oil than we have in twenty. Our housing market is healing, our stock market is rebounding, and consumers, patients, and homeowners enjoy stronger protections than ever before.

So, together, we have cleared away the rubble of crisis, and we can say with renewed confidence that the State of our Union is stronger.

But we gather here knowing that there are millions of Americans whose hard work and dedication have not yet been rewarded. Our economy is adding jobs—but too many people still can't find full-time employment. Corporate profits have skyrocketed to all-time highs—but for more than a decade, wages and incomes have barely budged.

It is our generation's task, then, to reignite the true engine of America's economic growth—a rising, thriving middle class.

It is our unfinished task to restore the basic bargain that built this country—the idea that if you work hard and meet your responsibilities, you can get ahead, no matter where you come from, no matter what you look like, or who you love.

It is our unfinished task to make sure that this government works on behalf of the many, and not just the few; that it encourages free enterprise, rewards individual initiative, and opens the doors of opportunity to every child across this great nation.

The American people don't expect government to solve every problem. They don't expect those of us in this chamber to agree on every issue. But they do expect us to put the nation's interests before party. They do expect us to forge reasonable compromise where we can. For they know that America moves forward only when we do so together, and that the responsibility of improving this union remains the task of us all.

Our work must begin by making some basic decisions about our budget—decisions that will have a huge impact on the strength of our recovery.

Over the last few years, both parties have worked together to reduce the deficit by more than $2.5 trillion—mostly through spending cuts, but also by raising tax rates on the wealthiest 1 percent of Americans. As a result, we are more than halfway towards the goal of $4 trillion in deficit reduction that economists say we need to stabilize our finances.

Now we need to finish the job. And the question is, how?

In 2011, Congress passed a law saying that if both parties couldn't agree on a plan to reach our deficit goal, about a trillion dollars' worth of budget cuts would automatically go into effect this year. These sudden, harsh, arbitrary cuts would jeopardize our military readiness. They'd devastate priorities like education, and energy, and medical research. They would certainly slow our recovery, and cost us hundreds of thousands of jobs. That's why Democrats, Republicans, business leaders, and economists have already said that these cuts, known here in Washington as the sequester, are a really bad idea.

Now, some in Congress have proposed preventing only the defense cuts by making even bigger cuts to things like education and job training, Medicare and Social Security benefits. That idea is even worse.

Yes, the biggest driver of our long-term debt is the rising cost of health care for an aging population. And those of us who care deeply about programs like Medicare must embrace the need for modest reforms—otherwise, our retirement programs will crowd out the investments we need for our children, and jeopardize the promise of a secure retirement for future generations.

But we can't ask senior citizens and working families to shoulder the entire burden of deficit reduction while asking nothing more from the wealthiest and the most powerful. We won't grow the middle class simply by shifting the cost of health care or college onto families that are already struggling, or by forcing communities to lay off more teachers and more cops and more firefighters. Most Americans—Democrats, Republicans, and independents—understand that we can't just cut our way to prosperity. They know that broad-based economic growth requires a balanced approach to deficit reduction, with spending cuts and revenue, and with everybody doing their fair share. And that's the approach I offer tonight.

On Medicare, I'm prepared to enact reforms that will achieve the same amount of health care savings by the beginning of the next decade as the reforms proposed by the bipartisan Simpson-Bowles commission.

Already, the Affordable Care Act is helping to slow the growth of health care costs. And the reforms I'm proposing go even further. We'll reduce taxpayer subsidies to prescription drug companies and ask more from the wealthiest seniors. We'll bring down costs by changing the way our government pays for Medicare, because our medical bills shouldn't be based on the number of tests ordered or days spent in the hospital; they should be based on the quality of care that our seniors receive. And I am open to additional reforms from both parties, so long as they don't violate the guarantee of a secure retirement. Our government shouldn't make promises we cannot keep—but we must keep the promises we've already made.

To hit the rest of our deficit reduction target, we should do what leaders in both parties have already suggested, and save hundreds of billions of dollars by getting rid of tax loopholes and deductions for the well-off and the well-connected. After all, why would we choose to make deeper cuts to education and Medicare just to protect special interest tax breaks? How is that fair? Why is it that deficit reduction is a big emergency justifying making cuts in Social Security benefits but not closing some loopholes? How does that promote growth?

Now is our best chance for bipartisan, comprehensive tax reform that encourages job creation and helps bring down the deficit. We can get this done. The American people deserve a tax code that helps small businesses spend less time filling out complicated forms, and more time expanding and hiring—a tax code that ensures billionaires with high-powered accountants can't work the system and pay a lower rate than their hardworking secretaries; a tax code that lowers incentives to move jobs overseas, and lowers tax rates for businesses and manufacturers that are creating jobs right here in the United States of America. That's what tax reform can deliver. That's what we can do together.

I realize that tax reform and entitlement reform will not be easy. The politics will be hard for both sides. None of us will get 100 percent of what we want. But the alternative will cost us jobs, hurt our economy, visit hardship on millions of hard-working Americans. So let's set party interests aside and work to pass a budget that replaces reckless cuts with smart savings and wise investments in our future. And let's do it without the brinksmanship that stresses consumers and scares off investors. The greatest nation on Earth cannot keep conducting its business by drifting from one manufactured crisis to the next. We can't do it.

Let's agree right here, right now to keep the people's government open, and pay our bills on time, and always uphold the full faith and credit of the United States of America. The American people have worked too hard, for too long, rebuilding from one crisis to see their elected officials cause another.

Now, most of us agree that a plan to reduce the deficit must be part of our agenda. But let's be clear, deficit reduction alone is not an economic plan. A growing economy that creates good, middle-class jobs—that must be the North Star that guides our efforts. Every day, we should ask ourselves three questions as a nation: How do we attract more jobs to our shores? How do we equip our people with the skills they need to get those jobs? And how do we make sure that hard work leads to a decent living?

A year and a half ago, I put forward an American Jobs Act that independent economists said would create more than one million new jobs. And I thank the last Congress for passing some of that agenda. I urge this Congress to pass the rest. But tonight, I'll lay out additional proposals that are fully paid for and fully consistent with the budget framework both parties agreed to just eighteen months ago. Let me repeat—nothing I'm proposing tonight should increase our deficit by a single dime. It is not a bigger government we need, but a smarter government that sets priorities and invests in broad-based growth. That's what we should be looking for.

Our first priority is making America a magnet for new jobs and manufacturing. After shedding jobs for more than ten years, our manufacturers have added about five hundred thousand jobs over the past three. Caterpillar is bringing jobs back from Japan. Ford is bringing jobs back from Mexico. And this year, Apple will start making Macs in America again.

There are things we can do, right now, to accelerate this trend. Last year, we created our first manufacturing innovation institute in Youngstown, Ohio. A once-shuttered warehouse is now a state-of-the art lab where new workers are mastering the 3-D printing that has the potential to revolutionize the way we make almost everything. There's no reason this can't happen in other towns.

So tonight, I'm announcing the launch of three more of these manufacturing hubs, where businesses will partner with the Department of Defense and Energy to turn regions left behind by globalization into global centers of high-tech jobs. And I ask this Congress to help create a network of fifteen of these hubs and guarantee that the next revolution in manufacturing is made right here in America. We can get that done.

Now, if we want to make the best products, we also have to

invest in the best ideas. Every dollar we invested to map the human genome returned $140 to our economy—every dollar. Today, our scientists are mapping the human brain to unlock the answers to Alzheimer's. They're developing drugs to regenerate damaged organs; devising new material to make batteries ten times more powerful. Now is not the time to gut these job-creating investments in science and innovation. Now is the time to reach a level of research and development not seen since the height of the Space Race. We need to make those investments.

Today, no area holds more promise than our investments in American energy. After years of talking about it, we're finally poised to control our own energy future. We produce more oil at home than we have in ten years. We have doubled the distance our cars will go on a gallon of gas, and the amount of renewable energy we generate from sources like wind and solar—with tens of thousands of good American jobs to show for it. We produce more natural gas than ever before—and nearly everyone's energy bill is lower because of it. And over the last four years, our emissions of the dangerous carbon pollution that threatens our planet have actually fallen.

But for the sake of our children and our future, we must do more to combat climate change. Now, it's true that no single event makes a trend. But the fact is the twelve hottest years on record have all come in the last fifteen. Heat waves, droughts, wildfires, floods—all are now more frequent and more intense. We can choose to believe that Superstorm Sandy, and the most severe drought in decades, and the worst wildfires some states have ever seen were all just a freak coincidence. Or we can choose to believe in the overwhelming judgment of science—and act before it's too late.

Now, the good news is we can make meaningful progress on this issue while driving strong economic growth. I urge this Congress to get together, pursue a bipartisan, market-based solution to climate change, like the one John McCain and Joe Lieberman worked on together a few years ago. But if Congress won't act soon to protect future generations, I will. I will direct my Cabinet to come up with executive actions we can take, now and in the future, to reduce pollution, prepare our communities for the consequences of climate change, and speed the transition to more sustainable sources of energy.

Four years ago, other countries dominated the clean energy market and the jobs that came with it. And we've begun to change that. Last year, wind energy added nearly half of all new power capacity in America. So let's generate even more. Solar energy gets cheaper by the year—let's drive down costs even further. As long as countries like China keep going all in on clean energy, so must we.

Now, in the meantime, the natural gas boom has led to cleaner power and greater energy independence. We need to encourage that. And that's why my administration will keep cutting red tape and speeding up new oil and gas permits. That's got to be part of an all-of-the-above plan. But I also want to work with this Congress to encourage the research and technology that helps natural gas burn even cleaner and protects our air and our water.

In fact, much of our new-found energy is drawn from lands and waters that we, the public, own together. So tonight, I propose we use some of our oil and gas revenues to fund an Energy Security Trust that will drive new research and technology to shift our cars and trucks off oil for good. If a nonpartisan coalition of CEOs and retired generals and admirals can get behind this idea, then so can we. Let's take their advice and free our families and businesses from the painful spikes in gas prices we've put up with for far too long.

I'm also issuing a new goal for America: Let's cut in half the energy wasted by our homes and businesses over the next twenty years. We'll work with the states to do it. Those states with the best ideas to create jobs and lower energy bills by constructing more efficient buildings will receive federal support to help make that happen.

America's energy sector is just one part of an aging infrastructure badly in need of repair. Ask any CEO where they'd rather locate and hire—a country with deteriorating roads and bridges, or one with high-speed rail and Internet; high-tech schools, self-healing power grids. The CEO of Siemens America—a company that brought hundreds of new jobs to North Carolina—said that if we upgrade our infrastructure, they'll bring even more jobs. And that's the attitude of a lot of companies all around the world. And I know you want these job-creating projects in your district. I've seen all those ribbon-cuttings.

So tonight, I propose a "Fix-It-First" program to put people to work as soon as possible on our most urgent repairs, like the nearly seventy thousand structurally deficient bridges across the country. And to make sure taxpayers don't shoulder the whole burden, I'm also proposing a Partnership to Rebuild America that attracts private capital to upgrade what our businesses need most: modern ports to move our goods, modern pipelines to withstand a storm, modern schools worthy of our children. Let's prove that there's no better place to do business than here in the United States of America, and let's start right away. We can get this done.

And part of our rebuilding effort must also involve our housing sector. The good news is our housing market is finally healing from the collapse of 2007. Home prices are rising at the fastest pace in six years. Home purchases are up nearly 50 percent, and construction is expanding again.

But even with mortgage rates near a fifty-year low, too many families with solid credit who want to buy a home are being rejected. Too many families who never missed a payment and want to refinance are being told no. That's holding our entire economy back. We need to fix it.

Right now, there's a bill in this Congress that would give every responsible homeowner in America the chance to save three thousand dollars a year by refinancing at today's rates. Democrats and Republicans have supported it before, so what are we waiting for? Take a vote, and send me that bill. Why would we be against that? Why would that be a partisan issue, helping folks refinance? Right now, overlapping regulations keep responsible young families from buying their first home. What's holding us back? Let's streamline the process, and help our economy grow.

These initiatives in manufacturing, energy, infrastructure, housing—all these things will help entrepreneurs and small business owners expand and create new jobs. But none of it will matter unless we also equip our citizens with the skills and training to fill those jobs.

And that has to start at the earliest possible age. Study after study shows that the sooner a child begins learning, the better he or she does down the road. But today, fewer than three in ten four-year-olds are enrolled in a high-quality preschool program. Most middle-class parents can't afford a few hundred bucks a week for a private preschool. And for poor kids who need help the most, this lack of access to preschool education can shadow them for the rest of their lives. So tonight, I propose working with states to make high-quality preschool available to every single child in America. That's something we should be able to do.

Every dollar we invest in high-quality early childhood education can save more than seven dollars later on—by boosting graduation rates, reducing teen pregnancy, even reducing violent crime. In states that make it a priority to educate our youngest children, like Georgia or Oklahoma, studies show students grow up more likely to read and do math at grade level, graduate high school, hold a job, form more stable families of their own. We know this works. So let's do what works and make sure none of our children start the race of life already behind. Let's give our kids that chance.

Let's also make sure that a high school diploma puts our kids on a path to a good job. Right now, countries like Germany focus on graduating their high school students with the equivalent of a technical degree from one of our community colleges. So those German kids, they're ready for a job when they graduate high school. They've been trained for the jobs that are there. Now at schools like P-Tech in Brooklyn, a collaboration between New York Public Schools and City University of New York and IBM, students will graduate with a high school diploma and an associate's degree in computers or engineering.

We need to give every American student opportunities like this.

And four years ago, we started Race to the Top—a competition that convinced almost every state to develop smarter curricula and higher standards, all for about 1 percent of what we spend on education each year. Tonight, I'm announcing a new challenge to redesign America's high schools so they better equip graduates for the demands of a high-tech economy. And we'll reward schools that develop new partnerships with colleges and employers, and create classes that focus on science, technology, engineering, and math—the skills today's employers are looking for to fill the jobs that are there right now and will be there in the future.

Now, even with better high schools, most young people will need some higher education. It's a simple fact the more education you've got, the more likely you are to have a good job and work your way into the middle class. But today, skyrocketing costs price too many young people out of a higher education, or saddle them with unsustainable debt.

Through tax credits, grants, and better loans, we've made college more affordable for millions of students and families over the last few years. But taxpayers can't keep on subsidizing higher and higher and higher costs for higher education. Colleges must do their part to keep costs down, and it's our job to make sure that they do.

So tonight, I ask Congress to change the Higher Education Act so that affordability and value are included in determining which colleges receive certain types of federal aid. And tomorrow, my administration will release a new "College Scorecard" that parents and students can use to compare schools based on a simple criteria—where you can get the most bang for your educational buck.

Now, to grow our middle class, our citizens have to have access to the education and training that today's jobs require. But we also have to make sure that America remains a place where everyone who's willing to work hard has the chance to get ahead.

Our economy is stronger when we harness the talents and ingenuity of striving, hopeful immigrants. And right now, leaders from the business, labor, law enforcement, faith communities— they all agree that the time has come to pass comprehensive immigration reform. Now is the time to do it. Now is the time to get it done. Now is the time to get it done.

Real reform means strong border security, and we can build on the progress my administration has already made—putting more boots on the Southern border than at any time in our history and reducing illegal crossings to their lowest levels in forty years.

Real reform means establishing a responsible pathway to earned citizenship—a path that includes passing a background check, paying taxes and a meaningful penalty, learning English, and going to the back of the line behind the folks trying to come here legally.

And real reform means fixing the legal immigration system to cut waiting periods and attract the highly-skilled entrepreneurs and engineers that will help create jobs and grow our economy.

In other words, we know what needs to be done. And as we speak, bipartisan groups in both chambers are working diligently to draft a bill, and I applaud their efforts. So let's get this done. Send me a comprehensive immigration reform bill in the next few months, and I will sign it right away. And America will be better for it. Let's get it done. Let's get it done.

But we can't stop there. We know our economy is stronger when our wives, our mothers, our daughters can live their lives free from discrimination in the workplace, and free from the fear of domestic violence. Today, the Senate passed the Violence Against Women Act that Joe Biden originally wrote almost twenty years ago. And I now urge the House to do the same. Good job, Joe. And I ask this Congress to declare that women should earn a living equal to their efforts, and finally pass the Paycheck Fairness Act this year.

We know our economy is stronger when we reward an honest day's work with honest wages. But today, a full-time worker making the minimum wage earns $14,500 a year. Even with the tax relief we put in place, a family with two kids that earns the minimum wage still lives below the poverty line. That's wrong. That's why, since the last time this Congress raised the minimum wage, nineteen states have chosen to bump theirs even higher.

Tonight, let's declare that in the wealthiest nation on Earth, no one who works full-time should have to live in poverty, and raise the federal minimum wage to nine dollars an hour. We should be able to get that done.

This single step would raise the incomes of millions of working families. It could mean the difference between groceries or the food bank; rent or eviction; scraping by or finally getting ahead. For businesses across the country, it would mean customers with more money in their pockets. And a whole lot of folks out there would probably need less help from government. In fact, working folks shouldn't have to wait year after year for the minimum wage to go up while CEO pay has never been higher. So here's an idea that Governor Romney and I actually agreed on last year—let's tie the minimum wage to the cost of living, so that it finally becomes a wage you can live on.

Tonight, let's also recognize that there are communities in this country where no matter how hard you work, it is virtually impossible to get ahead. Factory towns decimated from years of plants packing up. Inescapable pockets of poverty, urban and rural, where young adults are still fighting for their first job. America is not a place where the chance of birth or circumstance should decide our destiny. And that's why we need to build new ladders of opportunity into the middle class for all who are willing to climb them.

Let's offer incentives to companies that hire Americans who've got what it takes to fill that job opening, but have been out of work so long that no one will give them a chance anymore. Let's put people back to work rebuilding vacant homes in run-down neighborhoods. And this year, my administration will begin to partner with twenty of the hardest-hit towns in America to get these communities back on their feet. We'll work with local leaders to target resources at public safety, and education, and housing.

We'll give new tax credits to businesses that hire and invest. And we'll work to strengthen families by removing the financial deterrents to marriage for low-income couples, and do more to encourage fatherhood—because what makes you a man isn't the ability to conceive a child; it's having the courage to raise one. And we want to encourage that. We want to help that.

Stronger families. Stronger communities. A stronger America. It is this kind of prosperity—broad, shared, built on a thriving middle class—that has always been the source of our progress at home. It's also the foundation of our power and influence throughout the world.

Tonight, we stand united in saluting the troops and civilians who sacrifice every day to protect us. Because of them, we can say with confidence that America will complete its mission in Afghanistan and achieve our objective of defeating the core of al Qaeda.

Already, we have brought home thirty-three thousand of our brave servicemen and women. This spring, our forces will move into a support role, while Afghan security forces take the lead. Tonight, I can announce that over the next year, another thirty-four thousand American troops will come home from Afghanistan. This drawdown will continue and by the end of next year, our war in Afghanistan will be over.

Beyond 2014, America's commitment to a unified and sovereign Afghanistan will endure, but the nature of our commitment will change. We're negotiating an agreement with the Afghan government that focuses on two missions—training and equipping Afghan forces so that the country does not again slip into chaos, and counterterrorism efforts that allow us to pursue the remnants of al Qaeda and their affiliates.

Today, the organization that attacked us on 9/11 is a shadow of its former self. It's true, different al Qaeda affiliates and extremist groups have emerged—from the Arabian Peninsula to Africa. The threat these groups pose is evolving. But to meet this threat, we don't need to send tens of thousands of our sons and daughters abroad or occupy other nations. Instead, we'll need to help countries like Yemen, and Libya, and Somalia provide for their own security, and help allies who take the fight to terrorists, as we have in Mali. And where necessary, through a range of capabilities, we will continue to take direct action against those terrorists who pose the gravest threat to Americans.

Now, as we do, we must enlist our values in the fight. That's why my administration has worked tirelessly to forge a durable legal and policy framework to guide our counterterrorism efforts. Throughout, we have kept Congress fully informed of our efforts. I recognize that in our democracy, no one should just take my word for it that we're doing things the right way. So in the months ahead, I will continue to engage Congress to ensure not only that our targeting, detention, and prosecution of terrorists remains consistent with our laws and system of checks and balances, but that our efforts are even more transparent to the American people and to the world.

Of course, our challenges don't end with al Qaeda. America will continue to lead the effort to prevent the spread of the world's most dangerous weapons. The regime in North Korea must know they will only achieve security and prosperity by meeting their international obligations. Provocations of the sort we saw last night will only further isolate them, as we stand by our allies, strengthen our own missile defense, and lead the world in taking firm action in response to these threats.

Likewise, the leaders of Iran must recognize that now is the time for a diplomatic solution, because a coalition stands united in demanding that they meet their obligations, and we will do what is necessary to prevent them from getting a nuclear weapon.

At the same time, we'll engage Russia to seek further reductions in our nuclear arsenals, and continue leading the global effort to secure nuclear materials that could fall into the wrong hands—because our ability to influence others depends on our willingness to lead and meet our obligations.

America must also face the rapidly growing threat from cyber-attacks. Now, we know hackers steal people's identities and infiltrate private e-mails. We know foreign countries and companies swipe our corporate secrets. Now our enemies are also seeking the ability to sabotage our power grid, our financial institutions, our air traffic control systems. We cannot look back years from now and wonder why we did nothing in the face of real threats to our security and our economy.

And that's why, earlier today, I signed a new executive order that will strengthen our cyber defenses by increasing information sharing, and developing standards to protect our national security, our jobs, and our privacy.

But now Congress must act as well, by passing legislation to give our government a greater capacity to secure our networks and deter attacks. This is something we should be able to get done on a bipartisan basis.

Now, even as we protect our people, we should remember that today's world presents not just dangers, not just threats, it presents opportunities. To boost American exports, support American jobs, and level the playing field in the growing markets of Asia, we intend to complete negotiations on a Trans-Pacific Partnership. And tonight, I'm announcing that we will launch talks on a comprehensive Transatlantic Trade and Investment Partnership with the European Union—because trade that is fair and free across the Atlantic supports millions of good-paying American jobs.

We also know that progress in the most impoverished parts

of our world enriches us all—not only because it creates new markets, more stable order in certain regions of the world, but also because it's the right thing to do. In many places, people live on little more than a dollar a day. So the United States will join with our allies to eradicate such extreme poverty in the next two decades by connecting more people to the global economy; by empowering women; by giving our young and brightest minds new opportunities to serve, and helping communities to feed, and power, and educate themselves; by saving the world's children from preventable deaths; and by realizing the promise of an AIDS-free generation, which is within our reach.

You see, America must remain a beacon to all who seek freedom during this period of historic change. I saw the power of hope last year in Rangoon, in Burma, when Aung San Suu Kyi welcomed an American president into the home where she had been imprisoned for years; when thousands of Burmese lined the streets, waving American flags, including a man who said, "There is justice and law in the United States. I want our country to be like that."

In defense of freedom, we'll remain the anchor of strong alliances from the Americas to Africa; from Europe to Asia. In the Middle East, we will stand with citizens as they demand their universal rights, and support stable transitions to democracy.

We know the process will be messy, and we cannot presume to dictate the course of change in countries like Egypt, but we can—and will—insist on respect for the fundamental rights of all people. We'll keep the pressure on a Syrian regime that has murdered its own people, and support opposition leaders that respect the rights of every Syrian. And we will stand steadfast with Israel in pursuit of security and a lasting peace.

These are the messages I'll deliver when I travel to the Middle East next month. And all this work depends on the courage and sacrifice of those who serve in dangerous places at great personal risk—our diplomats, our intelligence officers, and the men and women of the United States Armed Forces. As long as I'm commander in chief, we will do whatever we must to protect those who serve their country abroad, and we will maintain the best military the world has ever known.

We'll invest in new capabilities, even as we reduce waste and wartime spending. We will ensure equal treatment for all service members, and equal benefits for their families—gay and straight. We will draw upon the courage and skills of our sisters and daughters and moms, because women have proven under fire that they are ready for combat.

We will keep faith with our veterans, investing in world-class care, including mental health care, for our wounded warriors—supporting our military families; giving our veterans the benefits and education and job opportunities that they have earned. And I want to thank my wife, Michelle, and Dr. Jill Biden for their continued dedication to serving our military families as well as they have served us. Thank you, honey. Thank you, Jill.

Defending our freedom, though, is not just the job of our military alone. We must all do our part to make sure our God-given rights are protected here at home. That includes one of the most fundamental rights of a democracy: the right to vote. When any American, no matter where they live or what their party, are denied that right because they can't afford to wait for five or six or seven hours just to cast their ballot, we are betraying our ideals.

So tonight, I'm announcing a nonpartisan commission to improve the voting experience in America. And it definitely needs improvement. I'm asking two long-time experts in the field—who, by the way, recently served as the top attorneys for my campaign and for Governor Romney's campaign—to lead it. We can fix this, and we will. The American people demand it, and so does our democracy.

Of course, what I've said tonight matters little if we don't come together to protect our most precious resource: our children. It has been two months since Newtown. I know this is not the first time this country has debated how to reduce gun violence. But this time is different. Overwhelming majorities of Americans—Americans who believe in the Second Amendment—have come together around common-sense reform, like background checks that will make it harder for criminals to get their hands on a gun. Senators of both parties are working together on tough new laws to prevent anyone from buying guns for resale to criminals. Police chiefs are asking our help to get weapons of war and massive ammunition magazines off our streets, because these police chiefs, they're tired of seeing their guys and gals being outgunned.

Each of these proposals deserves a vote in Congress. Now, if you want to vote no, that's your choice. But these proposals deserve a vote. Because in the two months since Newtown, more than a thousand birthdays, graduations, anniversaries have been stolen from our lives by a bullet from a gun—more than a thousand.

One of those we lost was a young girl named Hadiya

Pendleton. She was fifteen years old. She loved Fig Newtons and lip gloss. She was a majorette. She was so good to her friends they all thought they were her best friend. Just three weeks ago, she was here, in Washington, with her classmates, performing for her country at my inauguration. And a week later, she was shot and killed in a Chicago park after school, just a mile away from my house.

Hadiya's parents, Nate and Cleo, are in this chamber tonight, along with more than two dozen Americans whose lives have been torn apart by gun violence. They deserve a vote. They deserve a vote. Gabby Giffords deserves a vote. The families of Newtown deserve a vote. The families of Aurora deserve a vote. The families of Oak Creek and Tucson and Blacksburg, and the countless other communities ripped open by gun violence—they deserve a simple vote. They deserve a simple vote.

Our actions will not prevent every senseless act of violence in this country. In fact, no laws, no initiatives, no administrative acts will perfectly solve all the challenges I've outlined tonight. But we were never sent here to be perfect. We were sent here to make what difference we can, to secure this nation, expand opportunity, uphold our ideals through the hard, often frustrating, but absolutely necessary work of self-government.

We were sent here to look out for our fellow Americans the same way they look out for one another, every single day, usually without fanfare, all across this country. We should follow their example.

We should follow the example of a New York City nurse named Menchu Sanchez. When Hurricane Sandy plunged her hospital into darkness, she wasn't thinking about how her own home was faring. Her mind was on the twenty precious newborns in her care and the rescue plan she devised that kept them all safe.

We should follow the example of a North Miami woman named Desiline Victor. When Desiline arrived at her polling place, she was told the wait to vote might be six hours. And as time ticked by, her concern was not with her tired body or aching feet, but whether folks like her would get to have their say. And hour after hour, a throng of people stayed in line to support her—because Desiline is 102 years old. And they erupted in cheers when she finally put on a sticker that read, "I voted."

We should follow the example of a police officer named Brian Murphy. When a gunman opened fire on a Sikh temple in Wisconsin and Brian was the first to arrive, he did not consider his own safety. He fought back until help arrived and ordered his fellow officers to protect the safety of the Americans worshiping inside, even as he lay bleeding from twelve bullet wounds. And when asked how he did that, Brian said, "That's just the way we're made."

That's just the way we're made. We may do different jobs and wear different uniforms, and hold different views than the person beside us. But as Americans, we all share the same proud title—we are citizens. It's a word that doesn't just describe our nationality or legal status. It describes the way we're made. It describes what we believe. It captures the enduring idea that this country only works when we accept certain obligations to one another and to future generations, that our rights are wrapped up in the rights of others; and that well into our third century as a nation, it remains the task of us all, as citizens of these United States, to be the authors of the next great chapter of our American story.

Thank you. God bless you, and God bless these United States of America.

"TRAYVON MARTIN . . . COULD HAVE BEEN MY SON"

Remarks on Trayvon Martin
WASHINGTON, D.C., JULY 19, 2013

The death of Trayvon Martin had a profound personal impact on Barack Obama, inspiring him to create his My Brother's Keeper initiative to lift up and inspire black boys and teens (and eventually girls). It also led him to one of the most controversial but powerful statements of his presidency, in March of 2012, when Obama said in the Rose Garden that if he had a son, he'd have looked like the slain Florida youth. A year later, following the acquittal of Martin's killer, Obama offered these more extended remarks about the case, his own struggles growing up, and the stark realities facing young men of color in America.

I WANTED TO COME out here, first of all, to tell you that Jay is prepared for all your questions and is very much looking forward to the session. The second thing is I want to let you know that over the next couple of weeks, there's going to obviously be a whole range of issues—immigration, economics, et cetera—we'll try to arrange a fuller press conference to address your questions.

The reason I actually wanted to come out today is not to take questions, but to speak to an issue that obviously has gotten a lot of attention over the course of the last week—the issue of the Trayvon Martin ruling. I gave a preliminary statement right after the ruling on Sunday. But watching the debate over the course of the last week, I thought it might be useful for me to expand on my thoughts a little bit.

First of all, I want to make sure that, once again, I send my thoughts and prayers, as well as Michelle's, to the family of Trayvon Martin, and to remark on the incredible grace and dignity with which they've dealt with the entire situation. I can only imagine what they're going through, and it's remarkable how they've handled it.

The second thing I want to say is to reiterate what I said on Sunday, which is there's going to be a lot of arguments about the legal issues in the case—I'll let all the legal analysts and talking heads address those issues. The judge conducted the trial in a professional manner. The prosecution and the defense made their arguments. The juries were properly instructed that in a case such as this reasonable doubt was relevant, and they rendered a verdict. And once the jury has spoken, that's how our system works. But I did want to just talk a little bit about context and how people have responded to it and how people are feeling.

You know, when Trayvon Martin was first shot I said that this could have been my son. Another way of saying that is Trayvon Martin could have been me thirty-five years ago. And when you think about why, in the African American community at least, there's a lot of pain around what happened here, I think it's important to recognize that the African American community is looking at this issue through a set of experiences and a history that doesn't go away.

There are very few African American men in this country who haven't had the experience of being followed when they were shopping in a department store. That includes me. There are very few African American men who haven't had the experience of walking across the street and hearing the locks click on the doors of cars. That happens to me—at least before I was a senator. There are very few African Americans who haven't had the experience of getting on an elevator and a woman clutching her purse nervously and holding her breath until she had a chance to get off. That happens often.

And I don't want to exaggerate this, but those sets of experiences inform how the African American community interprets what happened one night in Florida. And it's inescapable for people to bring those experiences to bear. The African American community is also knowledgeable that there is a history of racial disparities in the application of our criminal laws—everything from the death penalty to enforcement of our drug laws. And that ends up having an impact in terms of how people interpret the case.

Now, this isn't to say that the African American community is naïve about the fact that African American young men are disproportionately involved in the criminal justice system; that they're disproportionately both victims and perpetrators of violence. It's not to make excuses for that fact—although black folks do interpret the reasons for that in a historical context. They understand that some of the violence that takes place in poor black neighborhoods around the country is born out of a very violent past in this country, and that the poverty and dysfunction that we see in those communities can be traced to a very difficult history.

And so the fact that sometimes that's unacknowledged adds to the frustration. And the fact that a lot of African American boys are painted with a broad brush and the excuse is given, well, there are these statistics out there that show that African American boys are more violent—using that as an excuse to then see sons treated differently causes pain.

I think the African American community is also not naïve in understanding that, statistically, somebody like Trayvon Martin was statistically more likely to be shot by a peer than he was by somebody else. So folks understand the challenges that exist for African American boys. But they get frustrated, I think, if they feel that there's no context for it and that context is being denied. And that all contributes I think to a sense that if a white male teen was involved in the same kind of scenario, that, from top to bottom, both the outcome and the aftermath might have been different.

Now, the question for me at least, and I think for a lot of folks, is where do we take this? How do we learn some lessons from this and move in a positive direction? I think it's understandable that there have been demonstrations and vigils and protests, and some of that stuff is just going to have to work its way through, as long as it remains nonviolent. If I see any violence, then I will remind folks that that dishonors what happened to Trayvon Martin and his family. But beyond protests or vigils, the question is, are there some concrete things that we might be able to do.

I know that Eric Holder is reviewing what happened down there, but I think it's important for people to have some clear expectations here. Traditionally, these are issues of state and local government, the criminal code. And law enforcement is traditionally done at the state and local levels, not at the federal levels.

That doesn't mean, though, that as a nation we can't do some things that I think would be productive. So let me just give a couple of specifics that I'm still bouncing around with my staff, so we're not rolling out some five-point plan, but some areas where I think all of us could potentially focus.

Number one, precisely because law enforcement is often determined at the state and local level, I think it would be productive for the Justice Department, governors, mayors to work with law enforcement about training at the state and local levels in order to reduce the kind of mistrust in the system that sometimes currently exists.

When I was in Illinois, I passed racial profiling legislation, and it actually did just two simple things. One, it collected data on traffic stops and the race of the person who was stopped. But the other thing was it resourced us training police departments across the state on how to think about potential racial bias and ways to further professionalize what they were doing.

And initially, the police departments across the state were resistant, but actually they came to recognize that if it was done in a fair, straightforward way that it would allow them to do their jobs better and communities would have more confidence in them and, in turn, be more helpful in applying the law. And obviously, law enforcement has got a very tough job.

So that's one area where I think there are a lot of resources and best practices that could be brought to bear if state and local governments are receptive. And I think a lot of them would be. And let's figure out are there ways for us to push out that kind of training.

Along the same lines, I think it would be useful for us to examine some state and local laws to see if they are designed in such a way that they may encourage the kinds of altercations and confrontations and tragedies that we saw in the Florida case, rather than defuse potential altercations.

I know that there's been commentary about the fact that the "stand your ground" laws in Florida were not used as a defense in the case. On the other hand, if we're sending a message as a society in our communities that someone who is armed potentially has the right to use those firearms even if there's a way for them to exit from a situation, is that really going to be contributing to the kind of peace and security and order that we'd like to see?

And for those who resist that idea that we should think about something like these "stand your ground" laws, I'd just ask people to consider, if Trayvon Martin was of age and armed, could he have stood his ground on that sidewalk? And do we actually think that he would have been justified in shooting Mr. Zimmerman who had followed him in a car because he felt threatened? And if the answer to that question is at least ambiguous, then it seems to me that we might want to examine those kinds of laws.

Number three—and this is a long-term project—we need to spend some time in thinking about how do we bolster and reinforce our African American boys. And this is something that Michelle and I talk a lot about. There are a lot of kids out there who need help who are getting a lot of negative rein-forcement. And is there more that we can do to give them the sense that their country cares about them and values them and is willing to invest in them?

I'm not naïve about the prospects of some grand, new federal program. I'm not sure that that's what we're talking about here. But I do recognize that as president, I've got some convening power, and there are a lot of good programs that are being done across the country on this front. And for us to be able to gather together business leaders and local elected officials and clergy and celebrities and athletes, and figure out how are we doing a better job helping young African American men feel that they're a full part of this society and that they've got path-ways and avenues to succeed—I think that would be a pretty good outcome from what was obviously a tragic situation. And we're going to spend some time working on that and thinking about that.

And then, finally, I think it's going to be important for all of us to do some soul-searching. There has been talk about should we convene a conversation on race. I haven't seen that be particularly productive when politicians try to organize conver-sations. They end up being stilted and politicized, and folks are locked into the positions they already have. On the other hand, in families and churches and workplaces, there's the possibility that people are a little bit more honest, and at least you ask yourself your own questions about, am I wringing as much bias out of myself as I can? Am I judging people as much as I can, based on not the color of their skin, but the content of their character? That would, I think, be an appropriate exercise in the wake of this tragedy.

And let me just leave you with a final thought that, as difficult and challenging as this whole episode has been for a lot of people, I don't want us to lose sight that things are getting better. Each successive generation seems to be making progress in changing attitudes when it comes to race. It doesn't mean we're in a post-racial society. It doesn't mean that racism is eliminated. But when I talk to Malia and Sasha, and I listen to their friends and I see them interact, they're better than we are—they're better than we were—on these issues. And that's true in every community that I've visited all across the country.

And so we have to be vigilant and we have to work on these issues. And those of us in authority should be doing everything we can to encourage the better angels of our nature, as opposed to using these episodes to heighten divisions. But we should also have confidence that kids these days, I think, have more sense than we did back then, and certainly more than our parents did or our grandparents did; and that along this long, difficult journey, we're becoming a more perfect union—not a perfect union, but a more perfect union.

"PUT ON LOVE"

Remarks at the National Prayer Breakfast

WASHINGTON, D.C., FEBRUARY 5, 2015

The National Prayer Breakfast is an annual event in Washington, D.C., that brings together thousands of religious people from around the world, including leaders of various faith denominations. Obama's 2015 speech at the breakfast may have been his most memorable, and the most debated. It opened with concern that religion was "being twisted and distorted, used as a wedge—or, worse, sometimes used as a weapon." These comments alone did not merit much attention, but it was what Obama said next that threw his political opponents into a frenzy. Recognizing the deep historical ties between religion and violence, Obama warned against getting "on our high horse" and specifically named the Crusades, slavery, and Jim Crow as examples in which extremist interpretations of Christianity were used to justify oppression. His comments sparked a national discussion about religion in the United States and around the world, and an exploration of the role of violence in Christianity and Islam.

GIVING ALL PRAISE and honor to God. It is wonderful to be back with you here. I want to thank our co-chairs, Bob and Roger. These two don't always agree in the Senate, but in coming together and uniting us all in prayer, they embody the spirit of our gathering today.

I also want to thank everybody who helped organize this breakfast. It's wonderful to see so many friends and faith leaders and dignitaries. And Michelle and I are truly honored to be joining you here today.

I want to offer a special welcome to a good friend, His Holiness the Dalai Lama— who is a powerful example of what it means to practice compassion, who inspires us to speak up for the freedom and dignity of all human beings. I've been pleased to welcome him to the White House on many occasions, and we're grateful that he's able to join us here today.

There aren't that many occasions that bring His Holiness under the same roof as NASCAR. This may be the first. But God works in mysterious ways. And so I want to thank Darrell [Waltrip] for that wonderful presentation. Darrell knows that when you're going two hundred miles an hour, a little prayer cannot hurt. I suspect that more than once, Darrell has had the same thought as many of us have in our own lives—Jesus, take the wheel. Although I hope that you kept your hands on the wheel when you were thinking that.

He and I obviously share something in having married up. And we are so grateful to Stevie for the incredible work that they've done together to build a ministry where the fastest drivers can slow down a little bit, and spend some time in prayer and reflection and thanks. And we certainly want to wish Darrell a happy birthday. Happy birthday.

I will note, though, Darrell, when you were reading that list of things folks were saying about you, I was thinking, well, you're a piker. I mean, that—I mean, if you really want a list, come talk to me. Because that ain't nothing. That's the best they can do in NASCAR?

Slowing down and pausing for fellowship and prayer—that's what this breakfast is about. I think it's fair to say Washington moves a lot slower than NASCAR. Certainly my agenda does sometimes. But still, it's easier to get caught up in the rush of our lives, and in the political back-and-forth that can take over this city. We get sidetracked with distractions, large and small. We can't go ten minutes without checking our smartphones— and for my staff, that's every ten seconds. And so for sixty-three years, this prayer tradition has brought us together, giving us the opportunity to come together in humility before the Almighty and to be reminded of what it is that we share as children of God.

And certainly for me, this is always a chance to reflect on my own faith journey. Many times as president, I've been reminded of a line of prayer that Eleanor Roosevelt was fond of. She said, "Keep us at tasks too hard for us that we may be driven to Thee for strength." Keep us at tasks too hard for us that we may be driven to Thee for strength. I've wondered at times if maybe God was answering that prayer a little too literally. But no matter the challenge, He has been there for all of us. He's certainly strengthened me "with the power through his Spirit," as I've sought His guidance not just in my own life but in the life of our nation.

Now, over the last few months, we've seen a number of challenges—certainly over the last six years. But part of what

I want to touch on today is the degree to which we've seen professions of faith used both as an instrument of great good, but also twisted and misused in the name of evil.

As we speak, around the world, we see faith inspiring people to lift up one another—to feed the hungry and care for the poor, and comfort the afflicted and make peace where there is strife. We heard the good work that Sister has done in Philadelphia, and the incredible work that Dr. Brantly and his colleagues have done. We see faith driving us to do right.

But we also see faith being twisted and distorted, used as a wedge—or, worse, sometimes used as a weapon. From a school in Pakistan to the streets of Paris, we have seen violence and terror perpetrated by those who profess to stand up for faith, their faith, professed to stand up for Islam, but, in fact, are betraying it. We see ISIL, a brutal, vicious death cult that, in the name of religion, carries out unspeakable acts of barbarism—terrorizing religious minorities like the Yezidis, subjecting women to rape as a weapon of war, and claiming the mantle of religious authority for such actions.

We see sectarian war in Syria, the murder of Muslims and Christians in Nigeria, religious war in the Central African Republic, a rising tide of anti-Semitism and hate crimes in Europe, so often perpetrated in the name of religion.

So how do we, as people of faith, reconcile these realities—the profound good, the strength, the tenacity, the compassion and love that can flow from all of our faiths, operating alongside those who seek to hijack the religious for their own murderous ends?

Humanity has been grappling with these questions throughout human history. And lest we get on our high horse

and think this is unique to some other place, remember that
during the Crusades and the Inquisition, people committed
terrible deeds in the name of Christ. In our home country,
slavery and Jim Crow all too often was justified in the name of
Christ. Michelle and I returned from India—an incredible,
beautiful country, full of magnificent diversity—but a place
where, in past years, religious faiths of all types have, on occasion, been targeted by other peoples of faith, simply due to their
heritage and their beliefs—acts of intolerance that would have
shocked Gandhiji, the person who helped to liberate that
nation.

So this is not unique to one group or one religion. There is a
tendency in us, a sinful tendency that can pervert and distort
our faith. In today's world, when hate groups have their own
Twitter accounts and bigotry can fester in hidden places in
cyberspace, it can be even harder to counteract such intolerance. But God compels us to try. And in this mission, I believe
there are a few principles that can guide us, particularly those of
us who profess to believe.

And, first, we should start with some basic humility. I believe
that the starting point of faith is some doubt—not being so full
of yourself and so confident that you are right and that God
speaks only to us, and doesn't speak to others, that God only
cares about us and doesn't care about others, that somehow we
alone are in possession of the truth.

Our job is not to ask that God respond to our notion of
truth—our job is to be true to Him, His word, and His commandments. And we should assume humbly that we're confused and
don't always know what we're doing and we're staggering and
stumbling towards Him, and have some humility in that process.

And that means we have to speak up against those who would misuse His name to justify oppression, or violence, or hatred with that fierce certainty. No God condones terror. No grievance justifies the taking of innocent lives, or the oppression of those who are weaker or fewer in number.

And so, as people of faith, we are summoned to push back against those who try to distort our religion—any religion— for their own nihilistic ends. And here at home and around the world, we will constantly reaffirm that fundamental freedom— freedom of religion—the right to practice our faith how we choose, to change our faith if we choose, to practice no faith at all if we choose, and to do so free of persecution and fear and discrimination.

There's wisdom in our founders writing in those documents that help found this nation the notion of freedom of religion, because they understood the need for humility. They also understood the need to uphold freedom of speech, that there was a connection between freedom of speech and freedom of religion. For to infringe on one right under the pretext of protecting another is a betrayal of both.

But part of humility is also recognizing in modern, compli- cated, diverse societies, the functioning of these rights, the concern for the protection of these rights calls for each of us to exercise civility and restraint and judgment. And if, in fact, we defend the legal right of a person to insult another's religion, we're equally obligated to use our free speech to condemn such insults—and stand shoulder-to-shoulder with religious communities, particularly religious minorities who are the targets of such attacks. Just because you have the right to say something doesn't mean the rest of us shouldn't question those who would insult others in the name of free speech. Because we know that our nations are stronger when people of all faiths feel that they are welcome, that they, too, are full and equal members of our countries.

So humility I think is needed. And the second thing we need is to uphold the distinction between our faith and our governments. Between church and between state. The United States is one of the most religious countries in the world—far more religious than most Western developed countries. And one of the reasons is that our founders wisely embraced the separation of church and state. Our government does not sponsor a religion, nor does it pressure anyone to practice a particular faith, or any faith at all. And the result is a culture where people of all backgrounds and beliefs can freely and proudly worship, without fear, or coercion—so that when you listen to Darrell talk about his faith journey you know it's real. You know he's not saying it because it helps him advance, or because somebody told him to. It's from the heart.

That's not the case in theocracies that restrict people's choice of faith. It's not the case in authoritarian governments that elevate an individual leader or a political party above the people, or in some cases, above the concept of God Himself. So the freedom of religion is a value we will continue to protect here at home and stand up for around the world, and is one that we guard vigilantly here in the United States.

Last year, we joined together to pray for the release of Christian missionary Kenneth Bae, held in North Korea for two years. And today, we give thanks that Kenneth is finally back where he belongs—home, with his family.

Last year, we prayed together for Pastor Saeed Abedini,

detained in Iran since 2012. And I was recently in Boise, Idaho, and had the opportunity to meet with Pastor Abedini's beautiful wife and wonderful children and to convey to them that our country has not forgotten brother Saeed and that we're doing everything we can to bring him home. And then, I received an extraordinary letter from Pastor Abedini. And in it, he describes his captivity, and expressed his gratitude for my visit with his family, and thanked us all for standing in solidarity with him during his captivity.

And Pastor Abedini wrote, "Nothing is more valuable to the Body of Christ than to see how the Lord is in control, and moves ahead of countries and leadership through united prayer." And he closed his letter by describing himself as "prisoner for Christ, who is proud to be part of this great nation of the United States of America that cares for religious freedom around the world."

We're going to keep up this work—for Pastor Abedini and all those around the world who are unjustly held or persecuted because of their faith. And we're grateful to our new Ambassador-at-Large for International Religious Freedom, Rabbi David Saperstein—who has hit the ground running, and is heading to Iraq in a few days to help religious communities there address some of those challenges. Where's David? I know he's here somewhere. Thank you, David, for the great work you're doing.

Humility; a suspicion of government getting between us and our faiths, or trying to dictate our faiths, or elevate one faith over another. And, finally, let's remember that if there is one law that we can all be most certain of that seems to bind people of all faiths, and people who are still finding their way towards faith but have a sense of ethics and morality in them—that one law, that Golden Rule that we should treat one another as we wish to be treated. The Torah says "Love thy neighbor as yourself." In Islam, there is a Hadith that states: "None of you truly believes until he loves for his brother what he loves for himself." The Holy Bible tells us to "put on love, which binds everything together in perfect harmony." Put on love.

Whatever our beliefs, whatever our traditions, we must seek to be instruments of peace, and bringing light where there is darkness, and sowing love where there is hatred. And this is the loving message of His Holiness, Pope Francis. And like so many people around the world, I've been touched by his call to relieve suffering, and to show justice and mercy and compassion to the most vulnerable; to walk with the Lord and ask "Who am I to judge?" He challenges us to press on in what he calls our "march of living hope." And like millions of Americans, I am very much looking forward to welcoming Pope Francis to the United States later this year.

His Holiness expresses that basic law: Treat thy neighbor as yourself. The Dalai Lama—anybody who's had an opportunity to be with him senses that same spirit. Kent Brantly expresses that same spirit. Kent was with Samaritan's Purse, treating Ebola patients in Liberia, when he contracted the virus himself. And with world-class medical care and a deep reliance on faith—with God's help, Kent survived.

And then by donating his plasma, he helped others survive as well. And he continues to advocate for a global response in West Africa, reminding us that "our efforts need to be on loving the people there." And I could not have been prouder to welcome Kent and his wonderful wife, Amber, to the Oval

Office. We are blessed to have him here today—because he reminds us of what it means to really "love thy neighbor as thyself." Not just words, but deeds.

Each of us has a role in fulfilling our common, greater purpose—not merely to seek high position, but to plumb greater depths so that we may find the strength to love more fully. And this is perhaps our greatest challenge—to see our own reflection in each other; to be our brother's keepers and sister's keepers, and to keep faith with one another. As children of God, let's make that our work, together.

As children of God, let's work to end injustice—injustice of poverty and hunger. No one should ever suffer from such want amidst such plenty. As children of God, let's work to eliminate the scourge of homelessness, because, as Sister Mary says, "None of us are home until all of us are home." None of us are home until all of us are home.

As children of God, let's stand up for the dignity and value of every woman, and man, and child, because we are all equal in His eyes, and work to send the scourge and the sin of modern-day slavery and human trafficking, and "set the oppressed free."

If we are properly humble, if we drop to our knees on occasion, we will acknowledge that we never fully know God's purpose. We can never fully fathom His amazing grace. "We see through a glass, darkly"—grappling with the expanse of His awesome love. But even with our limits, we can heed that which is required: To do justice, and love kindness, and walk humbly with our God.

I pray that we will. And as we journey together on this "march of living hope," I pray that, in His name, we will run and not be weary, and walk and not be faint, and we'll heed those words and "put on love."

May the Lord bless you and keep you, and may He bless this precious country that we love.

"FOR WE WERE BORN OF CHANGE"

Remarks on the Fiftieth Anniversary of "Bloody Sunday"

SELMA, ALABAMA, MARCH 7, 2015

Obama's speech on the Edmund Pettus Bridge on the fiftieth anniversary of Bloody Sunday wasn't his first in Selma. Seven years earlier, he and Hillary Clinton had made dueling speeches in the city whose scenes of racist brutality helped secure passage of the Voting Rights Act in 1965. But Obama's 2015 speech ranks among his most beautiful. It is an American elegy —full of odes to the heroic battles of the civil rights era that Obama likens to the great battles of America's wars. It is poetic, quoting as generously from James Baldwin as from the Bible. It is hopeful. And it was delivered as the smoke barely had cleared from the uprising in Ferguson, Missouri, after another death, another acquittal of a police officer, and fresh evidence of the imperfections of our union.

AUDIENCE MEMBER: We love you, President Obama!
PRESIDENT: Well, you know I love you back.

It is a rare honor in this life to follow one of your heroes. And John Lewis is one of my heroes.

Now, I have to imagine that when a younger John Lewis woke up that morning fifty years ago and made his way to Brown Chapel, heroics were not on his mind. A day like this was not on his mind. Young folks with bedrolls and backpacks were milling about. Veterans of the movement trained newcomers in the tactics of non-violence; the right way to protect yourself when attacked. A doctor described what tear gas does to the body, while marchers scribbled down instructions for contacting their loved ones. The air was thick with doubt, anticipation, and fear. And they comforted themselves with the final verse of the final hymn they sung:

"No matter what may be the test, God will take care of you; Lean, weary one, upon His breast, God will take care of you."

And then, his knapsack stocked with an apple, a toothbrush, and a book on government—all you need for a night behind bars—John Lewis led them out of the church on a mission to change America.

President and Mrs. Bush, Governor Bentley, Mayor Evans, Sewell, Reverend Strong, members of Congress, elected officials, foot soldiers, friends, fellow Americans:

As John noted, there are places and moments in America where this nation's destiny has been decided. Many are sites of war—Concord and Lexington, Appomattox, Gettysburg. Others are sites that symbolize the daring of America's character—Independence Hall and Seneca Falls, Kitty Hawk and Cape Canaveral.

Selma is such a place. In one afternoon fifty years ago, so much of our turbulent history—the stain of slavery and anguish of civil war; the yoke of segregation and tyranny of Jim Crow; the death of four little girls in Birmingham; and the dream of a Baptist preacher—all that history met on this bridge.

It was not a clash of armies, but a clash of wills; a contest to determine the true meaning of America. And because of men and women like John Lewis, Joseph Lowery, Hosea Williams, Amelia Boynton, Diane Nash, Ralph Abernathy, C. T. Vivian, Andrew Young, Fred Shuttlesworth, Dr. Martin Luther King Jr., and so many others, the idea of a just America and a fair America, an inclusive America, and a generous America—that idea ultimately triumphed.

As is true across the landscape of American history, we cannot examine this moment in isolation. The march on Selma was part of a broader campaign that spanned generations; the leaders that day part of a long line of heroes.

We gather here to celebrate them. We gather here to honor the courage of ordinary Americans willing to endure billy clubs and the chastening rod; tear gas and the trampling hoof; men and women who despite the gush of blood and splintered bone would stay true to their North Star and keep marching towards justice.

They did as Scripture instructed: "Rejoice in hope, be patient in tribulation, be constant in prayer." And in the days to come, they went back again and again. When the trumpet call sounded for more to join, the people came—black and white, young and old, Christian and Jew, waving the American flag and singing the same anthems full of faith and hope. A white newsman, Bill Plante, who covered the marches then and who is with us here today, quipped that the growing number of white people lowered the quality of the singing. To those who marched, though, those old gospel songs must have never sounded so sweet.

In time, their chorus would well up and reach President Johnson. And he would send them protection, and speak to the nation, echoing their call for America and the world to hear: "We shall overcome." What enormous faith these men and women had. Faith in God, but also faith in America.

The Americans who crossed this bridge, they were not physically imposing. But they gave courage to millions. They held no elected office. But they led a nation. They marched as Americans who had endured hundreds of years of brutal violence, countless daily indignities—but they didn't seek special treatment, just the equal treatment promised to them almost a century before.

What they did here will reverberate through the ages. Not because the change they won was preordained; not because their victory was complete; but because they proved that nonviolent change is possible, that love and hope can conquer hate.

As we commemorate their achievement, we are well-served to remember that at the time of the marches, many in power condemned rather than praised them. Back then, they were called Communists, or half-breeds, or outside agitators, sexual and moral degenerates, and worse—they were called everything but the name their parents gave them. Their faith was questioned. Their lives were threatened. Their patriotism challenged.

And yet, what could be more American than what happened in this place? What could more profoundly vindicate the idea of America than plain and humble people—unsung, the downtrodden, the dreamers not of high station, not born to wealth or privilege, not of one religious tradition but many, coming together to shape their country's course?

What greater expression of faith in the American experiment than this, what greater form of patriotism is there than the belief that America is not yet finished, that we are strong enough to be self-critical, that each successive generation can look upon our imperfections and decide that it is in our power to remake this nation to more closely align with our highest ideals?

That's why Selma is not some outlier in the American experience. That's why it's not a museum or a static monument to behold from a distance. It is instead the manifestation of a creed written into our founding documents: "We the People . . . in order to form a more perfect union." "We hold these truths to be self-evident, that all men are created equal."

These are not just words. They're a living thing, a call to action, a roadmap for citizenship and an insistence in the capacity of free men and women to shape our own destiny. For founders like Franklin and Jefferson, for leaders like Lincoln and FDR, the success of our experiment in self-government rested on engaging all of our citizens in this work. And that's what we celebrate here in Selma. That's what this movement was all about, one leg in our long journey toward freedom.

The American instinct that led these young men and women to pick up the torch and cross this bridge, that's the same instinct that moved patriots to choose revolution over tyranny. It's the same instinct that drew immigrants from across oceans and the Rio Grande; the same instinct that led women to reach for the ballot, workers to organize against an unjust status quo; the same instinct that led us to plant a flag at Iwo Jima and on the surface of the Moon.

It's the idea held by generations of citizens who believed that America is a constant work in progress; who believed that loving this country requires more than singing its praises or avoiding uncomfortable truths. It requires the occasional disruption, the willingness to speak out for what is right, to shake up the status quo. That's America.

That's what makes us unique. That's what cements our reputation as a beacon of opportunity. Young people behind the Iron Curtain would see Selma and eventually tear down that wall. Young people in Soweto would hear Bobby Kennedy talk about ripples of hope and eventually banish the scourge of apartheid. Young people in Burma went to prison rather than submit to military rule. They saw what John Lewis had done. From the streets of Tunis to the Maidan in Ukraine, this generation of young people can draw strength from this place, where the powerless could change the world's greatest power and push their leaders to expand the boundaries of freedom.

They saw that idea made real right here in Selma, Alabama. They saw that idea manifest itself here in America.

Because of campaigns like this, a Voting Rights Act was passed. Political and economic and social barriers came down. And the change these men and women wrought is visible here today in the presence of African Americans who run boardrooms, who sit on the bench, who serve in elected office from small towns to big cities; from the Congressional Black Caucus all the way to the Oval Office.

Because of what they did, the doors of opportunity swung open not just for black folks, but for every American. Women marched through those doors. Latinos marched through those doors. Asian Americans, gay Americans, Americans with disabilities—they all came through those doors. Their endeavors gave the entire South the chance to rise again, not by reasserting the past, but by transcending the past.

What a glorious thing, Dr. King might say. And what a solemn debt we owe. Which leads us to ask, just how might we repay that debt?

First and foremost, we have to recognize that one day's commemoration, no matter how special, is not enough. If Selma taught us anything, it's that our work is never done. The American experiment in self-government gives work and purpose to each generation.

Selma teaches us, as well, that action requires that we shed our cynicism. For when it comes to the pursuit of justice, we can afford neither complacency nor despair.

Just this week, I was asked whether I thought the Department of Justice's Ferguson report shows that, with respect to race, little has changed in this country. And I understood the question; the report's narrative was sadly familiar. It evoked the kind of abuse and disregard for citizens that spawned the Civil Rights Movement. But I rejected the notion that nothing's changed. What happened in Ferguson may not be unique, but it's no longer endemic. It's no longer sanctioned by law or by custom. And before the Civil Rights Movement, it most surely was.

We do a disservice to the cause of justice by intimating that bias and discrimination are immutable, that racial division is inherent to America. If you think nothing's changed in the past fifty years, ask somebody who lived through the Selma or Chicago or Los Angeles of the 1950s. Ask the female CEO who once might have been assigned to the secretarial pool if nothing's changed. Ask your gay friend if it's easier to be out and proud in America now than it was thirty years ago. To deny this progress, this hard-won progress—our progress—would be to rob us of our own agency, our own capacity, our responsibility to do what we can to make America better.

Of course, a more common mistake is to suggest that Ferguson is an isolated incident; that racism is banished; that the work that drew men and women to Selma is now complete, and that whatever racial tensions remain are a consequence of those seeking to play the "race card" for their own purposes. We don't need the Ferguson report to know that's not true. We just need to open our eyes, and our ears, and our hearts to know that this nation's racial history still casts its long shadow upon us.

We know the march is not yet over. We know the race is not yet won. We know that reaching that blessed destination where we are judged, all of us, by the content of our character requires admitting as much, facing up to the truth. "We are capable of bearing a great burden," James Baldwin once wrote, "once we discover that the burden is reality and arrive where reality is."

There's nothing America can't handle if we actually look squarely at the problem. And this is work for all Americans, not just some. Not just whites. Not just blacks. If we want to honor the courage of those who marched that day, then all of us are called to possess their moral imagination. All of us will need to feel as they did the fierce urgency of now. All of us need to recognize as they did that change depends on our actions, on our attitudes, the things we teach our children. And if we make such an effort, no matter how hard it may sometimes seem, laws can be passed, and consciences can be stirred, and consensus can be built.

With such an effort, we can make sure our criminal justice system serves all and not just some. Together, we can raise the level of mutual trust that policing is built on—the idea that police officers are members of the community they risk their lives to protect, and citizens in Ferguson and New York and Cleveland, they just want the same thing young people here marched for fifty years ago—the protection of the law. Together, we can address unfair sentencing and overcrowded prisons, and the stunted circumstances that rob too many boys of the chance to become men, and rob the nation of too many men who could be good dads, and good workers, and good neighbors.

With effort, we can roll back poverty and the roadblocks to opportunity. Americans don't accept a free ride for anybody, nor do we believe in equality of outcomes. But we do expect equal opportunity. And if we really mean it, if we're not just giving lip service to it, but if we really mean it and are willing to sacrifice for it, then, yes, we can make sure every child gets an education suitable to this new century, one that expands imaginations and lifts sights and gives those children the skills they need. We can make sure every person willing to work has the dignity of a job, and a fair wage, and a real voice, and sturdier rungs on that ladder into the middle class.

And with effort, we can protect the foundation stone of our democracy for which so many marched across this bridge—and that is the right to vote. Right now, in 2015, fifty years after Selma, there are laws across this country designed to make it harder for people to vote. As we speak, more of such laws are being proposed. Meanwhile, the Voting Rights Act, the culmination of so much blood, so much sweat and tears, the product of so much sacrifice in the face of wanton violence, the Voting Rights Act stands weakened, its future subject to political rancor.

How can that be? The Voting Rights Act was one of the crowning achievements of our democracy, the result of Republican and Democratic efforts. President Reagan signed its renewal when he was in office. President George W. Bush signed its renewal when he was in office. One hundred members of Congress have come here today to honor people who were willing to die for the right to protect it. If we want to honor this day, let that hundred go back to Washington and gather four hundred more, and together, pledge to make it their mission to restore that law this year. That's how we honor those on this bridge.

Of course, our democracy is not the task of Congress alone, or the courts alone, or even the president alone. If every new voter-suppression law was struck down today, we would still have, here in America, one of the lowest voting rates among free peoples. Fifty years ago, registering to vote here in Selma and much of the South meant guessing the number of jelly-beans in a jar, the number of bubbles on a bar of soap. It meant risking your dignity, and sometimes, your life.

What's our excuse today for not voting? How do we so casually discard the right for which so many fought? How do we so fully give away our power, our voice, in shaping America's future? Why are we pointing to somebody else when we could take the time just to go to the polling places? We give away our power.

Fellow marchers, so much has changed in fifty years. We have endured war and we've fashioned peace. We've seen technological wonders that touch every aspect of our lives. We take for granted conveniences that our parents could have scarcely imagined. But what has not changed is the imperative of citizenship; that willingness of a twenty-six-year-old deacon, or a Unitarian minister, or a young mother of five to decide they loved this country so much that they'd risk everything to realize its promise.

That's what it means to love America. That's what it means to believe in America. That's what it means when we say America is exceptional.

For we were born of change. We broke the old aristocracies, declaring ourselves entitled not by bloodline, but endowed by our Creator with certain inalienable rights. We secure our rights and responsibilities through a system of self-government, of and by and for the people. That's why we argue and fight with so much passion and conviction—because we know our efforts matter. We know America is what we make of it.

Look at our history. We are Lewis and Clark and Sacajawea, pioneers who braved the unfamiliar, followed by a stampede of farmers and miners, and entrepreneurs and hucksters. That's our spirit. That's who we are.

We are Sojourner Truth and Fannie Lou Hamer, women who could do as much as any man and then some. And we're Susan B. Anthony, who shook the system until the law reflected that truth. That is our character.

We're the immigrants who stowed away on ships to reach these shores, the huddled masses yearning to breathe free— Holocaust survivors, Soviet defectors, the Lost Boys of Sudan.

We're the hopeful strivers who cross the Rio Grande because we want our kids to know a better life. That's how we came to be.

We're the slaves who built the White House and the economy of the South. We're the ranch hands and cowboys who opened up the West, and countless laborers who laid rail, and raised skyscrapers, and organized for workers' rights.

We're the fresh-faced GIs who fought to liberate a continent. And we're the Tuskegee Airmen, and the Navajo code-talkers, and the Japanese Americans who fought for this country even as their own liberty had been denied.

We're the firefighters who rushed into those buildings on 9/11, the volunteers who signed up to fight in Afghanistan and Iraq. We're the gay Americans whose blood ran in the streets of San Francisco and New York, just as blood ran down this bridge.

We are storytellers, writers, poets, artists who abhor unfairness, and despise hypocrisy, and give voice to the voiceless, and tell truths that need to be told.

We're the inventors of gospel and jazz and blues, bluegrass and country, and hip-hop and rock and roll, and our very own sound with all the sweet sorrow and reckless joy of freedom.

We are Jackie Robinson, enduring scorn and spiked cleats and pitches coming straight to his head, and stealing home in the World Series anyway.

We are the people Langston Hughes wrote of who "build our temples for tomorrow, strong as we know how." We are the people Emerson wrote of, "who for truth and honor's sake stand fast and suffer long"; who are "never tired, so long as we can see far enough."

That's what America is. Not stock photos or airbrushed

history, or feeble attempts to define some of us as more American than others. We respect the past, but we don't pine for the past. We don't fear the future; we grab for it. America is not some fragile thing. We are large, in the words of Whitman, containing multitudes. We are boisterous and diverse and full of energy, perpetually young in spirit. That's why someone like John Lewis at the ripe old age of twenty-five could lead a mighty march.

And that's what the young people here today and listening all across the country must take away from this day. You are America. Unconstrained by habit and convention. Unencumbered by what is, because you're ready to seize what ought to be.

For everywhere in this country, there are first steps to be taken, there's new ground to cover, there are more bridges to be crossed. And it is you, the young and fearless at heart, the most diverse and educated generation in our history, who the nation is waiting to follow.

Because Selma shows us that America is not the project of any one person. Because the single-most powerful word in our democracy is the word "We." "We the People." "We Shall Overcome." "Yes, We Can." That word is owned by no one. It belongs to everyone. Oh, what a glorious task we are given, to continually try to improve this great nation of ours.

Fifty years from Bloody Sunday, our march is not yet finished, but we're getting closer. Two hundred and thirty-nine years after this nation's founding our union is not yet perfect, but we are getting closer. Our job's easier because somebody already got us through that first mile. Somebody already got us over that bridge. When it feels the road is too hard, when the torch we've been passed feels too heavy, we will remember these early travelers, and draw strength from their example, and hold firmly the words of the prophet Isaiah: "Those who hope in the Lord will renew their strength. They will soar on [the] wings like eagles. They will run and not grow weary. They will walk and not be faint."

We honor those who walked so we could run. We must run so our children soar. And we will not grow weary. For we believe in the power of an awesome God, and we believe in this country's sacred promise.

May He bless those warriors of justice no longer with us, and bless the United States of America.

"AMAZING GRACE"

Eulogy for the Honorable Reverend Clementa Pinckney

CHARLESTON, SOUTH CAROLINA, JUNE 26, 2015

President Obama's eulogy for the Reverend Clementa Pinckney—whom Obama befriended as he campaigned in South Carolina in the 2008 primaries and who was slaughtered, along with eight of his parishioners, inside the historic Mother Emanuel AME church in the summer of 2015—is best known not for its text, but for the moment when the president veered from it, spontaneously leading the mourning congregation in a chorus of "Amazing Grace." But the speech itself is notable for its scope and its grandeur. It is not just a tribute to the martyred "Charleston Nine," but to the unbroken spirit of the country Obama led.

GIVING ALL PRAISE and honor to God. The Bible calls us to hope. To persevere, and have faith in things not seen.

"They were still living by faith when they died," Scripture tells us. "They did not receive the things promised; they only saw them and welcomed them from a distance, admitting that they were foreigners and strangers on Earth."

We are here today to remember a man of God who lived by faith. A man who believed in things not seen. A man who believed there were better days ahead, off in the distance. A man of service who persevered, knowing full well he would not receive all those things he was promised, because he believed his efforts would deliver a better life for those who followed.

To Jennifer, his beloved wife; to Eliana and Malana, his beautiful, wonderful daughters; to the Mother Emanuel family and the people of Charleston, the people of South Carolina.

I cannot claim to have the good fortune to know Reverend Pinckney well. But I did have the pleasure of knowing him and meeting him here in South Carolina, back when we were both a little bit younger. Back when I didn't have visible gray hair. The first thing I noticed was his graciousness, his smile, his reassuring baritone, his deceptive sense of humor—all qualities that helped him wear so effortlessly a heavy burden of expectation.

Friends of his remarked this week that when Clementa Pinckney entered a room, it was like the future arrived; that even from a young age, folks knew he was special. Anointed. He was the progeny of a long line of the faithful—a family of preachers who spread God's word, a family of protesters who sowed change to expand voting rights and desegregate the South. Clem heard their instruction, and he did not forsake their teaching.

He was in the pulpit by thirteen, pastor by eighteen, public servant by twenty-three. He did not exhibit any of the cockiness of youth, nor youth's insecurities; instead, he set an example worthy of his position, wise beyond his years, in his speech, in his conduct, in his love, faith, and purity.

As a senator, he represented a sprawling swath of the Lowcountry, a place that has long been one of the most neglected in America. A place still wracked by poverty and inadequate schools; a place where children can still go hungry and the sick can go without treatment. A place that needed somebody like Clem.

His position in the minority party meant the odds of winning more resources for his constituents were often long. His calls for greater equity were too often unheeded, the votes he cast were sometimes lonely. But he never gave up. He stayed true to his convictions. He would not grow discouraged. After a full day at the capitol, he'd climb into his car and head to the church to draw sustenance from his family, from his ministry, from the community that loved and needed him. There he would fortify his faith, and imagine what might be.

Reverend Pinckney embodied a politics that was neither mean, nor small. He conducted himself quietly, and kindly, and diligently. He encouraged progress not by pushing his ideas alone, but by seeking out your ideas, partnering with you to make things happen. He was full of empathy and fellow feeling, able to walk in somebody else's shoes and see through their eyes. No wonder one of his Senate colleagues remembered Senator Pinckney as "the most gentle of the forty-six of us— the best of the forty-six of us."

Clem was often asked why he chose to be a pastor and a public servant. But the person who asked probably didn't know the history of the AME church. As our brothers and sisters in the AME church know, we don't make those distinctions. "Our calling," Clem once said, "is not just within the walls of the congregation, but . . . the life and community in which our congregation resides."

He embodied the idea that our Christian faith demands deeds and not just words; that the "sweet hour of prayer" actually lasts the whole week long—that to put our faith in action is more than individual salvation, it's about our collective salvation; that to feed the hungry and clothe the naked and house the homeless is not just a call for isolated charity but the imperative of a just society.

What a good man. Sometimes I think that's the best thing to hope for when you're eulogized—after all the words and recitations and resumes are read, to just say someone was a good man.

You don't have to be of high station to be a good man. Preacher by thirteen. Pastor by eighteen. Public servant by twenty-three. What a life Clementa Pinckney lived. What an example he set. What a model for his faith. And then to lose him at forty-one—slain in his sanctuary with eight wonderful members of his flock, each at different stages in life but bound together by a common commitment to God.

Cynthia Hurd. Susie Jackson. Ethel Lance. DePayne Middleton-Doctor. Tywanza Sanders. Daniel L. Simmons. Sharonda Coleman-Singleton. Myra Thompson. Good people. Decent people. God-fearing people. People so full of life and so full of kindness. People who ran the race, who persevered. People of great faith.

To the families of the fallen, the nation shares in your grief. Our pain cuts that much deeper because it happened in a church. The church is and always has been the center of African American life—a place to call our own in a too often hostile world, a sanctuary from so many hardships.

Over the course of centuries, black churches served as "hush harbors" where slaves could worship in safety; praise houses where their free descendants could gather and shout hallelujah; rest stops for the weary along the Underground Railroad; bunkers for the foot soldiers of the Civil Rights Movement. They have been, and continue to be, community centers where we organize for jobs and justice; places of scholarship and network; places where children are loved and fed and kept out of harm's way, and told that they are beautiful and smart, and taught that they matter. That's what happens in church.

That's what the black church means. Our beating heart. The place where our dignity as a people is inviolate. When there's no better example of this tradition than Mother Emanuel—a church built by blacks seeking liberty, burned to the ground because its founder sought to end slavery, only to rise up again, a Phoenix from these ashes.

When there were laws banning all-black church gatherings, services happened here anyway, in defiance of unjust laws. When there was a righteous movement to dismantle Jim Crow, Dr. Martin Luther King Jr. preached from its pulpit, and marches began from its steps. A sacred place, this church. Not just for blacks, not just for Christians, but for every American who cares about the steady expansion of human rights and human dignity in this country; a foundation stone for liberty and justice for all. That's what the church meant.

We do not know whether the killer of Reverend Pinckney and eight others knew all of this history. But he surely sensed the meaning of his violent act. It was an act that drew on a long history of bombs and arson and shots fired at churches, not random, but as a means of control, a way to terrorize and oppress. An act that he imagined would incite fear and recrimination; violence and suspicion. An act that he presumed would deepen divisions that trace back to our nation's original sin.

Oh, but God works in mysterious ways. God has different ideas.

He didn't know he was being used by God. Blinded by hatred, the alleged killer could not see the grace surrounding Reverend Pinckney and that Bible study group—the light of love that shone as they opened the church doors and invited a stranger to join in their prayer circle. The alleged killer could have never anticipated the way the families of the fallen would respond when they saw him in court—in the midst of unspeakable grief, with words of forgiveness. He couldn't imagine that.

The alleged killer could not imagine how the city of Charleston, under the good and wise leadership of Mayor Riley—how the state of South Carolina, how the United States of America would respond—not merely with revulsion at his evil act, but with big-hearted generosity and, more importantly, with a thoughtful introspection and self-examination that we so rarely see in public life.

Blinded by hatred, he failed to comprehend what Reverend Pinckney so well understood—the power of God's grace.

This whole week, I've been reflecting on this idea of grace. The grace of the families who lost loved ones. The grace that Reverend Pinckney would preach about in his sermons. The grace described in one of my favorite hymnals—the one we all know: Amazing grace, how sweet the sound that saved a wretch like me. I once was lost, but now I'm found; was blind but now I see.

According to the Christian tradition, grace is not earned. Grace is not merited. It's not something we deserve. Rather, grace is the free and benevolent favor of God as manifested in the salvation of sinners and the bestowal of blessings. Grace.

As a nation, out of this terrible tragedy, God has visited grace upon us, for he has allowed us to see where we've been blind. He has given us the chance, where we've been lost, to find our best selves. We may not have earned it, this grace, with our rancor and complacency, and short-sightedness and fear of each other—but we got it all the same. He gave it to us anyway. He's once more given us grace. But it is up to us now to make the most of it, to receive it with gratitude, and to prove ourselves worthy of this gift.

For too long, we were blind to the pain that the Confederate flag stirred in too many of our citizens. It's true, a flag did not cause these murders. But as people from all walks of life, Republicans and Democrats, now acknowledge—including Governor Haley, whose recent eloquence on the subject is worthy of praise—as we all have to acknowledge, the flag has always represented more than just ancestral pride. For many, black and white, that flag was a reminder of systemic oppression and racial subjugation. We see that now.

Removing the flag from this state's capitol would not be an act of political correctness; it would not be an insult to the valor of Confederate soldiers. It would simply be an acknowledgment that the cause for which they fought—the cause of slavery—was wrong, the imposition of Jim Crow after the Civil War, the resistance to civil rights for all people was wrong.

It would be one step in an honest accounting of America's history; a modest but meaningful balm for so many unhealed wounds. It would be an expression of the amazing changes that have transformed this state and this country for the better, because of the work of so many people of goodwill, people of all races striving to form a more perfect union. By taking down that flag, we express God's grace.

But I don't think God wants us to stop there. For too long, we've been blind to the way past injustices continue to shape the present. Perhaps we see that now. Perhaps this tragedy causes us to ask some tough questions about how we can permit so many of our children to languish in poverty, or attend dilapidated schools, or grow up without prospects for a job or for a career.

Perhaps it causes us to examine what we're doing to cause some of our children to hate. Perhaps it softens hearts towards those lost young men, tens and tens of thousands caught up in the criminal justice system, and leads us to make sure that that system is not infected with bias; that we embrace changes in how we train and equip our police so that the bonds of trust between law enforcement and the communities they serve make us all safer and more secure.

Maybe we now realize the way racial bias can infect us even when we don't realize it, so that we're guarding against not just racial slurs, but we're also guarding against the subtle impulse to call Johnny back for a job interview but not Jamal. So that we search our hearts when we consider laws to make it harder for some of our fellow citizens to vote. By recognizing our common humanity by treating every child as important, regardless of the color of their skin or the station into which they were born, and to do what's necessary to make opportunity real for every American—by doing that, we express God's grace.

For too long—

AUDIENCE: For too long!

PRESIDENT: For too long, we've been blind to the unique mayhem that gun violence inflicts upon this nation. Sporadically, our eyes are open: When eight of our brothers and sisters are cut down in a church basement, twelve in a movie theater, twenty-six in an elementary school. But I hope we also see the thirty precious lives cut short by gun violence in this country every single day; the countless more whose lives are forever changed— the survivors crippled, the children traumatized and fearful every day as they walk to school, the husband who will never feel his wife's warm touch, the entire communities whose grief over- flows every time they have to watch what happened to them happen to some other place.

The vast majority of Americans—the majority of gun owners—want to do something about this. We see that now. And I'm convinced that by acknowledging the pain and loss of others, even as we respect the traditions and ways of life that make up this beloved country—by making the moral choice to change, we express God's grace.

We don't earn grace. We're all sinners. We don't deserve it. But God gives it to us anyway. And we choose how to receive it. It's our decision how to honor it.

None of us can or should expect a transformation in race relations overnight. Every time something like this happens, somebody says we have to have a conversation about race. We talk a lot about race. There's no shortcut. And we don't need more talk. None of us should believe that a handful of gun safety measures will prevent every tragedy. It will not. People of goodwill will continue to debate the merits of various policies, as our democracy requires—this is a big, raucous place, America is. And there are good people on both sides of these debates. Whatever solutions we find will necessarily be incomplete.

But it would be a betrayal of everything Reverend Pinckney stood for, I believe, if we allowed ourselves to slip into a comfortable silence again. Once the eulogies have been delivered, once the TV cameras move on, to go back to business as usual—that's what we so often do to avoid uncomfortable truths about the prejudice that still infects our society. To settle for symbolic gestures without following up with the hard work of more lasting change—that's how we lose our way again.

It would be a refutation of the forgiveness expressed by those families if we merely slipped into old habits, whereby those who disagree with us are not merely wrong but bad; where we shout instead of listen; where we barricade ourselves behind preconceived notions or well-practiced cynicism.

Reverend Pinckney once said, "Across the South, we have a deep appreciation of history—we haven't always had a deep appreciation of each other's history." What is true in the South is true for America. Clem understood that justice grows out of recognition of ourselves in each other. That my liberty depends on you being free, too. That history can't be a sword to justify injustice, or a shield against progress, but must be a manual for how to avoid repeating the mistakes of the past—how to break the cycle. A roadway toward a better world. He knew that the path of grace involves an open mind—but, more importantly, an open heart.

That's what I've felt this week—an open heart. That, more

than any particular policy or analysis, is what's called upon right now, I think—what a friend of mine, the writer Marilyn Robinson, calls "that reservoir of goodness, beyond, and of another kind, that we are able to do each other in the ordinary cause of things."

That reservoir of goodness. If we can find that grace, anything is possible. If we can tap that grace, everything can change.

Amazing grace. Amazing grace.

[*Begins to sing*] Amazing grace, how sweet the sound, that saved a wretch like me; I once was lost, but now I'm found; was blind but now I see.

Clementa Pinckney found that grace.

Cynthia Hurd found that grace.

Susie Jackson found that grace.

Ethel Lance found that grace.

DePayne Middleton-Doctor found that grace.

Tywanza Sanders found that grace.

Daniel L. Simmons, Sr. found that grace.

Sharonda Coleman-Singleton found that grace.

Myra Thompson found that grace.

Through the example of their lives, they've now passed it on to us. May we find ourselves worthy of that precious and extraordinary gift, as long as our lives endure. May grace now lead them home. May God continue to shed His grace on the United States of America.

"A WORLD THAT IS WORTHY OF OUR CHILDREN"

Remarks at the First Session of COP21

PARIS, FRANCE, NOVEMBER 30, 2015

Of all of the initiatives that will come to form a part of Obama's legacy, his work to address climate change may be the most enduring—even if Congress denied him the legislation he sought. From his earliest days in office, Obama advanced a comprehensive plan of environmental protection and green energy promotion that departed radically from Bush-era policies and contrasted sharply with conservative views on Capitol Hill. And, while Obama made some important gains domestically (almost entirely from executive and state action), his most important breakthrough was international, notably an historic 2014 agreement with China to cut carbon emissions. The following year, the United States joined hundreds of other countries at the United Nations Climate Change Conference in Paris to work out a new environmental framework. At the opening of the meeting, Obama delivered this speech arguing that greater international cooperation was needed to respond to a crisis that would affect all of humankind for generations to

*come. The conference ultimately produced the Paris
Agreement, which, while not without its fair share of
critics, was widely heralded as a turning point in the
struggle to halt global warming.*

PRESIDENT HOLLANDE, MR. Secretary General, fellow
leaders. We have come to Paris to show our resolve.

We offer our condolences to the people of France for the
barbaric attacks on this beautiful city. We stand united in solidarity not only to deliver justice to the terrorist network
responsible for those attacks but to protect our people and
uphold the enduring values that keep us strong and keep us
free. And we salute the people of Paris for insisting this crucial
conference go on—an act of defiance that proves nothing will
deter us from building the future we want for our children.
What greater rejection of those who would tear down our
world than marshaling our best efforts to save it?

Nearly two hundred nations have assembled here this
week—a declaration that for all the challenges we face, the
growing threat of climate change could define the contours of
this century more dramatically than any other. What should
give us hope that this is a turning point, that this is the moment
we finally determined we would save our planet, is the fact that
our nations share a sense of urgency about this challenge and a
growing realization that it is within our power to do something
about it.

Our understanding of the ways human beings disrupt the
climate advances by the day. Fourteen of the fifteen warmest
years on record have occurred since the year 2000—and 2015 is

on pace to be the warmest year of all. No nation—large or small, wealthy or poor—is immune to what this means.

This summer, I saw the effects of climate change firsthand in our northernmost state, Alaska, where the sea is already swallowing villages and eroding shorelines; where permafrost thaws and the tundra burns; where glaciers are melting at a pace unprecedented in modern times. And it was a preview of one possible future—a glimpse of our children's fate if the climate keeps changing faster than our efforts to address it. Submerged countries. Abandoned cities. Fields that no longer grow. Political disruptions that trigger new conflict, and even more floods of desperate peoples seeking the sanctuary of nations not their own.

That future is not one of strong economies, nor is it one where fragile states can find their footing. That future is one that we have the power to change. Right here. Right now. But only if we rise to this moment. As one of America's governors has said, "We are the first generation to feel the impact of climate change, and the last generation that can do something about it."

I've come here personally, as the leader of the world's largest economy and the second-largest emitter, to say that the United States of America not only recognizes our role in creating this problem, we embrace our responsibility to do something about it.

Over the last seven years, we've made ambitious investments in clean energy, and ambitious reductions in our carbon emissions. We've multiplied wind power threefold, and solar power more than twentyfold, helping create parts of America where these clean power sources are finally cheaper than dirtier, conventional power. We've invested in energy efficiency in every way imaginable. We've said no to infrastructure that would pull high-carbon fossil fuels from the ground, and we've said yes to the first-ever set of national standards limiting the amount of carbon pollution our power plants can release into the sky.

The advances we've made have helped drive our economic output to all-time highs, and drive our carbon pollution to its lowest levels in nearly two decades.

But the good news is this is not an American trend alone. Last year, the global economy grew while global carbon emissions from burning fossil fuels stayed flat. And what this means can't be overstated. We have broken the old arguments for inaction. We have proved that strong economic growth and a safer environment no longer have to conflict with one another; they can work in concert with one another.

And that should give us hope. One of the enemies that we'll be fighting at this conference is cynicism, the notion we can't do anything about climate change. Our progress should give us hope during these two weeks—hope that is rooted in collective action.

Earlier this month in Dubai, after years of delay, the world agreed to work together to cut the super-pollutants known as HFCs. That's progress. Already, prior to Paris, more than 180 countries representing nearly 95 percent of global emissions have put forward their own climate targets. That is progress. For our part, America is on track to reach the emissions targets that I set six years ago in Copenhagen—we will reduce our carbon emissions in the range of 17 percent below 2005 levels by 2020. And that's why, last year, I set a new target: America will reduce our emissions 26 to 28 percent below 2005 levels within ten years from now.

So our task here in Paris is to turn these achievements into an enduring framework for human progress—not a stopgap solution, but a long-term strategy that gives the world confidence in a low-carbon future.

Here, in Paris, let's secure an agreement that builds in ambition, where progress paves the way for regularly updated targets—targets that are not set for each of us but by each of us, taking into account the differences that each nation is facing.

Here in Paris, let's agree to a strong system of transparency that gives each of us the confidence that all of us are meeting our commitments. And let's make sure that the countries who don't yet have the full capacity to report on their targets receive the support that they need.

Here in Paris, let's reaffirm our commitment that resources will be there for countries willing to do their part to skip the dirty phase of development. And I recognize this will not be easy. It will take a commitment to innovation and the capital to continue driving down the cost of clean energy. And that's why, this afternoon, I'll join many of you to announce an historic joint effort to accelerate public and private clean energy innovation on a global scale.

Here in Paris, let's also make sure that these resources flow to the countries that need help preparing for the impacts of climate change that we can no longer avoid. We know the truth that many nations have contributed little to climate change but will be the first to feel its most destructive effects. For some, particularly island nations—whose leaders I'll meet with tomorrow—climate change is a threat to their very existence. And that's why today, in concert with other nations, America confirms our strong and ongoing commitment to the Least Developed Countries Fund. And tomorrow, we'll pledge new contributions to risk insurance initiatives that help vulnerable populations rebuild stronger after climate-related disasters.

And finally, here in Paris, let's show businesses and investors that the global economy is on a firm path towards a low-carbon future. If we put the right rules and incentives in place, we'll unleash the creative power of our best scientists and engineers and entrepreneurs to deploy clean energy technologies and the new jobs and new opportunities that they create all around the world. There are hundreds of billions of dollars ready to deploy to countries around the world if they get the signal that we mean business this time. Let's send that signal.

That's what we seek in these next two weeks. Not simply an agreement to roll back the pollution we put into our skies, but an agreement that helps us lift people from poverty without condemning the next generation to a planet that's beyond its capacity to repair. Here, in Paris, we can show the world what is possible when we come together, united in common effort and by a common purpose.

And let there be no doubt, the next generation is watching what we do. Just over a week ago, I was in Malaysia, where I held a town hall with young people, and the first question I received was from a young Indonesian woman. And it wasn't about terrorism, it wasn't about the economy, it wasn't about human rights. It was about climate change. And she asked whether I was optimistic about what we can achieve here in Paris, and what young people like her could do to help.

I want our actions to show her that we're listening. I want

our actions to be big enough to draw on the talents of all our people—men and women, rich and poor—I want to show her passionate, idealistic young generation that we care about their future.

For I believe, in the words of Dr. Martin Luther King Jr., that there is such a thing as being too late. And when it comes to climate change, that hour is almost upon us. But if we act here, if we act now, if we place our own short-term interests behind the air that our young people will breathe, and the food that they will eat, and the water that they will drink, and the hopes and dreams that sustain their lives, then we won't be too late for them.

And, my fellow leaders, accepting this challenge will not reward us with moments of victory that are clear or quick. Our progress will be measured differently—in the suffering that is averted, and a planet that's preserved. And that's what's always made this so hard. Our generation may not even live to see the full realization of what we do here. But the knowledge that the next generation will be better off for what we do here—can we imagine a more worthy reward than that? Passing that on to our children and our grandchildren, so that when they look back and they see what we did here in Paris, they can take pride in our achievement.

Let that be the common purpose here in Paris. A world that is worthy of our children. A world that is marked not by conflict, but by cooperation; and not by human suffering, but by human progress. A world that's safer, and more prosperous, and more secure, and more free than the one that we inherited.

Let's get to work.

"YOU SEE, CHANGE REQUIRES MORE THAN RIGHTEOUS ANGER"

Remarks at Howard University Commencement

WASHINGTON, D.C., MAY 7, 2016

Although Obama established himself as a politician who was comfortable talking about race, he sometimes drew criticism from prominent black writers and commentators for what they read as a patronizing attitude toward African American youth. Heading into the second half of his second term, Obama began to speak more forcefully about the lingering inequalities between black and white Americans and returned to a theme he had explored in the past: the significance of racial identity in the United States. His May 2016 commencement address at Howard University was a prime example of this shifting racial discourse, combining a deep pride in African American history and identity with praise for young black leaders and measured advice for effectively advancing social justice. It also reflected his ongoing insistence on a cross-racial dialogue and his impatience with those who called for change but were unwilling to engage in the messy and often frustrating work of politics.

THANK YOU! HELLO, Howard! H-U!

AUDIENCE: You know!

PRESIDENT: H-U!

AUDIENCE: You know!

PRESIDENT: Thank you so much, everybody. Please, please, have a seat. Oh, I feel important now. Got a degree from Howard. Cicely Tyson said something nice about me.

AUDIENCE MEMBER: I love you, President!

PRESIDENT: I love you back.

To President Frederick, the Board of Trustees, faculty and staff, fellow recipients of honorary degrees, thank you for the honor of spending this day with you. And congratulations to the Class of 2016! Four years ago, back when you were just freshmen, I understand many of you came by my house the night I was reelected. So I decided to return the favor and come by yours.

To the parents, the grandparents, aunts, uncles, brothers, sisters, all the family and friends who stood by this class, cheered them on, helped them get here today—this is your day, as well. Let's give them a big round of applause, as well.

I'm not trying to stir up any rivalries here; I just want to see who's in the house. We got Quad? Annex. Drew. Carver. Slow. Towers. And Meridian. Rest in peace, Meridian. Rest in peace.

I know you're all excited today. You might be a little tired, as well. Some of you were up all night making sure your credits were in order. Some of you stayed up too late, ended up at HoChi at 2:00 A.M. Got some mambo sauce on your fingers.

But you got here. And you've all worked hard to reach this day. You've shuttled between challenging classes and Greek life. You've led clubs, played an instrument or a sport. You volunteered, you interned. You held down one, two, maybe three jobs. You've made lifelong friends and discovered exactly what you're made of. The "Howard Hustle" has strengthened your sense of purpose and ambition.

Which means you're part of a long line of Howard graduates. Some are on this stage today. Some are in the audience. That spirit of achievement and special responsibility has defined this campus ever since the Freedman's Bureau established Howard just four years after the Emancipation Proclamation; just two years after the Civil War came to an end. They created this university with a vision—a vision of uplift; a vision for an America where our fates would be determined not by our race, gender, religion or creed, but where we would be free—in every sense—to pursue our individual and collective dreams.

It is that spirit that's made Howard a centerpiece of African American intellectual life and a central part of our larger American story. This institution has been the home of many firsts: The first black Nobel Peace Prize winner. The first black Supreme Court justice. But its mission has been to ensure those firsts were not the last. Countless scholars, professionals, artists, and leaders from every field received their training here. The generations of men and women who walked through this yard helped reform our government, cure disease, grow a black middle class, advance civil rights, shape our culture. The seeds of change—for all Americans—were sown here. And that's what I want to talk about today.

As I was preparing these remarks, I realized that when I was first elected president, most of you—the Class of 2016—were just starting high school. Today, you're graduating college. I used to joke about being old. Now I realize I'm old. It's not a joke anymore.

But seeing all of you here gives me some perspective. It makes me reflect on the changes that I've seen over my own lifetime. So let me begin with what may sound like a controversial statement—a hot take.

Given the current state of our political rhetoric and debate, let me say something that may be controversial, and that is this: America is a better place today than it was when I graduated from college. Let me repeat: America is by almost every measure better than it was when I graduated from college. It also happens to be better off than when I took office—but that's a longer story. That's a different discussion for another speech.

But think about it. I graduated in 1983. New York City, America's largest city, where I lived at the time, had endured a decade marked by crime and deterioration and near bankruptcy. And many cities were in similar shape. Our nation had gone through years of economic stagnation, the stranglehold of foreign oil, a recession where unemployment nearly scraped 11 percent. The auto industry was getting its clock cleaned by foreign competition. And don't even get me started on the clothes and the hairstyles. I've tried to eliminate all photos of me from this period. I thought I looked good. I was wrong.

Since that year—since the year I graduated—the poverty rate is down. Americans with college degrees, that rate is up. Crime rates are down. America's cities have undergone a renaissance. There are more women in the workforce. They're earning more money. We've cut teen pregnancy in half. We've slashed the African American dropout rate by almost 60 percent, and all of you have a computer in your pocket that gives you the world at the touch of a button. In 1983, I was part of fewer than 10 percent of African Americans who graduated with a bachelor's degree. Today, you're part of the more than 20 percent who will. And more than half of blacks say we're better off than our parents were at our age—and that our kids will be better off, too.

So America is better. And the world is better, too. A wall came down in Berlin. An Iron Curtain was torn asunder. The obscenity of apartheid came to an end. A young generation in Belfast and London have grown up without ever having to think about IRA bombings. In just the past sixteen years, we've come from a world without marriage equality to one where it's a reality in nearly two dozen countries. Around the world, more people live in democracies. We've lifted more than one billion people from extreme poverty. We've cut the child mortality rate worldwide by more than half.

America is better. The world is better. And stay with me now—race relations are better since I graduated. That's the truth. No, my election did not create a post-racial society. I don't know who was propagating that notion. That was not mine. But the election itself—and the subsequent one—because the first one, folks might have made a mistake. The second one, they knew what they were getting. The election itself was just one indicator of how attitudes had changed.

In my inaugural address, I remarked that just sixty years earlier, my father might not have been served in a D.C. restaurant— at least not certain of them. There were no black CEOs of Fortune 500 companies. Very few black judges. Shoot, as Larry

Wilmore pointed out last week, a lot of folks didn't even think blacks had the tools to be a quarterback. Today, former Bull Michael Jordan isn't just the greatest basketball player of all time—he owns the team. When I was graduating, the main black hero on TV was Mr. T. Rap and hip hop were counterculture, underground. Now, Shonda Rhimes owns Thursday night, and Beyoncé runs the world. We're no longer only entertainers, we're producers, studio executives. No longer small business owners—we're CEOs, we're mayors, representatives, presidents of the United States.

I am not saying gaps do not persist. Obviously, they do. Racism persists. Inequality persists. Don't worry—I'm going to get to that. But I wanted to start, Class of 2016, by opening your eyes to the moment that you are in. If you had to choose one moment in history in which you could be born, and you didn't know ahead of time who you were going to be—what nationality, what gender, what race, whether you'd be rich or poor, gay or straight, what faith you'd be born into—you wouldn't choose one hundred years ago. You wouldn't choose the fifties, or the sixties, or the seventies. You'd choose right now. If you had to choose a time to be, in the words of Lorraine Hansberry, "young, gifted, and black" in America, you would choose right now.

I tell you all this because it's important to note progress. Because to deny how far we've come would do a disservice to the cause of justice, to the legions of foot soldiers; to not only the incredibly accomplished individuals who have already been mentioned, but your mothers and your dads, and grandparents and great grandparents, who marched and toiled and suffered and overcame to make this day possible. I tell you this not to lull you into complacency, but to spur you into action—because there's still so much more work to do, so many more miles to travel. And America needs you to gladly, happily take up that work. You all have some work to do. So enjoy the party, because you're going to be busy.

Yes, our economy has recovered from crisis stronger than almost any other in the world. But there are folks of all races who are still hurting—who still can't find work that pays enough to keep the lights on, who still can't save for retirement. We've still got a big racial gap in economic opportunity. The overall unemployment rate is 5 percent, but the black unemployment rate is almost nine. We've still got an achievement gap when black boys and girls graduate high school and college at lower rates than white boys and white girls. Harriet Tubman may be going on the twenty, but we've still got a gender gap when a black woman working full-time still earns just 66 percent of what a white man gets paid.

We've got a justice gap when too many black boys and girls pass through a pipeline from underfunded schools to over-crowded jails. This is one area where things have gotten worse. When I was in college, about half a million people in America were behind bars. Today, there are about 2.2 million. Black men are about six times likelier to be in prison right now than white men.

Around the world, we've still got challenges to solve that threaten everybody in the twenty-first century—old scourges like disease and conflict, but also new challenges, from terrorism and climate change.

So make no mistake, Class of 2016—you've got plenty of work to do. But as complicated and sometimes intractable as these challenges may seem, the truth is that your generation is better positioned than any before you to meet those challenges, to flip the script.

Now, how you do that, how you meet these challenges, how you bring about change will ultimately be up to you. My generation, like all generations, is too confined by our own experience, too invested in our own biases, too stuck in our ways to provide much of the new thinking that will be required. But us old-heads have learned a few things that might be useful in your journey. So with the rest of my time, I'd like to offer some suggestions for how young leaders like you can fulfill your destiny and shape our collective future—bend it in the direction of justice and equality and freedom.

First of all—and this should not be a problem for this group—be confident in your heritage. Be confident in your blackness. One of the great changes that's occurred in our country since I was your age is the realization there's no one way to be black. Take it from somebody who's seen both sides of debate about whether I'm black enough. In the past couple months, I've had lunch with the Queen of England and hosted Kendrick Lamar in the Oval Office. There's no straitjacket, there's no constraints, there's no litmus test for authenticity.

Look at Howard. One thing most folks don't know about Howard is how diverse it is. When you arrived here, some of you were like, oh, they've got black people in Iowa? But it's true—this class comes from big cities and rural communities, and some of you crossed oceans to study here. You shatter stereotypes. Some of you come from a long line of Bison. Some of you are the first in your family to graduate from college. You all talk different, you all dress different. You're Lakers fans, Celtics fans, maybe even some hockey fans.

And because of those who've come before you, you have models to follow. You can work for a company, or start your own. You can go into politics, or run an organization that holds politicians accountable. You can write a book that wins the National Book Award, or you can write the new run of Black Panther. Or, like one of your alumni, Ta-Nehisi Coates, you can go ahead and just do both. You can create your own style, set your own standard of beauty, embrace your own sexuality. Think about an icon we just lost—Prince. He blew up categories. People didn't know what Prince was doing. And folks loved him for it.

You need to have the same confidence. Or as my daughters tell me all the time, "You be you, Daddy." Sometimes Sasha puts a variation on it—"You do you, Daddy." And because you're a black person doing whatever it is that you're doing, that makes it a black thing. Feel confident.

Second, even as we each embrace our own beautiful, unique, and valid versions of our blackness, remember the tie that does bind us as African Americans—and that is our particular awareness of injustice and unfairness and struggle. That means we cannot sleepwalk through life. We cannot be ignorant of history. We can't meet the world with a sense of entitlement. We can't walk by a homeless man without asking why a society as wealthy as ours allows that state of affairs to occur. We can't just lock up a low-level dealer without asking why this boy, barely out of childhood, felt he had no other options. We have cousins and uncles and brothers and sisters who we remember were just as smart and just as talented as we were, but somehow got ground down by structures that are unfair and unjust.

And that means we have to not only question the world as it is, and stand up for those African Americans who haven't been so lucky—because, yes, you've worked hard, but you've also been lucky. That's a pet peeve of mine: People who have been successful and don't realize they've been lucky. That God may have blessed them; it wasn't nothing you did. So don't have an attitude. But we must expand our moral imaginations to understand and empathize with all people who are struggling, not just black folks who are struggling—the refugee, the immigrant, the rural poor, the transgender person, and yes, the middle-aged white guy who you may think has all the advantages, but over the last several decades has seen his world upended by economic and cultural and technological change, and feels powerless to stop it. You got to get in his head, too.

Number three: You have to go through life with more than just passion for change; you need a strategy. I'll repeat that. I want you to have passion, but you have to have a strategy. Not just awareness, but action. Not just hashtags, but votes.

You see, change requires more than righteous anger. It requires a program, and it requires organizing. At the 1964 Democratic Convention, Fannie Lou Hamer—all five-feet-four-inches tall—gave a fiery speech on the national stage. But then she went back home to Mississippi and organized cotton pickers. And she didn't have the tools and technology where you can whip up a movement in minutes. She had to go door to door. And I'm so proud of the new guard of black civil rights leaders who understand this. It's thanks in large part to the activism of young people like many of you, from Black Twitter to Black Lives Matter, that America's eyes have been opened—white, black, Democrat, Republican—to the real problems, for example, in our criminal justice system.

But to bring about structural change, lasting change, awareness is not enough. It requires changes in law, changes in custom. If you care about mass incarceration, let me ask you: How are you pressuring members of Congress to pass the criminal justice reform bill now pending before them? If you care about better policing, do you know who your district attorney is? Do you know who your state's attorney general is? Do you know the difference? Do you know who appoints the police chief and who writes the police training manual? Find out who they are, what their responsibilities are. Mobilize the community, present them with a plan, work with them to bring about change, hold them accountable if they do not deliver. Passion is vital, but you've got to have a strategy.

And your plan better include voting—not just some of the time, but all the time. It is absolutely true that fifty years after the Voting Rights Act, there are still too many barriers in this country to vote. There are too many people trying to erect new barriers to voting. This is the only advanced democracy on Earth that goes out of its way to make it difficult for people to vote. And there's a reason for that. There's a legacy to that.

But let me say this: Even if we dismantled every barrier to voting, that alone would not change the fact that America has some of the lowest voting rates in the free world. In 2014, only 36 percent of Americans turned out to vote in the midterms—the second-lowest participation rate on record. Youth turnout—that would be you—was less than 20 percent. Less than 20 percent. Four out of five did not vote. In 2012, nearly two in three African Americans turned out. And then, in 2014, only two in five turned out. You don't think that made a difference in terms of the Congress I've got to deal with? And then people are wondering, well, how come Obama hasn't gotten this done? How come he didn't get that done? You don't think that made a difference? What would have happened if you had turned out at 50, 60, 70 percent, all across this country? People try to make this political thing really complicated. Like, what kind of reforms do we need? And how do we need to do that? You know what, just vote. It's math. If you have more votes than the other guy, you get to do what you want. It's not that complicated.

And you don't have excuses. You don't have to guess the number of jellybeans in a jar or bubbles on a bar of soap to register to vote. You don't have to risk your life to cast a ballot. Other people already did that for you. Your grandparents, your great grandparents might be here today if they were working on it. What's your excuse? When we don't vote, we give away our power, disenfranchise ourselves—right when we need to use the power that we have; right when we need your power to stop others from taking away the vote and rights of those more vulnerable than you are—the elderly and the poor, the formerly incarcerated trying to earn their second chance.

So you got to vote all the time, not just when it's cool, not just when it's time to elect a president, not just when you're inspired. It's your duty. When it's time to elect a member of Congress or a city councilman, or a school board member, or a sheriff. That's how we change our politics—by electing people at every level who are representative of and accountable to us. It is not that complicated. Don't make it complicated.

And finally, change requires more than just speaking out—it

requires listening, as well. In particular, it requires listening to those with whom you disagree, and being prepared to compromise. When I was a state senator, I helped pass Illinois's first racial profiling law, and one of the first laws in the nation requiring the videotaping of confessions in capital cases. And we were successful because, early on, I engaged law enforcement. I didn't say to them, oh, you guys are so racist, you need to do something. I understood, as many of you do, that the overwhelming majority of police officers are good, and honest, and courageous, and fair, and love the communities they serve.

And we knew there were some bad apples, and that even the good cops with the best of intentions—including, by the way, African American police officers—might have unconscious biases, as we all do. So we engaged and we listened, and we kept working until we built consensus. And because we took the time to listen, we crafted legislation that was good for the police—because it improved the trust and cooperation of the community—and it was good for the communities, who were less likely to be treated unfairly. And I can say this unequivocally: Without at least the acceptance of the police organizations in Illinois, I could never have gotten those bills passed. Very simple. They would have blocked them.

The point is, you need allies in a democracy. That's just the way it is. It can be frustrating and it can be slow. But history teaches us that the alternative to democracy is always worse. That's not just true in this country. It's not a black or white thing. Go to any country where the give and take of democracy has been repealed by one-party rule, and I will show you a country that does not work.

And democracy requires compromise, even when you are

100 percent right. This is hard to explain sometimes. You can be completely right, and you still are going to have to engage folks who disagree with you. If you think that the only way forward is to be as uncompromising as possible, you will feel good about yourself, you will enjoy a certain moral purity, but you're not going to get what you want. And if you don't get what you want long enough, you will eventually think the whole system is rigged. And that will lead to more cynicism, and less participation, and a downward spiral of more injustice and more anger and more despair. And that's never been the source of our progress. That's how we cheat ourselves of progress.

We remember Dr. King's soaring oratory, the power of his letter from a Birmingham jail, the marches he led. But he also sat down with President Johnson in the Oval Office to try and get a Civil Rights Act and a Voting Rights Act passed. And those two seminal bills were not perfect—just like the Emancipation Proclamation was a war document as much as it was some clarion call for freedom. Those mileposts of our progress were not perfect. They did not make up for centuries of slavery or Jim Crow or eliminate racism or provide for forty acres and a mule. But they made things better. And you know what, I will take better every time. I always tell my staff— better is good, because you consolidate your gains and then you move on to the next fight from a stronger position.

Brittany Packnett, a member of the Black Lives Matter movement and Campaign Zero, one of the Ferguson protest organizers, she joined our Task Force on 21st Century Policing. Some of her fellow activists questioned whether she should participate. She rolled up her sleeves and sat at the same table with big city police chiefs and prosecutors. And because she did, she ended up shaping many of the recommendations of that task force. And those recommendations are now being adopted across the country—changes that many of the protesters called for. If young activists like Brittany had refused to participate out of some sense of ideological purity, then those great ideas would have just remained ideas. But she did participate. And that's how change happens.

America is big and it is boisterous and it is more diverse than ever. The president told me that we've got a significant Nepalese contingent here at Howard. I would not have guessed that. Right on. But it just tells you how interconnected we're becoming. And with so many folks from so many places, converging, we are not always going to agree with each other.

Another Howard alum, Zora Neale Hurston, once said— this is a good quote here: "Nothing that God ever made is the same thing to more than one person." Think about that. That's why our democracy gives us a process designed for us to settle our disputes with argument and ideas and votes instead of violence and simple majority rule.

So don't try to shut folks out, don't try to shut them down, no matter how much you might disagree with them. There's been a trend around the country of trying to get colleges to disinvite speakers with a different point of view, or disrupt a politician's rally. Don't do that—no matter how ridiculous or offensive you might find the things that come out of their mouths. Because as my grandmother used to tell me, every time a fool speaks, they are just advertising their own ignorance. Let them talk. Let them talk. If you don't, you just make them a victim, and then they can avoid accountability.

That doesn't mean you shouldn't challenge them. Have the confidence to challenge them, the confidence in the rightness of your position. There will be times when you shouldn't compromise your core values, your integrity, and you will have the responsibility to speak up in the face of injustice. But listen. Engage. If the other side has a point, learn from them. If they're wrong, rebut them. Teach them. Beat them on the battlefield of ideas. And you might as well start practicing now, because one thing I can guarantee you—you will have to deal with ignorance, hatred, racism, foolishness, trifling folks. I promise you, you will have to deal with all that at every stage of your life. That may not seem fair, but life has never been completely fair. Nobody promised you a crystal stair. And if you want to make life fair, then you've got to start with the world as it is.

So that's my advice. That's how you change things. Change isn't something that happens every four years or eight years; change is not placing your faith in any particular politician and then just putting your feet up and saying, okay, go. Change is the effort of committed citizens who hitch their wagons to something bigger than themselves and fight for it every single day.

That's what Thurgood Marshall understood—a man who once walked this yard, graduated from Howard Law; went home to Baltimore, started his own law practice. He and his mentor, Charles Hamilton Houston, rolled up their sleeves and they set out to overturn segregation. They worked through the NAACP. Filed dozens of lawsuits, fought dozens of cases. And after nearly twenty years of effort—twenty years—Thurgood Marshall ultimately succeeded in bringing his righteous cause before the Supreme Court, and securing the ruling in *Brown v.*

Board of Education that separate could never be equal. Twenty years.

Marshall, Houston—they knew it would not be easy. They knew it would not be quick. They knew all sorts of obstacles would stand in their way. They knew that even if they won, that would just be the beginning of a longer march to equality. But they had discipline. They had persistence. They had faith— and a sense of humor. And they made life better for all Americans.

And I know you graduates share those qualities. I know it because I've learned about some of the young people graduating here today. There's a young woman named Ciearra Jefferson, who's graduating with you. And I'm just going to use her as an example. I hope you don't mind, Ciearra. Ciearra grew up in Detroit and was raised by a poor single mom who worked seven days a week in an auto plant. And for a time, her family found themselves without a place to call home. They bounced around between friends and family who might take them in. By her senior year, Ciearra was up at 5:00 A.M. every day, juggling homework, extracurricular activities, volunteering, all while taking care of her little sister. But she knew that education was her ticket to a better life. So she never gave up. Pushed herself to excel. This daughter of a single mom who works on the assembly line turned down a full scholarship to Harvard to come to Howard.

And today, like many of you, Ciearra is the first in her family to graduate from college. And then, she says, she's going to go back to her hometown, just like Thurgood Marshall did, to make sure all the working folks she grew up with have access to the health care they need and deserve. As she puts it, she's going to be a "change agent." She's going to reach back and help folks like her succeed.

And people like Ciearra are why I remain optimistic about America. Young people like you are why I never give in to despair.

James Baldwin once wrote, "Not everything that is faced can be changed, but nothing can be changed until it is faced."

Graduates, each of us is only here because someone else faced down challenges for us. We are only who we are because someone else struggled and sacrificed for us. That's not just Thurgood Marshall's story, or Ciearra's story, or my story, or your story—that is the story of America. A story whispered by slaves in the cotton fields, the song of marchers in Selma, the dream of a King in the shadow of Lincoln. The prayer of immigrants who set out for a new world. The roar of women demanding the vote. The rallying cry of workers who built America. And the GIs who bled overseas for our freedom.

Now it's your turn. And the good news is, you're ready. And when your journey seems too hard, and when you run into a chorus of cynics who tell you that you're being foolish to keep believing or that you can't do something, or that you should just give up, or you should just settle—you might say to yourself a little phrase that I've found handy these last eight years: Yes, we can.

Congratulations, Class of 2016! Good luck! God bless you. God bless the United States of America. I'm proud of you.

"WE MUST GO FORWARD"

Remarks at the United Nations General Assembly
NEW YORK CITY, NEW YORK, SEPTEMBER 20, 2016

Obama's final speech before the United Nations as president was a thoughtful valedictory and an appropriate close to his eight years in office. In his remarks, Obama reflected on some of the domestic and foreign policy accomplishments of his administration. He also acknowledged the many challenges that remain and offered a road map for greater international cooperation. He touched on many of the signature issues of his presidency, from climate change and terrorism to racism, economic injustice, and religious persecution. Using his own biography, Obama lifted up the achievements of America's democratic system. The United States, he said, was not entitled to dictate the paths of other nations, but he insisted that development, security, and peace could be most successfully attained through democracy and integration. The speech was also notable for its indirect but clear reference to Donald Trump, the 2016 presidential election, and the threat to the global liberal order. "Today," Obama said pointedly, "a nation ringed by walls would only imprison itself."

M R. PRESIDENT; MR. Secretary General; fellow dele-gates; ladies and gentlemen: As I address this hall as president for the final time, let me recount the progress that we've made these last eight years.

From the depths of the greatest financial crisis of our time, we coordinated our response to avoid further catastrophe and return the global economy to growth. We've taken away terrorist safe havens, strengthened the nonproliferation regime, resolved the Iranian nuclear issue through diplomacy. We opened relations with Cuba, helped Colombia end Latin America's longest war, and we welcome a democratically elected leader of Myanmar to this Assembly. Our assistance is helping people feed them-selves, care for the sick, power communities across Africa, and promote models of development rather than dependence. And we have made international institutions like the World Bank and the International Monetary Fund more representative, while establishing a framework to protect our planet from the ravages of climate change.

This is important work. It has made a real difference in the lives of our people. And it could not have happened had we not worked together. And yet, around the globe we are seeing the same forces of global integration that have made us interdependent also expose deep fault lines in the existing international order.

We see it in the headlines every day. Around the world, refugees flow across borders in flight from brutal conflict. Financial disruptions continue to weigh upon our workers and entire communities. Across vast swaths of the Middle East, basic security, basic order has broken down. We see too many governments muzzling journalists, and quashing dissent, and censoring the flow of information. Terrorist networks use social media to prey upon the minds of our youth, endangering open societies and spurring anger against innocent immigrants and Muslims. Powerful nations contest the constraints placed on them by international law.

This is the paradox that defines our world today. A quarter century after the end of the Cold War, the world is by many measures less violent and more prosperous than ever before, and yet our societies are filled with uncertainty, and unease, and strife. Despite enormous progress, as people lose trust in institutions, governing becomes more difficult and tensions between nations become more quick to surface.

And so I believe that at this moment we all face a choice. We can choose to press forward with a better model of cooperation and integration. Or we can retreat into a world sharply divided, and ultimately in conflict, along age-old lines of nation and tribe and race and religion.

I want to suggest to you today that we must go forward, and not backward. I believe that as imperfect as they are, the principles of open markets and accountable governance, of democracy and human rights and international law that we have forged, remain the firmest foundation for human progress in this century. I make this argument not based on theory or ideology, but on facts—facts that all too often we forget in the immediacy of current events.

Here's the most important fact: The integration of our global economy has made life better for billions of men, women, and children. Over the last twenty-five years, the number of people living in extreme poverty has been cut from nearly 40 percent of humanity to under 10 percent. That's unprecedented. And it's not an abstraction. It means children have enough to eat; mothers don't die in childbirth.

Meanwhile, cracking the genetic code promises to cure diseases that have plagued us for centuries. The Internet can deliver the entirety of human knowledge to a young girl in a remote village on a single handheld device. In medicine and in manufacturing, in education and communications, we're experiencing a transformation of how human beings live on a scale that recalls the revolutions in agriculture and industry. And as a result, a person born today is more likely to be healthy, to live longer, and to have access to opportunity than at any time in human history.

Moreover, the collapse of colonialism and communism has allowed more people than ever before to live with the freedom to choose their leaders. Despite the real and troubling areas where freedom appears in retreat, the fact remains that the number of democracies around the world has nearly doubled in the last twenty-five years.

In remote corners of the world, citizens are demanding respect for the dignity of all people no matter their gender, or race, or religion, or disability, or sexual orientation, and those who deny others dignity are subject to public reproach. An explosion of social media has given ordinary people more ways to express themselves, and has raised people's expectations for those of us in power. Indeed, our international order has been so successful that we take it as a given that great powers no longer fight world wars; that the end of the Cold War lifted the shadow of nuclear Armageddon; that the battlefields of Europe have been replaced by peaceful union; that China and India remain on a path of remarkable growth.

I say all this not to whitewash the challenges we face, or to suggest complacency. Rather, I believe that we need to acknowledge these achievements in order to summon the confidence to carry this progress forward and to make sure that we do not abandon those very things that have delivered this progress.

In order to move forward, though, we do have to acknowledge that the existing path to global integration requires a course correction. As too often, those trumpeting the benefits of globalization have ignored inequality within and among nations; have ignored the enduring appeal of ethnic and sectarian identities; have left international institutions ill-equipped, underfunded, under-resourced, in order to handle transnational challenges.

And as these real problems have been neglected, alternative visions of the world have pressed forward both in the wealthiest countries and in the poorest: religious fundamentalism; the politics of ethnicity, or tribe, or sect; aggressive nationalism; a crude populism—sometimes from the far left, but more often from the far right—which seeks to restore what they believe was a better, simpler age free of outside contamination.

We cannot dismiss these visions. They are powerful. They reflect dissatisfaction among too many of our citizens. I do not believe those visions can deliver security or prosperity over the long term, but I do believe that these visions fail to recognize, at a very basic level, our common humanity. Moreover, I believe that the acceleration of travel and technology and telecommunications—together with a global economy that depends on a global supply chain—makes it self-defeating ultimately for those who seek to reverse this progress. Today, a nation ringed by walls would only imprison itself.

So the answer cannot be a simple rejection of global integration. Instead, we must work together to make sure the benefits of such integration are broadly shared, and that the disruptions—economic, political, and cultural—that are caused by integration are squarely addressed. This is not the place for a detailed policy blueprint, but let me offer in broad strokes those areas where I believe we must do better together.

It starts with making the global economy work better for all people and not just for those at the top. While open markets, capitalism have raised standards of living around the globe, globalization combined with rapid progress and technology has also weakened the position of workers and their ability to secure a decent wage. In advanced economies like my own, unions have been undermined, and many manufacturing jobs have disappeared. Often, those who benefit most from global-ization have used their political power to further undermine the position of workers.

In developing countries, labor organizations have often been suppressed, and the growth of the middle class has been held back by corruption and underinvestment. Mercantilist policies pursued by governments with export-driven models threaten to under-mine the consensus that underpins global trade. And meanwhile, global capital is too often unaccountable—nearly eight trillion dollars stashed away in tax havens, a shadow banking system that grows beyond the reach of effective oversight.

A world in which 1 percent of humanity controls as much wealth as the other 99 percent will never be stable. I understand that the gaps between rich and poor are not new, but just as the child in a slum today can see the skyscraper nearby, technology now allows any person with a smartphone to see how the most privileged among us live and the contrast between their own lives and others. Expectations rise, then, faster than governments can deliver, and a pervasive sense of injustice undermines people's faith in the system.

So how do we fix this imbalance? We cannot unwind integration any more than we can stuff technology back into a box. Nor can we look to failed models of the past. If we start resorting to trade wars, market-distorting subsidies, beggar thy neighbor policies, an overreliance on natural resources instead of innovation—these approaches will make us poorer, collectively, and they are more likely to lead to conflict. And the stark contrast between, say, the success of the Republic of Korea and the wasteland of North Korea shows that central, planned control of the economy is a dead end.

But I do believe there's another path—one that fuels growth and innovation, and offers the clearest route to individual opportunity and national success. It does not require succumbing to a soulless capitalism that benefits only the few, but rather recognizes that economies are more successful when we close the gap between rich and poor, and growth is broadly based. And that means respecting the rights of workers so they can organize into independent unions and earn a living wage. It means investing in our people—their skills, their education, their capacity to take an idea and turn it into a business. It means strengthening the safety net that protects our people from hardship and allows them to take more risks—to look for a new job, or start a new venture.

These are the policies that I've pursued here in the United States, and with clear results. American businesses have created now fifteen million new jobs. After the recession, the top

1 percent of Americans were capturing more than 90 percent of income growth. But today, that's down to about half. Last year, poverty in this country fell at the fastest rate in nearly fifty years. And with further investment in infrastructure and early childhood education and basic research, I'm confident that such progress will continue.

So just as I've pursued these measures here at home, so has the United States worked with many nations to curb the excesses of capitalism—not to punish wealth, but to prevent repeated crises that can destroy it. That's why we've worked with other nations to create higher and clearer standards for banking and taxation—because a society that asks less of oligarchs than ordinary citizens will rot from within. That's why we've pushed for transparency and cooperation in rooting out corruption, and tracking illicit dollars, because markets create more jobs when they're fueled by hard work, and not the capacity to extort a bribe. That's why we've worked to reach trade agreements that raise labor standards and raise environmental standards, as we've done with the Trans-Pacific Partnership, so that the benefits are more broadly shared.

And just as we benefit by combatting inequality within our countries, I believe advanced economies still need to do more to close the gap between rich and poor nations around the globe. This is difficult politically. It's difficult to spend on foreign assistance. But I do not believe this is charity. For the small fraction of what we spent at war in Iraq we could support institutions so that fragile states don't collapse in the first place, and invest in emerging economies that become markets for our goods. It's not just the right thing to do, it's the smart thing to do.

And that's why we need to follow through on our efforts to combat climate change. If we don't act boldly, the bill that could come due will be mass migrations, and cities submerged and nations displaced, and food supplies decimated, and conflicts born of despair. The Paris Agreement gives us a framework to act, but only if we scale up our ambition. And there must be a sense of urgency about bringing the agreement into force, and helping poorer countries leapfrog destructive forms of energy.

So, for the wealthiest countries, a Green Climate Fund should only be the beginning. We need to invest in research and provide market incentives to develop new technologies, and then make these technologies accessible and affordable for poorer countries. And only then can we continue lifting all people up from poverty without condemning our children to a planet beyond their capacity to repair.

So we need new models for the global marketplace, models that are inclusive and sustainable. And in the same way, we need models of governance that are inclusive and accountable to ordinary people.

I recognize not every country in this hall is going to follow the same model of governance. I do not think that America can—or should—impose our system of government on other countries. But there appears to be growing contest between authoritarianism and liberalism right now. And I want everybody to understand, I am not neutral in that contest. I believe in a liberal political order—an order built not just through elections and representative government, but also through respect for human rights and civil society, and independent judiciaries and the rule of law.

I know that some countries, which now recognize the power of free markets, still reject the model of free societies. And perhaps those of us who have been promoting democracy feel somewhat discouraged since the end of the Cold War, because we've learned that liberal democracy will not just wash across the globe in a single wave. It turns out building accountable institutions is hard work—the work of generations. The gains are often fragile. Sometimes we take one step forward and then two steps back. In countries held together by borders drawn by colonial powers, with ethnic enclaves and tribal divisions, politics and elections can sometimes appear to be a zero-sum game. And so, given the difficulty in forging true democracy in the face of these pressures, it's no surprise that some argue the future favors the strongman, a top-down model, rather than strong, democratic institutions.

But I believe this thinking is wrong. I believe the road of true democracy remains the better path. I believe that in the twenty-first century, economies can only grow to a certain point until they need to open up—because entrepreneurs need to access information in order to invent; young people need a global education in order to thrive; independent media needs to check the abuses of power. Without this evolution, ultimately expectations of people will not be met; suppression and stagnation will set in. And history shows that strongmen are then left with two paths—permanent crackdown, which sparks strife at home, or scapegoating enemies abroad, which can lead to war.

Now, I will admit, my belief that governments serve the individual, and not the other way around, is shaped by America's story. Our nation began with a promise of freedom that applied only to the few. But because of our democratic Constitution, because of our Bill of Rights, because of our ideals, ordinary people were able to organize, and march, and protest, and ultimately, those ideals won out—opened doors for women and minorities and workers in ways that made our economy more productive and turned our diversity into a strength; that gave innovators the chance to transform every area of human endeavor; that made it possible for someone like me to be elected president of the United States.

So, yes, my views are shaped by the specific experiences of America, but I do not think this story is unique to America. Look at the transformation that's taken place in countries as different as Japan and Chile, Indonesia, Botswana. The countries that have succeeded are ones in which people feel they have a stake.

In Europe, the progress of those countries in the former Soviet bloc that embraced democracy stand in clear contrast to those that did not. After all, the people of Ukraine did not take to the streets because of some plot imposed from abroad. They took to the streets because their leadership was for sale and they had no recourse. They demanded change because they saw life get better for people in the Baltics and in Poland, societies that were more liberal, and democratic, and open than their own.

So those of us who believe in democracy, we need to speak out forcefully, because both the facts and history, I believe, are on our side. That doesn't mean democracies are without flaws. It does mean that the cure for what ails our democracies is greater engagement by our citizens—not less.

Yes, in America, there is too much money in politics; too much entrenched partisanship; too little participation by citizens, in part because of a patchwork of laws that makes it harder to vote. In Europe, a well-intentioned Brussels often became too isolated from the normal push and pull of national politics. Too often, in capitals, decision-makers have forgotten that democracy needs to be driven by civic engagement from the bottom up, not governance by experts from the top down. And so these are real problems, and as leaders of democratic governments make the case for democracy abroad, we better strive harder to set a better example at home.

Moreover, every country will organize its government informed by centuries of history, and the circumstances of geography, and the deeply held beliefs of its people. So I recognize a traditional society may value unity and cohesion more than a diverse country like my own, which was founded upon what, at the time, was a radical idea—the idea of the liberty of individual human beings endowed with certain God-given rights. But that does not mean that ordinary people in Asia, or Africa, or the Middle East somehow prefer arbitrary rule that denies them a voice in the decisions that can shape their lives. I believe that spirit is universal. And if any of you doubt the universality of that desire, listen to the voices of young people everywhere who call out for freedom, and dignity, and the opportunity to control their own lives.

This leads me to the third thing we need to do: We must reject any forms of fundamentalism, or racism, or a belief in ethnic superiority that makes our traditional identities irreconcilable with modernity. Instead we need to embrace the tolerance that results from respect of all human beings.

It's a truism that global integration has led to a collision of cultures; trade, migration, the Internet, all these things can challenge and unsettle our most cherished identities. We see liberal societies express opposition when women choose to cover themselves. We see protests responding to Western newspaper cartoons that caricature the Prophet Muhammad. In a world that left the age of empire behind, we see Russia attempting to recover lost glory through force. Asian powers debate competing claims of history. And in Europe and the United States, you see people wrestle with concerns about immigration and changing demographics, and suggesting that somehow people who look different are corrupting the character of our countries.

Now, there's no easy answer for resolving all these social forces, and we must respect the meaning that people draw from their own traditions—from their religion, from their ethnicity, from their sense of nationhood. But I do not believe progress is possible if our desire to preserve our identities gives way to an impulse to dehumanize or dominate another group. If our religion leads us to persecute those of another faith, if we jail or beat people who are gay, if our traditions lead us to prevent girls from going to school, if we discriminate on the basis of race or tribe or ethnicity, then the fragile bonds of civilization will fray. The world is too small, we are too packed together, for us to be able to resort to those old ways of thinking.

We see this mindset in too many parts of the Middle East. There, so much of the collapse in order has been fueled because leaders sought legitimacy not because of policies or programs but by resorting to persecuting political opposition, or demonizing other religious sects, by narrowing the public space to the mosque, where in too many places perversions of a great faith were tolerated. These forces built up for years, and are now at work helping to fuel both Syria's tragic civil war and the mind-less, medieval menace of ISIL.

The mindset of sectarianism, and extremism, and bloodlet-ting, and retribution that has been taking place will not be quickly reversed. And if we are honest, we understand that no external power is going to be able to force different religious communities or ethnic communities to coexist for long. But I do believe we have to be honest about the nature of these conflicts, and our international community must continue to work with those who seek to build rather than to destroy.

And there is a military component to that. It means being united and relentless in destroying networks like ISIL, which show no respect for human life. But it also means that in a place like Syria, where there's no ultimate military victory to be won, we're going to have to pursue the hard work of diplomacy that aims to stop the violence, and deliver aid to those in need, and support those who pursue a political settlement and can see those who are not like themselves as worthy of dignity and respect.

Across the region's conflicts, we have to insist that all parties recognize a common humanity and that nations end proxy wars that fuel disorder. Because until basic questions are answered about how communities coexist, the embers of extremism will continue to burn, countless human beings will suffer—most of all in that region—but extremism will continue to be exported overseas. And the world is too small for us to simply be able to build a wall and prevent it from affecting our own societies.

And what is true in the Middle East is true for all of us. Surely, religious traditions can be honored and upheld while teaching young people science and math, rather than intolerance. Surely, we can sustain our unique traditions while giving women their full and rightful role in the politics and economics of a nation. Surely, we can rally our nations to solidarity while recognizing equal treatment for all communities—whether it's a religious minority in Myanmar, or an ethnic minority in Burundi, or a racial minority right here in the United States. And surely, Israelis and Palestinians will be better off if Palestinians reject incitement and recognize the legitimacy of Israel, but Israel recognizes that it cannot permanently occupy and settle Palestinian land. We all have to do better as leaders in tamping down, rather than encouraging, a notion of identity that leads us to diminish others.

And this leads me to the fourth and final thing we need to do, and that is sustain our commitment to international cooperation rooted in the rights and responsibilities of nations.

As president of the United States, I know that for most of human history, power has not been unipolar. The end of the Cold War may have led too many to forget this truth. I've noticed as president that at times, both America's adversaries and some of our allies believe that all problems were either caused by Washington or could be solved by Washington—and perhaps too many in Washington believed that as well. But I believe America has been a rare superpower in human history insofar as it has been willing to think beyond narrow self-interest; that while we've made our share of mistakes over these last twenty-five years—and I've acknowledged some—we have strived, sometimes at great sacrifice, to align better our actions with our ideals. And as a consequence, I believe we have been a force for good.

We have secured allies. We've acted to protect the vulnerable. We supported human rights and welcomed scrutiny of our own actions. We've bound our power to international laws and institutions. When we've made mistakes, we've tried to acknowledge them. We have worked to roll back poverty and hunger and disease beyond our borders, not just within our borders.

I'm proud of that. But I also know that we can't do this alone. And I believe that if we're to meet the challenges of this century, we are all going to have to do more to build up international capacity. We cannot escape the prospect of nuclear war unless we all commit to stopping the spread of nuclear weapons and pursuing a world without them.

When Iran agrees to accept constraints on its nuclear program, that enhances global security and enhances Iran's ability to work with other nations. On the other hand, when North Korea tests a bomb, that endangers all of us. And any country that breaks this basic bargain must face consequences. And those nations with these weapons, like the United States, have a unique responsibility to pursue the path of reducing our stockpiles, and reaffirming basic norms like the commitment to never test them again.

We can't combat a disease like Zika that recognizes no borders—mosquitos don't respect walls—unless we make permanent the same urgency that we brought to bear against Ebola—by strengthening our own systems of public health, by investing in cures and rolling back the root causes of disease, and helping poorer countries develop a public health infrastructure.

We can only eliminate extreme poverty if the sustainable development goals that we have set are more than words on paper. Human ingenuity now gives us the capacity to feed the hungry and give all of our children—including our girls—the education that is the foundation for opportunity in our world. But we have to put our money where our mouths are.

And we can only realize the promise of this institution's founding—to replace the ravages of war with cooperation—if powerful nations like my own accept constraints. Sometimes I'm criticized in my own country for professing a belief in international norms and multilateral institutions. But I am convinced that in the long run, giving up some freedom of action—not giving up our ability to protect ourselves or pursue our core interests, but binding ourselves to international rules over the long term—enhances our security. And I think that's not just true for us.

If Russia continues to interfere in the affairs of its neighbors, it may be popular at home, it may fuel nationalist fervor for a time, but over time it is also going to diminish its stature and make its borders less secure. In the South China Sea, a peaceful resolution of disputes offered by law will mean far greater stability than the militarization of a few rocks and reefs.

We are all stakeholders in this international system, and it calls upon all of us to invest in the success of institutions to which we belong. And the good news is that many nations have shown what kind of progress is possible when we make those commitments. Consider what we've accomplished here over the past few years.

Together, we mobilized some fifty thousand additional troops for UN peacekeeping, making them nimble, better equipped, better prepared to deal with emergencies. Together, we established an Open Government Partnership so that, increasingly, transparency empowers more and more people around the globe. And together, now, we have to open our hearts and do more to help refugees who are desperate for a home.

We should all welcome the pledges of increased assistance that have been made at this General Assembly gathering. I'll be discussing that more this afternoon. But we have to follow through, even when the politics are hard. Because in the eyes of innocent men and women and children who, through no fault of their own, have had to flee everything that they know, everything that they love, we have to have the empathy to see ourselves. We have to imagine what it would be like for our family, for our children, if the unspeakable happened to us. And we should all understand that, ultimately, our world will be more secure if we are prepared to help those in need and the nations who are carrying the largest burden with respect to accommodating these refugees.

There are a lot of nations right now that are doing the right thing. But many nations—particularly those blessed with wealth and the benefits of geography—that can do more to offer a hand, even if they also insist that refugees who come to our countries have to do more to adapt to the customs and conventions of the communities that are now providing them a home.

Let me conclude by saying that I recognize history tells a different story than the one that I've talked about here today. There's a much darker and more cynical view of history that we can adopt. Human beings are too often motivated by greed and by power. Big countries for most of history have pushed smaller ones around. Tribes and ethnic groups and nation states have very often found it most convenient to define themselves by what they hate and not just those ideas that bind them together.

Time and again, human beings have believed that they finally arrived at a period of enlightenment only to repeat, then, cycles of conflict and suffering. Perhaps that's our fate. We have to remember that the choices of individual human beings led to repeated world war. But we also have to remember that the choices of individual human beings created a United Nations, so that a war like that would never happen again. Each of us as leaders, each nation can choose to reject those who appeal to our worst impulses and embrace those who appeal to our best. For we have shown that we can choose a better history.

Sitting in a prison cell, a young Martin Luther King Jr. wrote that "human progress never rolls on the wheels of inevitability; it comes through the tireless efforts of men willing to be co-workers with God." And during the course of these eight years, as I've traveled to many of your nations, I have seen that spirit in our young people, who are more educated and more tolerant, and more inclusive and more diverse, and more creative than our generation; who are more empathetic and compassionate towards their fellow human beings than previous generations. And, yes, some of that comes with the idealism of youth. But it also comes with young people's access to information about other peoples and places—an understanding unique in human history that their future is bound with the fates of other human beings on the other side of the world.

I think of the thousands of health care workers from around the world who volunteered to fight Ebola. I remember the young entrepreneurs I met who are now starting new businesses in Cuba, the parliamentarians who used to be just a few years ago political prisoners in Myanmar. I think of the girls who have braved taunts or violence just to go to school in

Afghanistan, and the university students who started programs online to reject the extremism of organizations like ISIL. I draw strength from the young Americans—entrepreneurs, activists, soldiers, new citizens—who are remaking our nation once again, who are unconstrained by old habits and old conventions, and unencumbered by what is, but are instead ready to seize what ought to be.

My own family is made up of the flesh and blood and traditions and cultures and faiths from a lot of different parts of the world—just as America has been built by immigrants from every shore. And in my own life, in this country, and as president, I have learned that our identities do not have to be defined by putting someone else down, but can be enhanced by lifting somebody else up. They don't have to be defined in opposition to others, but rather by a belief in liberty and equality and justice and fairness.

And the embrace of these principles as universal doesn't weaken my particular pride, my particular love for America—it strengthens it. My belief that these ideals apply everywhere doesn't lessen my commitment to help those who look like me, or pray as I do, or pledge allegiance to my flag. But my faith in those principles does force me to expand my moral imagination and to recognize that I can best serve my own people, I can best look after my own daughters, by making sure that my actions seek what is right for all people and all children, and your daughters and your sons.

This is what I believe: that all of us can be co-workers with God. And our leadership, and our governments, and this United Nations should reflect this irreducible truth.

Thank you very much.

ACKNOWLEDGMENTS

Above all, we thank Anton Mueller of Bloomsbury, who conceived of this collection and invited us to edit it. We appreciated his superb editorial instincts, his enthusiasm, his thoughtfulness, and his insight that many Americans would want to look back on President Obama's tenure by reexamining his own words. We also extend our deepest thanks to Adam Waters, whose gifts as a researcher and writer were absolutely essential to this project. Adam is blessed with unusual wisdom about politics and history—and with a beat reporter's awareness of the importance of deadlines. We couldn't have done this without him. Great thanks to our agents, Gail Ross and Suzanne Gluck. Finally, thanks to the Miller Center, the White House, and the numerous media outlets that provided transcripts for President Obama's speeches.

INDEX

"How Far We've Come"
(Atlanta, Feb., 2005),
14–20
human rights
as necessary for just peace,
159–61
U.S. support for, 134, 160–61,
228
Hussein, Saddam, 3, 128, 156

"I Am Here To Say They Are
Wrong" (Osawatomie,
Kan., Dec., 2011), xiv, xv,
xxi, 172–93
ideology, Obama's mistrust of, xv
Illinois State Senate campaign
(2003), 5
immigrants, Americans as,
263–64, 322
immigration reform, 84, 207, 222
Inaugural Address (Jan., 2009),
96–105
Inaugural Address (Jan., 2013),
201–8
India, religious violence in, 246
inequality of wealth/income
global, need to address, 307–9,
310
impact of, 180–81
racial discrimination and,
59–60
in U.S., 174–75, 180, 309–10
infrastructure
and job growth, 182, 218
spending on, 218–19
international order
challenges faced by, 304–5,
307–17
cooperation needed in, 317–19

and democracy, 311–14
progress made by, 304, 305–7,
319–20
as way forward, 305
Internet and social media, 137,
178, 218, 305, 306, 308–9
Iran, 82, 132–33, 159, 161, 226,
248–49, 304, 318
Iraq War, 91–92
and democracy promotion,
133–34
ending of, 128, 151–52
opposition to, 1–4, 10, 40, 81,
128
promise to end, 42–43, 48–49,
66–67, 81–82, 101
ISIL, 245, 316
Islam. *See also entries under*
Muslim
and religious tolerance, 123
Sunni-Shia conflict and, 135
Israel, 55, 82, 129, 229
Israeli-Palestinian conflict,
129–32, 317

Jefferson, Thomas, 123, 128,
257
Jefferson-Jackson Dinner speech
(Iowa, Nov., 2007),
xxvi–xxvii, 38–45
Jerusalem, 132
job creation, 182–84, 210, 214–16,
215, 218, 224, 309
Johnson, Lyndon B., 256, 298
"A Just and Lasting Peace" (Oslo,
Dec., 2009), 150–65
"Justice Has Been Done"
(Washington, May, 2011),
166–71